Dec 2019

D0907228

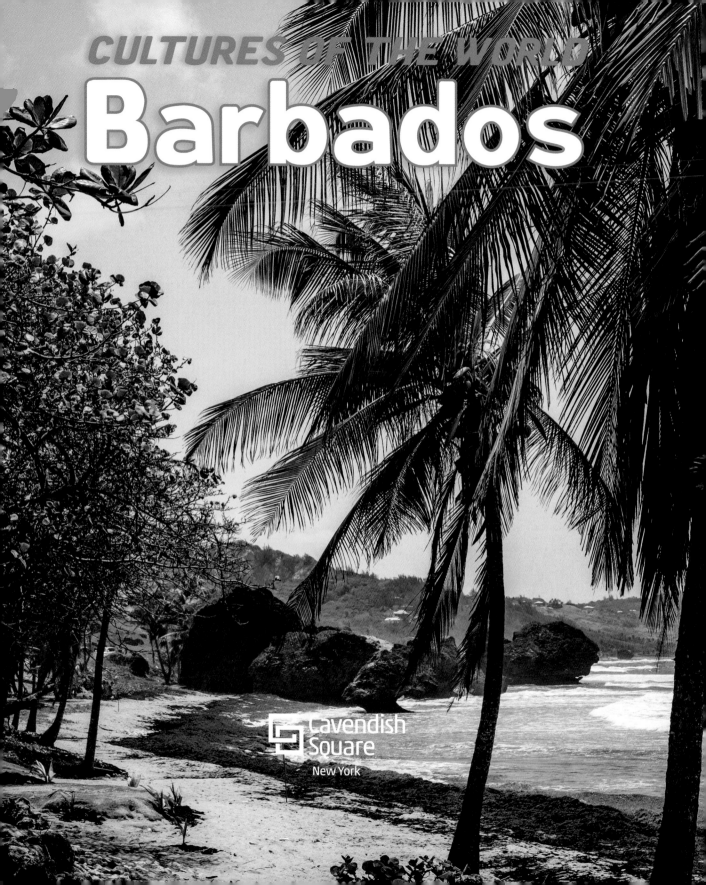

CULTURES OF THE WORLD

Barbados

Cavendish
Square
New York

Published in 2019 by Cavendish Square Publishing, LLC
243 5th Avenue, Suite 136, New York, NY 10016

Library of Congress Cataloging-in-Publication Data

Names: Elias, Marie Louise, author. | Elias, Josie, author. | Bryan, Bethany, author.
Title: Barbados / Marie Louise Elias, Josie Elias, and Bethany Bryan.
Description: New York : Cavendish Square, 2020. | Series: Cultures of the world |
Previous edition published in 2000. | Includes bibliographical references and index.
Identifiers: LCCN 2018043904 (print) | LCCN 2018045072 (ebook) |
ISBN 9781502647313 (ebook) | ISBN 9781502647306 (library bound)
Subjects: LCSH: Barbados--Juvenile literature.
Classification: LCC F2041 (ebook) | LCC F2041 .E45 2020 (print) | DDC 972.981--dc23
LC record available at https://lccn.loc.gov/2018043904

Editorial Director: David McNamara
Editor: Kristen Susienka
Copy Editor: Nathan Heidelberger
Associate Art Director: Alan Sliwinski
Designer: Jessica Nevins
Production Coordinator: Karol Szymczuk
Photo Research: J8 Media

CONTENTS

BARBADOS TODAY

BARBADOS IS A SMALL ISLAND IN THE CARIBBEAN, AROUND 166 square miles (430 square kilometers) in size, formed less than one million years ago when the Caribbean tectonic plate slid over the top of the South American plate, scraping away at its surface and leaving behind an enormous pile of sediment. Coral began to develop over the top of this pile over centuries, building up and up until it formed an island. Barbados is relatively small in size, only around 21 miles (34 kilometers) from north to south and 14 miles (23 km) from east to west. However, despite its small size, today Barbados boasts a population of around 292,000 people and a nature of perseverance that has taken the island from being one of the top sugarcane producers in the world to a hub of tourism and manufacturing.

THE ISLAND TODAY

Barbados was once covered with tropical rain forest, home to a number of animal and plant species, including the green monkey and the bearded fig tree, for which

the country is named. *Los barbados* is Portuguese for "bearded ones." The sugarcane industry took its toll, however, and by 1665 much of the forest was wiped out. Today, only a small patch of forest remains, and Barbados struggles with some of the ill effects of deforestation, like erosion and a reduction in natural plant and animal life. Tourism in Barbados is dependent on the beach areas for development of hotels and other attractions. But beaches in particular are affected by erosion, as natural beach sand washes away, leaving only craggy rocks behind. The biggest threat to Barbados's natural beauty and ecological well-being, however, is damage and destruction of the coral reefs due to pollution and sewage runoff. Work is being done to ensure the island's preservation, and to restore and maintain wildlife for many generations to come.

ECONOMIC EVOLUTION

From its early origins as the home of the Arawak and Carib people, Barbados has had a vast, often controversial and complicated history. The island was settled by Britain in 1627 and grew to be a top producer of sugarcane. Land was divided into sugar plantations where African slaves performed the intensive labor required to produce sugar and rum, cotton, and tobacco. Then, in 1834, slavery was abolished in all British territories. Without slave labor, the cost of producing sugar went up, and the sugar industry slowly began to decline. Today, some farmers still grow and produce sugar, although production continues to decrease each year. In 2016, Barbados produced only 91,899 tons (83,369 metric tons) of sugar; only ten years prior, this number was 383,935 tons (348,300 metric tons). Over the past century, as the sugar industry has slipped into history, tourism, services, and manufacturing have moved to the forefront of Barbados's economy.

Barbados's economy is in a precarious situation today, however. It never recovered from the global financial crisis of 2009, which sent the government deeply into debt as it worked to maintain the country's infrastructure and state-run businesses like the Barbados National Oil Company. The tourism industry has also taken a hit from travelers worried about hurricanes and from the influx of sargassum seaweed, which has recently begun to cause damage to beaches and kill sea life. With the most important industry in Barbados floundering, this makes it difficult to turn the economy around. With one of the highest debt-to-GDP ratios in the world, Barbados has a long way to go to economic recovery.

TODAY'S BARBADIANS

Despite current economic hardships, the people of Barbados have persevered for centuries, often leading the way when it comes to progress. Slave uprisings in Barbados during the seventeenth century set the stage for later slave rebellions in the United States. After slaves were emancipated in Barbados, it took another thirty years before the United States would follow. The independence movement

of the twentieth century carried Barbadians out of the colonial rule they had lived under for centuries and into a period where they had some say in choosing leadership for their country. Today, Barbados is ruled by a democratic parliament, with Queen Elizabeth II of England as the head of state. Many Barbadians support this type of government, while others would prefer complete independence.

Barbadians—or Bajans (Bay-jans), as they refer to themselves—today are fiercely unique. It's a point of pride to call yourself a Bajan, even after you've moved away from the island where you were born and raised. Barbadians are deeply religious and spiritual, the majority adopting their beliefs from the British. Britain continues to influence Barbadian language, food, art, sports, and architecture too. Barbadians enjoy cricket, a sport that originated in Britain, and they drive on the left-hand side

Crop Over is attended by people from all over the world, eager to see the colorful costumes and enjoy some Bajan culture.

of the road. However, Barbadians are also proud of their West African heritage and celebrate this through dance, storytelling, food, and other means. British and West African influences have melded in Barbados, creating a culture not found anywhere else in the Caribbean—or the world.

Barbadians tend to have a very laid-back style where they try to stay stress-free and enjoy life as much as possible. They love a party, apparent with the many festivals that take place across the island every year. Independence Day in Barbados is celebrated every year on November 30. This is the day that the country achieved independence from Britain in 1966. At the very first Independence Day ceremony, proud Barbadians raised their flag and heard their national anthem played publicly for the first time. However, modern

Barbadians don't just celebrate one day. The entire month of November is filled with festivals, community events, contests, and sports. At the Garrison Savannah horse-racing track just outside the capital city of Bridgetown, citizens hold a parade, and the surrounding government buildings are lit for the occasion. The biggest festival of the year, however, is Crop Over, celebrating the end of the sugarcane season. People from all over the world attend Crop Over to eat food, check out some colorful and elaborate costumes, and dance to calypso, the Afro-Caribbean style of music created by slaves as they grew and harvested sugarcane.

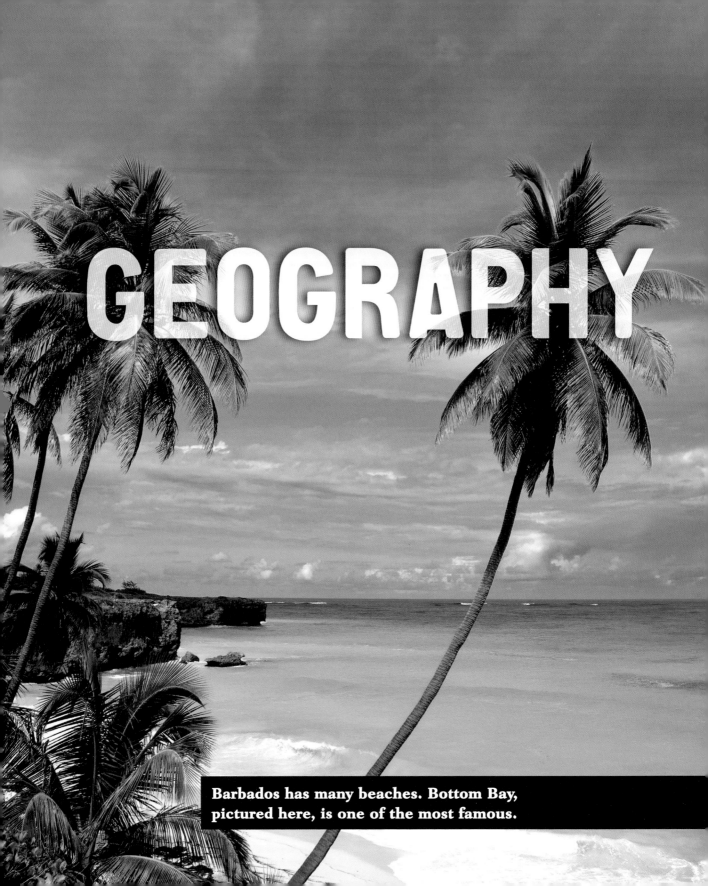

GEOGRAPHY

Barbados has many beaches. Bottom Bay, pictured here, is one of the most famous.

THE PEAR-SHAPED ISLAND OF Barbados is 21 miles (34 km) long and 14 miles (23 km) across at its widest, with a total land area of 166 square miles (430 sq km). Approximately 300 miles (483 km) north of Venezuela and 100 miles (161 km) east of the Caribbean chain, Barbados lies at 13°10' N, 59°32' W. This makes it the most easterly island of the West Indies.

"It is often said that beauty is in the eye of the beholder and nowhere is this more true than right here on the island of Barbados."
—Totally Barbados website

A YOUNG ISLAND

Geologically Barbados is a relatively young island—it is only about a million years old. Unlike its neighbors to the west, which were formed by volcanic activity, it is composed of coral limestone accumulations on a ridge of submarine debris on the seabed, which collected sand and grit from the Orinoco River in South America.

Tectonic forces pushed the coral out of the water, forming two small islands. Today's central plateau around Mount Hillaby, Barbados's highest point, was once divided from the southern ridge of Christ Church by a shallow sea covering what is now Saint George Valley. The landmass, covered by a cap of coral stone, tilted as it rose, forming high cliffs to the east and a series of ridges and terraces to the west. Water permeating

With 60 miles (97 km) of coastline, the island of Barbados is about three times the size of Washington, DC, and is the easternmost Caribbean island in the northern Atlantic Ocean. It has a tropical climate with a rainy season (June to October) and is relatively flat, rising to a central highland region, with the highest point, Mount Hillaby, at 1,102 feet (336 m) above sea level.

Hikers standing at the summit of Mount Hillaby might see a view like this one.

the island's porous limestone created underground streams, springs, and caverns. Surrounded by coral reefs, most of the island is relatively flat.

The west coast, with its white sandy beaches and calm blue waters, is traditionally the center of Barbados's tourist industry. Most of the island's resorts and hotels are located there or in the south. In contrast, high waves beat against the rocks and rugged cliffs of the less developed east coast. The undertow is also strong along the east coast, discouraging swimming. The north is the least populated region.

In the relatively hilly northeast, known as the Scotland District—called this name because it resembles mountains of the Scottish highlands—erosion has removed much of the thick coral cover found on the rest of the island. Mount Hillaby rises in the north-central part of the island.

The island is divided into eleven parishes, or local administrative units, and one city. The parishes are a legacy of the clergy's powerful influence in the past.

BARBADOS WEATHER

"With excellent weather year-round, it's always a great time to visit Barbados."
–Barbados.org

Barbados has a tropical climate. Temperatures in January range from 75 degrees Fahrenheit (24 degrees Celsius) to 84°F (29°C), and in July they increase only by a couple of degrees. Typically, the driest months are February to June. July is the wettest month, and annual rainfall averages 45 inches (114 centimeters). The country experiences high levels of humidity throughout the year as well.

In the east, Hackleton's Cliff towers 1,000 feet (305 m) over the coast and is several miles long. It was formed when the eastern side of the island rose and tilted gently to the west. Waves pounding at the base of the cliff and raging waterfalls dislodged enormous boulders, which tumbled to the sea at Bathsheba.

HURRICANE SEASON

The hurricane season in the Caribbean is from June to November, with hurricanes occurring most frequently in August and September. This region has one of the world's highest rates of hurricanes per year. Major hurricanes hit Barbados in 1667, 1731, 1780, 1831, and 1955, causing loss of life and extensive damage to property. However, usually the storms bypass the island to the north. In 2017, Barbados avoided major hurricanes Irma and Maria. The island nation's position in the Caribbean has made tourists reluctant to visit in recent years, despite it receiving less damage from the natural disasters than its neighbors.

Hurricane Ivan in 2004 damaged homes in Barbados and nearby Saint Vincent (shown here).

FLORA

Seeds of mangroves, sea coconuts, sea grapes, sea spurges, sea beans, French cotton, and manchineels (a poisonous tree) probably drifted to Barbados from South America hundreds of thousands of years ago. Once established, these plants stabilized the coastline. Coconuts, horse nicker plants, and lavender floated from Africa, while wind-borne seeds came with Sahara dust. Gradually, a forest developed. Most of the native forests were cleared by early settlers for farming. The landscape now consists predominantly of sugarcane fields, pastures, and scrubland. The remaining woodlands are mainly found where gullies and cliffs make the land unsuitable for agriculture.

FLOWERS ON BARBADOS

Barbados is home to a number of flower species, including the anthurium, the ground orchid, the blue lotus, and the red ginger lily. But scientists speculate that none of the flowers that grow on Barbados are actually indigenous to the island. Instead, they arrived there by accident aboard ships as the island was explored and colonized. The anthurium is native to the Americas, the ground orchid could originally be found in Australia and Asia, the blue lotus is native to parts of Africa and Asia, and the red ginger lily is native to Malaysia.

The bearded fig tree's aerial roots give it a "bearded" appearance.

Only a few areas, such as Grenade Hall Forest, have remained comparatively untouched. Turner's Hall Woods in the parish of Saint Andrew is a remnant of the dense tropical forest that covered the island at the time of the first settlement. Fine examples of silk cotton, sandbox tree, trumpet tree, cabbage palm, and the indigenous macaw palm grow there. Other trees common to Barbados include the giant bearded fig (*Ficus citrofolia*), casuarina, white cedar, poinciana, locust, and mahogany. Welchman Hall Gully, a deep ravine planted in the 1860s, is well known for its groves of citrus and spice-bearing trees, as well as many rare trees.

FAUNA

A few introduced species of mammals such as mongooses, green monkeys, vervet monkeys (*Cercopithecus aethiops*), hares, mice, and rats can be found in the wild. A nonpoisonous and rarely seen grass snake known as the Barbados racer (*Liophis perfuscus*) is found only on Barbados, but there are other harmless blind snakes, whistling frogs, lizards, red-footed tortoises, and eight species of bats. Hawksbill turtles lay their eggs on the sandy beaches, and the leatherback turtle is an occasional nester.

Although more than 272 species of birds have been sighted on Barbados, most are migrating shorebirds and waders that stop over from North America on their way to winter feeding grounds in South America. Only 31 species actually nest on Barbados, including wood doves, blackbirds, banana quits, guinea fowl, cattle egrets, herons, finches, and three kinds of hummingbirds.

While a number of snake species can be found on Barbados, one is particularly unique because of its size. The smallest snake species in the world, the Leptotyphlops carlae, *a variety of threadsnake, makes its home on the island. The Barbados threadsnake is as thin as a piece of spaghetti, and the average adult measures only 4 inches (10 cm) in length.*

The snake species was discovered in 2008 in a small, forested region of eastern Barbados, but it's thought that the species is very rare and potentially endangered because of development in this region. Almost no forest remains on the island because of the sugarcane industry and dense human population.

Because of its small size, the Barbados threadsnake has a diet limited to very tiny things like ant and termite larvae. It spends most of its time burrowed underground, where it can retain as much moisture as possible. The snake also only lays one egg at a time, and the average hatchling measures only 2 inches (5 cm) in length.

The seas around Barbados abound with more than fifty varieties of fish, providing a source of livelihood for many people. Surface-dwelling fish of the open seas (pelagic fish) are found 5 to 25 miles (8 to 40 km) offshore. Dolphins, kingfish, billfish, sharks, flying fish, and bonitos fall into this category. Big game fish include blue marlin—one weighing 524.5 pounds (238 kilograms) was caught off Barbados in 2015—white marlin, sailfish, and tuna. Coral reefs are home to a rich marine life, including ning-nings, lobsters, moray eels, octopuses, and gorgonias.

CULTURAL CENTERS

BRIDGETOWN, on the southwestern coast of Barbados, is the island's capital and commercial center. Today, it has a population of about eighty-nine thousand. It was founded in 1628 on Carlisle Bay, the island's only natural harbor.

In this image of Bridgetown from 1900, you can see the post office standing to the left, and the Council and Assembly Chambers at the right.

Bridgetown's main street includes some restored colonial buildings. The Careenage, an inlet now lined with recreational boats, cuts into the heart of the city. Inter-island schooners carrying fresh produce and other goods docked here for three hundred years, while sailing ships sought harbor in the outer basin or were careened (turned sideways so that their hull could be scraped and cleaned) in the inner basin. Before the construction of Bridgetown Harbour in 1961, large vessels and dreadnoughts anchored in Carlisle Bay.

Independence Arch, which commemorates Bajan, or Barbadian, independence, is at the south side of Chamberlain Bridge, which crosses the Careenage to National Heroes Square. This square marks the bustling center of the city's political, financial, commercial, and seafaring life. On Remembrance Day, or November 11, military parades fill the square, and poppy wreaths are laid at the Cenotaph, an obelisk monument erected in 1925 to honor those killed in World War I.

HOLETOWN is in the sophisticated parish of Saint James. It was originally called Jamestown by the first English visitors, who landed here in 1625 aboard the *Olive Blossom* and claimed the island in the name of King James I of England. An obelisk monument and a mural running along the main road in the town center commemorate this event, but the date on the monument, July 1605, is two decades early. The nearby post office and the police station incorporate a style reminiscent of life in colonial Barbados.

SPEIGHTSTOWN, in the parish of Saint Peter, was named after a 1639 member of Parliament, William Speight. It was once dubbed Little Bristol because it was the main shipping line to Bristol, England, when sugar was Barbados's mainstay. A quiet place, slightly off the beaten track, it is the only town on the island to retain many of its original small streets lined with simple two-story houses, some of which have Georgian-style balconies and overhanging galleries. Speightstown is the second-largest town on the island.

OISTINS, in the parish of Christ Church, is the center of the island's fishing industry. It has a large and bustling fish market open daily as long as the catch—dolphin, shark, barracuda, snapper, and flying fish—keeps arriving. The government built a Bds$10 million fisheries terminal to encourage modernization of the fishing industry. In 2016, work began to fix the landing jetty at Oistins. The jetty had been damaged in 2013, making it difficult to move fish from boats to the shore. The growing number of deep-sea fishing boats, which have replaced smaller vessels, make good use of the new ice machines in the terminal. Every Friday night, the city's restaurants draw crowds for excellent fish fries.

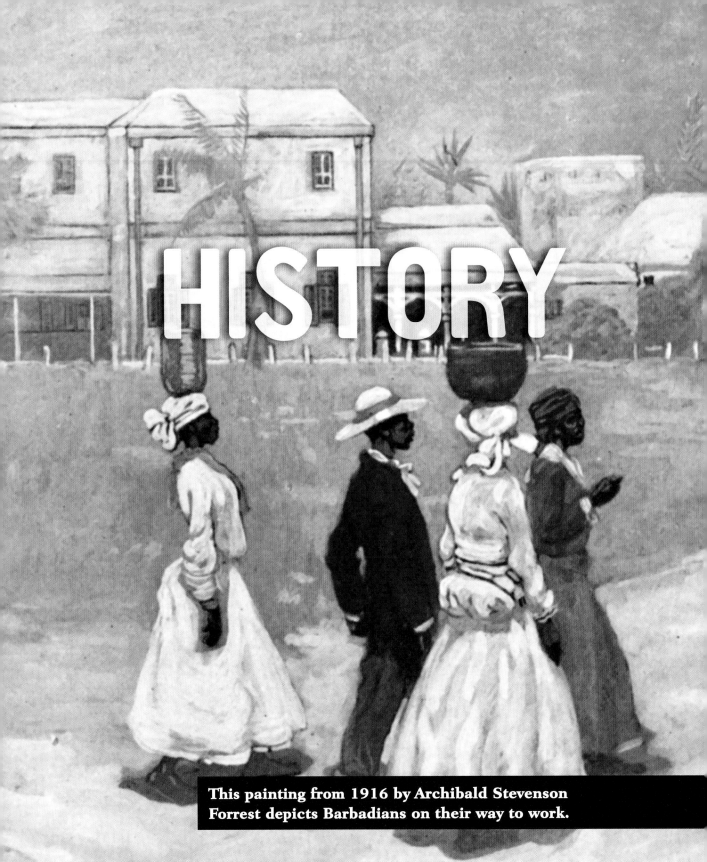

HISTORY

This painting from 1916 by Archibald Stevenson Forrest depicts Barbadians on their way to work.

U NLIKE SOME OF ITS CARIBBEAN neighbors, Barbados was never visited by Christopher Columbus, perhaps the most well-known explorer of the area. His renowned expeditions on behalf of Spanish monarchs Ferdinand and Isabella changed the course of human history, and started a trend of American colonization whose effects have continued to this day. Although the name Los Barbados is mentioned in Spanish *cedulas* (formal official orders) in 1511 and 1512, Columbus passed it by in favor of the larger islands nearby. The first Europeans to note the island on their maps were the Portuguese, but it was not until early in the seventeenth century that Barbados was claimed by English explorers.

"The advent of sugar cultivation made the Caribbean islands the most desirable American lands because of the riches they brought to the planters and to England."
—Richard Ligon, *A True and Exact History of the Island of Barbados*

EARLY BARBADIANS

The history of the early settlement of Barbados has been debated, but many suspect the area could have been inhabited as early as 1600 BCE. Artifacts and other evidence unearthed at Port Saint Charles point to a first settlement around 1623 BCE. Among the items unearthed were several stacks of pots that turned out to be a very primitive form of water well. This is thought to be the largest collection of stacks of pots ever found in the West Indies and Central America. Still, very little is known about the people who inhabited the settlement. However, this settlement certainly predates the Saladoid-Barrancoid Amerindians who came from Venezuela and were previously thought to be the earliest permanent settlers.

The Arawak tribe made up some of the first inhabitants of the island of Barbados.

A subsequent movement of Amerindian migrants known as the Arawaks arrived around 500 CE. The Arawaks were skilled farmers and fishermen and accomplished in the ceramic crafts, which they traded among other communities throughout the Caribbean area. They were short, olive-skinned, and handsome. Their villages, sited in sheltered freshwater bays, were strung along the coastline in areas where the fishing grounds were good, particularly at the northeastern tip of the island. The Arawaks cultivated cassava, potatoes, and corn. They made cassareep (ka-sa-REEP) from grated or ground cassava, a unique flavoring still used in Caribbean cuisine today.

These early settlers lived harmoniously in relative isolation in Barbados until about 1250, when the Caribs, a taller, stronger tribe, arrived. The Caribs were a warlike and savage group. The Spanish named this tribe Caribes, which means "cannibals" and which gave the region its name, Caribbean. In fact, the Caribs did practice cannibalism, but human flesh was not eaten as food; it was consumed in rituals to gain control over the dead enemies or to acquire the qualities of dead ancestors.

The Amerindians' existence was disrupted in 1492 when the Spanish conquistadors began raiding the island for slaves to work in the sugar estates and mines in Hispaniola. The raiders also brought with them European diseases to which the Amerindians had little or no resistance. Those who did not get sick and managed to evade the slave raids escaped to the neighboring Windward Islands, where they could consolidate their defenses against the Spaniards. Barbados was effectively abandoned by its early Native American settlers because the island's lack of mountains made it difficult for them to defend themselves from raiders.

In 1536, Portuguese explorer Pedro a Campos, on his way to Brazil, claimed that the island was uninhabited. He is said to have given the island its name of Los Barbados (the Bearded Ones), presumably after the fig trees with long-hanging aerial roots that have a beardlike appearance. Barbados's name is thus Portuguese in origin.

This map, which can be found in the British Museum, was drawn in 1683, several decades after the arrival of the British.

ENGLISH COLONIZATION

When Captain John Powell landed on Barbados in May 1625 and claimed it for King James I of England, all he found was a flourishing herd of wild hogs, descendants of those left behind by the Portuguese. The first English settlement was established in Jamestown (now Holetown) in February 1627 when Captain Henry Powell, John's brother, landed with a party of eighty settlers and ten black slaves.

Financed by merchant Sir William Courteen and associates, the pioneer colonists were employees rather than freehold farmers. They owned neither land nor stock. Helped by white indentured servants and meeting no armed resistance, these settlers were able to concentrate on the immediate task of planting crops and establishing trade systems. Because other English settlements in the West Indies were hampered by continuous native opposition, Barbados quickly surpassed them all, both in population growth and in commercial activity.

ESTABLISHING GOVERNMENT

In 1639, Governor Henry Hawley established the House of Assembly. The land tenure system was changed, and lands were issued to colonists in return for a quitrent (payment) of 40 pounds (18 kg) of tobacco annually. Only men

Barbados acquired the nickname "Little England" because it is the most British of the Caribbean islands. It was not conquered and reconquered many times, as were some of the other Caribbean islands, because winds and currents made it relatively difficult to reach by sail. British control lasted from 1625 until independence in 1966, but British influence remains apparent in school structure, the judicial system, and location names like Oxford, Cambridge, and Christ Church. The Queen of England is also the head of state.

with large amounts of capital (money) could afford to become substantial landholders, so a society dominated by a small, landed elite developed. Lands were effectively allocated to colonists with known financial and social connections in England. English law and tradition took hold quickly, and the island became known as "Little England."

COTTON AND TOBACCO

Barbados was described as a colony "built on smoke" because, at first, tobacco was its only export. By 1631, however, planters were cultivating cotton, which was fetching high prices in London. Boom conditions prevailed until 1639, when the London market was oversupplied with cotton. Prices fell sharply, and the colonists had to find a new crop.

THE INTRODUCTION OF INDENTURED SERVANTS

Evidence of indentured servitude on Barbados exists today in their descendants.

The production of tobacco, cotton, and indigo relied heavily on a labor force of British indentured servants. More than half of the whites who came to Barbados during the 1630s and 1640s were indentured servants. These men and women were contracted to serve their employers for five years (if over twenty-one years old) or up to seven years (if under twenty-one) in return for passage to the colony and subsistence on arrival.

Indentured servants were little more than slaves. They could be bought or sold, or even gambled away. They were not permitted to leave their plantations without a pass signed by their master. Their contracts gave them certain rights, such as the receipt of adequate food, clothing, and shelter and the right to complain to local magistrates of mistreatment by their masters.

Because planters believed they could treat their "property" in whatever way they wished within the limits of the "customs of the country," these rights were seldom exercised. The descendants of these Scottish, Irish, and Welsh indentured servants would later be known as "redlegs," the name coming from the sunburned skin on their kilt-exposed legs.

THE SUGARCANE INDUSTRY

Sugarcane was brought to the island in 1637 by a Dutchman who had learned how to grow and process it in Brazil. Defeated by the Portuguese in Brazil, the Dutch needed a market for their sugar-making machinery and their slave trade. Dutch merchants therefore helped struggling English colonists grow sugarcane so that these farmers would then need to purchase slaves to cultivate the crop and machinery to process it.

These women are working in a sugarcane field.

By 1645, Barbados was flourishing. Five years later, it was described as the richest spot in the New World. Barbadians dominated the sugar industry in the early years as the wealth of the planter class increased. Large sugarcane estates were formed by combining smaller ones that did not have access to sufficient capital.

During the next fifteen years the number of landholders declined substantially. Although they made up fewer than 10 percent of the island's population, the elite plantocracy dominated public life and civic organizations and made sure that only white, Anglo-Saxon Anglicans were allowed any political or legal power. Some of them received high honors like knighthoods or baronetcies in the second half of the century.

A FREELY ELECTED ASSEMBLY

The English Parliament, after the execution of King Charles I in 1649, decided planters in Barbados were rebels and launched an operation to subdue the colony. A fleet under Sir George Ayscue blockaded the island until early 1652,

when the colonists accepted the terms offered by Ayscue's delegation and signed articles of capitulation, agreeing to recognize the rule of Parliament and the colony's governor in return for continued self-government, free trade, and the restoration of confiscated properties.

This formed the basis for the Charter of Barbados, which guaranteed government by a governor and a freely elected assembly as well as freedom from taxation without local consent. When the monarchy was restored in England in 1660, this charter provided Barbados with a greater measure of independence from the monarchy than any of the other British colonies.

SLAVERY COMES TO BARBADOS

Large numbers of slaves had to be brought in to work in the sugar fields, mills, boiling houses, and distilleries. The plantations could not have existed without these slaves, who came to Barbados from West Africa. They were of many ethnic groups, speaking different languages.

The field slaves were housed in floorless huts, given meager food, and forced to work twelve hours a day, six days a week. Skilled slaves such as carpenters, blacksmiths, and tailors fared better, and domestic slaves were more trusted and better treated than field workers.

THE BARBADOS SLAVE CODES

During the sugar boom, the slave population changed. In the 1640s, the number of blacks stood at around six thousand. By 1684, the number had increased to forty-six thousand blacks, and by 1834, the number had risen further to eighty-eight thousand blacks. The white population had decreased, in turn, from thirty-seven thousand in 1640 to fifteen thousand in 1834. Acts were passed to control a vast labor force. The Barbados Slave Code of 1661 was passed to allegedly help owners protect slaves from harm and to offer a few protections to slaves, but the law strongly favored slave owners. The only real help offered to slaves was a requirement that masters provide their slaves with one new set of clothing each year. This law didn't include work standards, housing and dietary requirements, or even basic rights under English law. In fact, the Barbados

Slave Code of 1661 gave owners the right to legally harm or even murder slaves without repercussion.

This law was slightly updated in both 1676 and 1682, and then again in 1688. The 1688 act declared slaves to be "real estate," which legally tied them to specific plantations and meant that they could neither own property nor give evidence in court against whites. In addition, slaves could not leave their plantation without a ticket signed by their master, and they were forbidden to beat drums, blow horns, or use other loud instruments.

In this image, you can see slaves harvesting sugarcane at lower right. A boiling house and windmill are visible in the distance behind them.

SLAVE RESISTANCE AND REBELLION

From the very beginning, Africans resisted their enslavement in Barbados. Plantation houses were built to incorporate defenses against slave attacks. The first recorded incident was a small-scale uprising in 1649. In 1675, however, a planned revolt by African-born slaves involving a large number of plantations across the island was discovered, and the ringleaders were arrested and executed.

A more widespread conspiracy, which involved plans for slaves to form themselves into four regiments of foot soldiers and two mounted regiments with the intention of bringing the entire island under black control, was exposed in 1692. Of the two hundred to three hundred slaves who were arrested and brought to trial, ninety-two were executed.

No attempted rebellions were recorded in Barbados between 1702 and 1815, partly because the white community established and maintained a powerful island-wide system for the control of slaves, with dozens of forts strung along the coast. Slaves did run away, but they could not form large runaway communities, as slaves on some of the larger Caribbean islands did, because there was nowhere safe to establish them. Historical research has shown that there was a high level of slave resistance, but even so, there was only a single actual outbreak of armed revolt, which became known as Bussa's Rebellion, or the Rebellion of 1816.

Bussa's Rebellion (also called the Bussa Rebellion) was the result of a misunderstanding. In 1815, Britain passed a bill declaring that all slaves in the West Indies had to be registered. Believing this bill was a threat to their right of self-government, the Barbadian House of Assembly rejected it. The slaves thought the bill was not to register them but was intended to free them. It was the unfulfilled expectation of freedom that sparked the rebellion.

An African-born slave called Bussa was the primary leader. Not much is known about him, the man who is often known as the National Hero of Barbados, because detailed records were not often kept by slave owners. Even Bussa's birth name remains a mystery.

What is known about the rebellion is this: Rebel contingents assembled at Bussa's plantation in Saint Philip, where sugarcane fields were set alight. The revolt spread but was eventually suppressed by the British militia. Bussa is believed to have died in battle as the head of his contingent during the final showdown.

The event is commemorated by the Emancipation Statue. It goes simply by the name "Bussa" to many Barbadians. It stands in the St. Barnabus Roundabout in Bridgetown.

BARBADOS IN THE 1700s

Barbados languished during the eighteenth century. Trade competition from islands such as Jamaica and Saint Kitts intensified, and the price of sugar fell sharply. Britain was at war with France in the Americas, and that combined with the American War of Independence caused trade between Barbados and the British colonies in America to plummet, cutting off food supplies and material for the sugar industry. Food shortages became so serious that the poor died in the streets.

Barbados also suffered several other calamities. Yellow fever in 1703 caused many deaths. A hurricane in 1731 wreaked widespread damage and was followed by a drought two years later. An even more destructive hurricane struck in 1780, destroying crops and killing nearly 22,000 people in Barbados, Saint Lucia, Saint Vincent, and Martinique, with about 4,500 dead in Barbados alone.

Recognizing Barbados's strategic location, the English used the colony as part of a multi-island defense center. British regiments were stationed in imposing arched brick buildings in the garrison in Bridgetown. By 1795, Barbados had 22 forts, 450 guns, and a series of elevated signal stations that could relay signals to alert the entire island within minutes of sighting an aggressor to the north or the south. The victory of Vice Admiral Horatio Nelson at Trafalgar, Spain, in 1805 and the military success of English troops in the West Indies stabilized sugar markets.

SLAVERY ABOLISHED

The abolition of the slave trade in 1807 caused the plantocracy little concern, even though black Barbadians had become more aggressive after Haitian revolutionaries had declared independence in 1804. This was especially true of the artisan and domestic slaves, who were better informed than the field workers and considered themselves closer to freedom.

The Emancipation Act was passed into law in 1833 and took effect on August 1, 1834. All slaves under the age of six were unconditionally emancipated. Slaves over the age of six were freed but had to continue to serve their former owners as unpaid apprentices for six years. This was intended to give the slaves time to adjust gradually to freedom and the slave owners the opportunity to reorganize their plantations around wage laborers.

Instead of improving working conditions for the former slaves, the act had the opposite effect. The planters' attitude to their workforce hardened, and workers became sullen and unproductive. When the planters abandoned all responsibility for infants, workers had to struggle to provide for their children, and many of the fourteen thousand children who had been freed in 1834 joined the ranks of the destitute in the colony. It soon became clear that the apprenticeship system was a farce, and on August 1, 1838, all slaves were fully emancipated, two years ahead of schedule.

In addition to hurricane damage and destruction, a locust plague in 1663, a fire in Bridgetown in 1667, drought in 1668, and excessive rainfall in 1669 caused irreparable damage to the sugar industry. By 1720, both Jamaica and the Leeward Islands were producing more sugar than Barbados.

BARBADOS IN THE TWENTIETH CENTURY

Subsidized sugar beet production in Europe caused a crisis for Barbados's sugar industry during the mid-1890s, and many indebted estates were sold to the urban merchant class. Thus bolstered by the wealth of the merchant families, the plantocracy entered the twentieth century secure in their ability to rule in the difficult times ahead.

The British government's growing concern for the welfare of the working class found little support among the Barbadian planters, who remained determined to keep their plantation labor in line and restrict the education of black children to discourage them from seeking employment outside agriculture. Although ownership of their own piece of land was the ambition of nearly every plantation worker, very few succeeded in obtaining freehold.

THE PANAMA CANAL

The resumption of construction on the Panama Canal by the United States in 1904 provided male Barbadian workers with an opportunity to escape from plantation work. Planters subsequently employed women to do "men's work" at lower wages.

Some twenty thousand men emigrated to Panama. Former field hands returning from Panama had enough money to buy land, open shops, learn a craft, or acquire education for clerical or business professions. A slump in sugar prices forced indebted planters to sell some of their plantations in small lots to these "Panama men," and the pattern of landownership changed significantly.

Although many of the workers returning from Panama were able to achieve a better quality of life, for the majority of the working class, conditions deteriorated.

THE FIGHT FOR BLACK POWER

Education, societies for the working class, and the Barbados Labor Union (formed in 1919) provided the background for the development of a radical

A CONTROVERSIAL STATUE

The bronze statue of Horatio Nelson, who sailed into Barbados in 1805 a few months before dying at the Battle of Trafalgar, was erected in Bridgetown in 1813, two decades before its larger London counterpart. Over the years, the statue has been the subject of controversy among the islanders, as some feel it embraces the island's colonial past too closely. In the 1970s, the Mighty Gabby, a leading calypso singer, had a popular song called "Take Down Nelson" that suggested replacing Nelson with a Bajan man.

The statue continues to be a point of controversy. In 2017, it was splashed with blue and yellow paint representing the Barbadian flag. A sign placed at the base of the defaced statue read, in part, "Nelson must go!! Fear not Barbados. The people have spoken. Politicians have failed us!" The statue was quickly restored, but many Barbadians continue to call for its removal. The hashtag #nelsonmustfall, originated with a call to remove the statue in London, began to spread on Twitter. The square where the statue stands was renamed National Heroes Square (formerly Trafalgar Square) in 1999.

political movement in Barbados, abetted by Marcus Garvey's pan-Caribbean and international "black power" movement.

During the 1930s, the combination of a rapidly growing population, the rising cost of living, and dissatisfaction with wages fixed at the equivalent of 30 cents a day sparked street riots in Barbados. Fourteen people were killed and forty-seven were wounded in protests in 1937. The rioting spurred a man named Grantley Adams to found the Barbados Labour Party (BLP) in 1938. During the 1942 House of Assembly session, Adams led a fight for reforms that allowed more people to qualify to vote, increased direct taxation, and established a workers' compensation program. Adams became the island's first premier in 1954 and was knighted in 1957. He was posthumously named a national hero of Barbados in 1998.

GAINING INDEPENDENCE

Errol Walton Barrow was a fervent social reformer who replaced Sir Grantley Adams as premier in 1961 when the Democratic Labour Party (DLP) gained power as a liberal alternative to the more conservative but politically similar BLP. Barbados was able to function autonomously through a peaceful democratic process, and this resulted in the negotiation of its independence at a constitutional conference with the United Kingdom in 1966, at which point it became an independent nation within the British Commonwealth, today known as the Commonwealth of Nations.

BARBADOS MOVES INTO THE TWENTY-FIRST CENTURY

The turn of the century brought with it a lot of achievements for Barbados—women in particular. In 2005, Barbados native Rihanna was signed to Def Jam Recordings and released her first single, "Pon de Replay," which went to number two on Billboard's Hot 100 chart. However, it wasn't until 2007, with the release of her single "Umbrella," that Rihanna became a household name. Today, she is one of the most recognizable performers in the world.

In 2018, Mia Mottley became the first female prime minister in Barbados history when the Barbados Labour Party swept the general election, defeating the Democratic Labour Party (DLP) and picking up all thirty seats in the House of Assembly. Before being elected prime minister, Mottley held the position of attorney general and minister of home affairs. She became the Barbados Labour Party leader in 2008.

Relatively conservative Barbados has also made strides socially over the past fifty years, becoming slowly more accepting of its LGBTQ residents. In 2018, the first pride parade was held in Bridgetown. Many—especially in the religious community—are opposed to this type of change, but not all religious leaders feel this way. Clifford Hall of the Anglican Church addressed the crowd during the parade: "Don't let anyone bully you, or torment you or terrorize you. They have had their day, yours is now and tomorrow and forever."

Steps forward have also been taken for the country's environmental wellness. Pollution, erosion, and energy costs are longstanding issues in Barbados, but in the past twenty years, the country has been moving toward environmental consciousness and sustainability. More and more homes each year are being outfitted with solar technology, taking some of the burden off of fossil fuels. Furthermore, nonprofit organizations like Clean Up Barbados are working to change the habits of Barbadians to help reduce littering.

Prime Minister Mia Mottley of the Barbados Labour Party came into power in 2018.

INTERNET LINKS

http://news.bbc.co.uk/2/hi/americas/country_profiles/1154227.stm
This BBC websites provides a timeline of the history of Barbados.

http://futurecentretrust.org/main/projects-programmes/clean-up-barbados
This website explores Clean Up Barbados.

https://www.youtube.com/watch?v=UrCCyTJlSBk
This short animated film, narrated from the viewpoint of Bussa himself, provides some history of the Bussa Rebellion.

GOVERNMENT

Here, you can see the Parliament building in Bridgetown.

U NIQUE AMONG THE ISLANDS OF THE Caribbean, Barbados was ruled by Britain for more than three centuries. Today, as a member of the Commonwealth of Nations, its links to Britain remain strong. This has helped to create a foundation of stability in a country made up of different races and creeds.

Barbados is governed by a system of constitutional monarchy and parliamentary government with democratic traditions. The island is divided into thirty constituencies. The people of Barbados enjoy many constitutional safeguards, including freedom of speech, worship, press, movement, and association.

CONSTITUTIONAL MONARCHY

Barbados's political system is a constitutional monarchy, with the king or queen of England as head of state, represented in the country by a governor-general. The governor-general is appointed by the monarch. Barbados's constitution dates from 1966 and provides for a system of parliamentary government on the British model, with a prime minister and cabinet drawn from and responsible to the legislature, which consists of a Senate and a House of Assembly.

"As a predominantly Black country we can wear our economic and social achievements proudly."
—David, *Barbados Underground*

Queen Elizabeth II of England is also the queen of Barbados since she is the head of state there, but in 2015 then prime minister Freundel Stuart announced that he would like to remove the queen as head of state and turn Barbados into a parliamentary republic where all government leaders are chosen via election. A change like this would require a significant update to the constitution, which not all Barbadians support. Originally, Stuart's plan was to revisit this proposal and implement it in 2016, the country's fiftieth anniversary year, but in the end he did not follow through.

THE LEGISLATURE

The Senate consists of twenty-one members appointed by the governor-general: twelve on the advice of the prime minister, two on the advice of the leader of the opposition, and the remaining seven on the basis of wider consultations within the religious community and other social interests. The House of Assembly, which dates back to 1639, has thirty members elected by adult suffrage. The voting age is eighteen years.

Each legislature has a maximum tenure of five years and can be dissolved anytime during this period. The governor-general appoints the prime minister—on the basis of support in the House of Assembly—and the leader of the opposition. Cabinet ministers are also chosen by the governor-general, on the advice of the prime minister. In 2018, a record-breaking twenty-six cabinet members were appointed.

Dame Sandra Mason is the governor-general of Barbados, representing Britain's interests in the country.

GRANTLEY ADAMS AND THE BARBADOS LABOUR PARTY

The Barbados Labour Party (moderate left of center) won the first general election in 1951. It was formed in 1938 by Grantley Adams, who became premier in 1954 when a ministerial government was established.

Before Sir Grantley Adams became the most important figure in pre-independence politics, he was a lawyer who in 1918 won the Barbados Scholarship to Oxford University. This achievement granted young people from Barbados the opportunity to attend college in England. He rose to prominence through his testimony before Britain's Moyne Commission investigating regional disturbances in the late 1930s, claiming that the riots were caused mainly by economic distress.

Elected to the House of Assembly in 1940 and president-general of the Barbados Workers' Union in 1941, he became leader of the government in 1946. In 1951, in the first election conducted under universal adult suffrage with no property qualifications, the BLP won sixteen of the twenty-four seats, thus gaining a majority. Adams was knighted in 1957. He is the only person ever to hold the office of prime minister of the West Indies Federation, which was formed in 1958 but dissolved in 1962 when Jamaica and Trinidad and Tobago opted for independence.

Sir Grantley Adams is a much-celebrated figure in Barbados's history.

Under Adams's leadership, Barbados was transformed from an oligarchy into a democracy based on universal suffrage. A wide range of social reforms were introduced, and major construction projects, such as Bridgetown's Deep Water Harbour, were started.

After Adams's retirement from Parliament in 1970 and his death in 1971, others stepped up to fill his shoes. One of the most influential of his successors was his own son, Tom Adams, who became the second prime minister of Barbados. The younger Adams pushed for heightened military security and democracy, and enacted a number of social reforms.

Because of economic struggles in Barbados, by 2018, citizens were ready for a change from the rule of the Democratic Labour Party, which had been in power since 2008. The BLP swept the general election, filling all thirty seats of the House of Assembly and placing party leader Mia Mottley in the prime minister's seat.

ERROL BARROW AND THE DEMOCRATIC LABOUR PARTY

The Democratic Labour Party (moderate left of center) was formed in 1955. While both the DLP and BLP are broadly seen as center-left in their positions, the BLP is generally understood to be more conservative than the DLP.

When full internal self-government was achieved in 1961, the DLP won the general election under leader Errol Barrow. He became the first prime minister of an independent Barbados following its independence in 1966.

Barrow served in the British Royal Air Force during World War II and subsequently studied law in London. He returned to Barbados in 1950, joined the BLP, and was elected to the House of Assembly in 1951. He became the leader of a discontented BLP left wing, which felt that Adams was too close to the governor and not giving enough attention to the workers.

Errol Barrow (*right*) talks to Pierre Trudeau (*left*), then the prime minister of Canada.

In 1954, Barrow left the BLP. The following year, he founded the DLP, which he led for the next thirty-two years. He gained the support of sugar workers demanding higher wages, and his party won the 1961 elections. Between 1961 and 1966, the DLP replaced the legislative council with a senate appointed by the governor, increased workers' benefits, instituted a program for industrialization, and expanded free education.

The DLP won the November 1966 elections, and Barrow became the country's first prime minister when Barbados gained its independence on November 30, 1966. Significant achievements during his period in office included the introduction of free secondary and university education and the lowering of the voting age to eighteen.

The BLP won the election in 1976 under Sir Grantley Adams's son, Tom, who died suddenly in 1985 and was succeeded by Harold Bernard St. John. The following year the DLP, led by Barrow, returned to power with twenty-four of the twenty-seven seats in the House of Assembly. Barrow died suddenly in 1987 and was succeeded by the deputy prime minister, Lloyd Erskine Sandiford.

A new opposition party, the National Democratic Party (centrist), was formed in 1989 by Richard Haynes, a former minister of finance in Sandiford's cabinet.

In 1990, the Electoral and Boundaries Commission increased the number of seats in the House of Assembly from twenty-seven to twenty-eight (it was later further expanded to thirty seats). The DLP, under Sandiford, won the general election in 1991. In 1994, Owen Seymour Arthur became prime minister after leading the BLP to victory in nineteen of the twenty-eight seats in the House of Assembly, securing 48 percent of the vote. David Thompson became the sixth prime minister in January 2008 after the DLP won the general election with twenty seats against ten for the BLP. When Thompson became ill in 2010, deputy prime minister and longtime DLP member Freundel Stuart filled in temporarily and then assumed the post permanently after Thompson died later that year.

OAS MEMBERSHIP

The Organization of American States (OAS) was established as the International Union of American Republics at a meeting in Washington, DC, in 1890. It took on its current form in 1948. The main objectives of the OAS include strengthening the peace and security of North, Central, and South America; ensuring the peaceful settlement of disputes among member states; and promoting economic, social, and cultural development through cooperative action.

Most countries in North, South, and Central America, as well as the Caribbean, including the United States and Barbados, are members of the OAS. Until 2009, a notable exception was Cuba; its membership was suspended from 1962 to 2009. In 2009, a new resolution lifted the suspension, and membership was allowed on condition of negotiation. The OAS is headquartered in Washington, DC, and has an annual budget contributed by member governments. Every member nation has one vote, and unlike in the United Nations, no country has veto power. The OAS celebrated its seventieth anniversary in 2018.

Private Deweyne Green of the Barbados Defence Force monitors a vehicle checkpoint in Trinidad and Tobago in 2017.

THE BARBADOS DEFENCE FORCE

During the seventeenth and eighteenth centuries, Barbados was an important military base for the British, enabling them to protect their interests in the Caribbean. The many antiquated cannons still found on the island are a reminder of those turbulent times when Barbados held a vital role in regional power.

Today, Barbados is a peaceful island with little crime, and it no longer requires a large military force. The Barbados Defence Force, established in 1978, has a strength of 610 armed forces personnel, including around 500 army and 110 navy (coast guard) personnel, in addition to 430 reserve forces. Numbers go up or down depending on need. The coast guard tends to increase every year in order to combat drug trafficking.

INTER-AMERICAN DEVELOPMENT BANK

The Inter-American Development Bank (IDB) was founded in 1959 with the goal of providing development loans or grants to Latin American and Caribbean nations that may struggle with poverty, social inequality, or natural disasters and need help funding infrastructure, energy, or health reform projects. After the 2010 earthquake in Haiti, the IDB pledged $2.2 billion to the recovery effort. As of 2018, Barbados has received loans of $191 million from the IDB.

Barbados also has a police force of about 1,300 that includes the Harbour Police and the Corps of Writ Servers. As of 2017, it was in need of 200 more people—ideally younger men—to join the force, as many older members resigned or were removed from their positions. Female numbers were good, but younger men were needed, according to Assistant Commissioner of Police William Yearwood.

DIPLOMATIC RELATIONS

Both the DLP and the BLP are committed to maintaining free enterprise and alignment with the United States. In 1972, the DLP government reestablished diplomatic relations with Cuba while maintaining cordial relations with the United States. Today, Barbados maintains friendly diplomatic relations with the United States, from which it imports 40 percent of its goods.

In 1983, the BLP government participated in the US invasion of Grenada. This action, however, strained relations with Trinidad, which claimed that the operation was undertaken without proper consultation of all members of the Caribbean Community (CARICOM). Relations with Trinidad have been fragile in the twenty-first century over a dispute involving the fishing industry. In 2004, it was discovered that the Atlantic flying fish population, vital to the Barbadian fishing industry, had begun to migrate farther south, into Trinidad and Tobago territorial waters. Barbadian fishermen followed the fish south and were detained for fishing illegally in foreign waters. The

countries signed an agreement in 2014 to help establish protocols in case of this happening again.

Barbados is a member of several international organizations, including the United Nations (UN), the Organization of American States (OAS), CARICOM, the Commonwealth of Nations, and the Inter-American Development Bank (IDB). In 2008, Barbados and the other members of CARICOM signed an Economic Partnership Agreement (EPA) with the European Union (EU) and its European Commission. This deal covers CARICOM's membership in the Caribbean Forum (CARIFORUM). CARIFORUM is part of the Group of African, Caribbean, and Pacific (ACP) States. The agreement outlines Barbados's trade ties and future development with the EU. Countries with diplomatic representation in Barbados include Brazil, Canada, the People's Republic of China, Colombia, Costa Rica, the United Kingdom, the United States, and Venezuela. Barbados has established official diplomatic relations with 105 countries worldwide.

INTERNET LINKS

https://www.bdfbarbados.com/home
Readers can learn more about the Barbados Defence Force on the organization's website.

https://www.blp.org.bb
The Barbados Labour Party website offers insight on its history and some of the current goals it's working to achieve.

https://dlpbarbados.org
The website for the Democratic Labour Party provides news and some of the latest issues Barbados is facing.

ECONOMY

One of the top contributors to Barbados's economy is the tourism industry. Each year, people come from all over the world to enjoy beaches, sun, and fun times.

BARBADOS IS ONE OF THE wealthiest and most developed countries in the Caribbean. Its economy is based on three main sectors: agriculture, industry, and services. Agriculture includes cultivation of sugarcane, vegetables, and cotton, and makes up 1.4 percent of Barbados's gross domestic product (GDP). Industry, at 4.8 percent of the GDP, includes sugar processing, light manufacturing, and component assembly. Services make up the largest portion of the GDP, at 93.8 percent. This includes offshore financial services, tourism, and other business services.

RECESSION AND RECOVERY

Barbados has struggled to recover from the 2008 to 2009 recession because of fluctuating oil prices and a dip in the tourism industry. The government is currently in debt at 175 percent of the GDP, putting it at

"We needed to stabilize the country and stop the bleeding."
—Prime Minister Mia Mottley

one of the highest debt-to-GDP ratios in the world. In 2018, in order to get out of the debt crisis, the country began work on an emergency debt relief plan.

As part of the debt resolution strategy, Prime Minister Mia Mottley asked the International Monetary Fund (IMF) to step in. The IMF is an economic cooperative of 189 countries that work together to provide loans to countries in need. Financial assistance from the IMF helps countries to replenish their reserves and provide aid in paying for necessary imports. This helps to rebuild a climate of financial stability. The IMF will help to restructure Barbados's debts so that there's a plan in place for paying off money owed to creditors.

THE TOURISM INDUSTRY

The tourist industry had its origins in the years just before World War I, catering to winter visitors from North America and the United Kingdom, as well as visitors from Latin America, particularly Brazil. The colony owed its increasing prosperity to such visitors, but the tourist industry remained subordinate to the sugar industry until the 1970s.

Dover Beach, shown here, and other beaches along the west coast of Barbados are essential to the island's tourist industry.

In 1751, more than three decades before he became the first president of the United States, George Washington came to Barbados with his half-brother Lawrence, who suffered from tuberculosis and was hoping that the island's tropical climate would prove therapeutic. Unfortunately, Washington contracted smallpox while on Barbados, which left his face scarred, and Lawrence died the following year. The Barbados trip was the only overseas journey George Washington ever made.

Tourism is now crucial to the economy, with the service sector as a whole representing approximately 93.8 percent of GDP. About 9.7 percent of the working population—some fourteen thousand people—are employed in the tourism sector. In 2007, Barbados was one of several Caribbean nations to cohost the Cricket World Cup, which attracted visitors and helped improve growth figures of the construction, communication, utilities, and tourism sectors. Today, tourists visit Barbados's resorts with white sandy beaches for swimming and relaxation, to enjoy good food and entertaining festivals, and to see Barbados's sights.

INTERNATIONAL OFFSHORE COMPANIES

Barbados has been encouraging international offshore companies such as banks, insurers, trusts, and shipping registration companies to register in the country by exempting them from capital gains taxes and estate duties. Tax breaks and incentives make the island an attractive investment opportunity. The government agency responsible for the establishment and expansion of business enterprises is the Barbados Investment and Development Corporation (BIDC).

CASH CROPS

Although the government has adopted a policy of agricultural diversification to increase the production of fruits and vegetables, sugarcane is still the main cash crop and makes a large contribution to the island's export earnings.

About 30 percent of sugarcane sap is sucrose. During harvesting, the cane stalks are stripped of leaves and trimmed for easier handling. In the factory, the stalks are washed and cut into short lengths or shredded. The sugar is removed from the canes by a diffusion process, in which the finely cut stalks are dissolved in hot water, or by milling, which entails pressing the stalks between heavy rollers to squeeze out the juice. In the latter process, the rollers are arranged in sets of three, each set exerting a greater pressure than the previous one. Water is sprayed on the stalks as they pass through the rollers to help dissolve additional juice. The waste material remaining after the rolling is called bagasse.

The acidic liquid extracted from cane is dark gray or greenish and contains impurities that need to be clarified by the use of chemicals. Milk of lime (a mixture of calcium hydroxide and water) is added to the juice. It is immediately heated to the boiling point and then run into settling tanks, where the precipitated matter is separated from the clear juice. To produce white sugar directly from the cane juice, sulfur dioxide and sometimes phosphoric acid are added to the juice before the milk of lime.

The juice is evaporated into a thick syrup and then concentrated by vacuum boiling in several stages. The vacuum allows the mixture to boil at a relatively low temperature, which prevents the syrup from scorching. It is boiled until sugar crystalizes out of the liquid, forming a mixture known as massecuite. Special machines (centrifugal machines; perforated hollow cylinders that revolve rapidly) separate the raw sugar crystals from the massecuite.

THE OLD SUGAR MILL

The Morgan Lewis sugar mill is one of only two remaining sugar mills in the Caribbean. (The other, Betty's Hope Estate, is on Antigua, but it is no longer in use, even for tour demonstrations.) Today, the Morgan Lewis mill is a museum, offering tours and a view of the eastern coast of Barbados. Like other mills of its time, the Morgan Lewis was driven by wind power. The machinery that ground the cane is still intact, but the canvas sails that caught the wind and turned the grinding mechanism are no longer on the arms. Other windmill structures can be seen around Barbados, although many are in ruins. Others have been remodeled into homes!

Sugarcane (*Saccharum officinarum*) is a giant, thick perennial grass cultivated for its sweet sap. The plant grows in clumps of solid stalks and has graceful, sword-shaped leaves. Mature canes can grow from 10 to 26 feet (3 to 8 meters) tall and from 1 to 2 inches (2.5 to 5 cm) in diameter. The color of the stalk ranges from almost white to yellow to deep green, red, or violet.

Barbados is also an ideal location for growing cotton because of the climate and soil quality. The nation is known, particularly, for growing West Indian Sea Island cotton, one of the highest-quality and rarest cottons in the world. Records show West Indian Sea Island cotton growing in Barbados as far back as 1650, and Queen Victoria was known to be a fan. This type of cotton is known for its softness, strength, and resistance to natural wear. Today, only a small number of Barbadian farmers grow this cotton variety. It is sold for about five times the price of other high-quality cottons.

Some of the fruits and vegetables grown in Barbados include tomatoes, pumpkins, yams, cassava, bananas, mangoes, grapefruits, and guavas. They are sold both in supermarkets and at farmers' markets, and many are exported to other countries.

Farmers use machinery today to harvest sugarcane, producing tens of thousands of tons each year.

LIVESTOCK AND DAIRY

Also part of the agriculture industry in Barbados is livestock and dairy production. Farmers raise cows, pigs, sheep, chickens, and turkeys for meat. Most widely recognized of the livestock grown in Barbados is the Barbados blackbelly sheep, descended from similar breeds in Africa. This type of sheep thrives in hot and humid climates, resists disease well, and reproduces more often than some other breeds.

There is only one dairy processing plant on the island of Barbados, Pinehill, which collects an average of 4,000 gallons (15,000 liters) of milk every day. Their products are sold locally and shipped to other islands of the Caribbean, the United States, and Canada.

THE FISHING INDUSTRY

The fishing industry in Barbados includes not only fishermen but those who process, distribute, export, and sell fish, and those who build fishing vessels as well. This industry employs around six thousand people, or about 4.2 percent of the total workforce.

In 1983, new and expanded facilities opened at the main fishing port of Oistins, and small boats have been increasingly replaced by larger and more powerful boats with large ice-storage chests that enable fishermen to stay at sea longer. Closer to shore, reef fish are caught by simple lines from open boats or trapped in cage-like fish pots. Along the shore, nets of varying sizes are cast for fish such as fray, sprat, and pilcher.

This industry has faced many ups and downs over the years. Flying fish were found to be migrating southward and out of Barbados territorial waters around 2004, leading to some legal troubles for fishermen who pursued the fish into the waters around Trinidad and Tobago. More recently, catch rates have been affected by a massive invasion of sargassum seaweed, a brown seaweed that has overgrown beaches up to several feet in some places. A national emergency was called on June 7, 2018, while scientists tried to find a solution to this spreading issue.

THE ARAWAK CEMENT COMPANY

The Arawak Cement Company began production in 1984, but it struggled in the beginning. The company closed in 1991 because of financial losses but was sold and restructured. It reopened in 1997.

Today its main product is portland limestone cement, which carries a smaller carbon footprint than other types of cement because less carbon dioxide is produced when it's manufactured. To protect the environment, systems such as dust extraction guarantee that the operation has only a small effect on the environment. Orimulsion, a low-emission fuel, is used to fire the kiln.

In June 2016, Arawak Cement Company exported a record 22,046 tons (20,000 metric tons) of cement.

THE LAND OF THE FLYING FISH

Despite its name, the flying fish does not fly. It can, however, glide considerable distances out of the water by using its four "wings" (pectoral and ventral fins). Although thirteen species of flying fish are found in the waters surrounding Barbados, only one species, *Hirundichthys affinis*, is caught commercially. In May, when the fish spawn, they can often be scooped aboard by using a dip net. Flying fish make up the majority of fish caught by commercial fishermen, and Barbados has often been called the Land of the Flying Fish.

Fishermen in Barbados depend on catching the silvery flying fish. Many Bajans enjoy the fish fried.

PRODUCT MANUFACTURE

Manufacturing is an evolving industry. In the 1990s, it, along with tourism, surpassed the sugarcane industry in economic importance. Electronic components, clothing, cement and other building supplies, furniture, medical supplies, soap, and processed food are some of the products manufactured in Barbados.

THE MINING INDUSTRY

The limestone that covers more than two-thirds of the island contains few impurities and is well suited for the manufacture of cement and the production of slaked lime for the iron, steel, and chemical industries. Some limestone locations produce what is locally called soft stone, traditionally used in the building industry for making blocks.

Sand is mined for the production of green and amber glass, and for the building industry. Modern houses in Barbados are often built from cement or sandstone blocks.

IMPORTS AND EXPORTS

Sugar and its by-products, rum and molasses, together with electrical/electronic components, food and beverages, and chemicals, are the country's chief exports. Main imports include machinery, food and beverages, construction materials, fuel, and electrical components. The United States, Trinidad and Tobago, China, and the United Kingdom are Barbados's top import partners.

Solar energy is captured by the solar panels found on homes and businesses across Barbados.

PRODUCING ENERGY

Barbados produces both natural gas and crude oil to be used for energy, but there are no longer any oil refineries operating on the island. Instead, oil is shipped to refineries in Trinidad. The history of oil in Barbados stretches back several decades, however.

Production of petroleum started at Woodbourne in Saint Philip in 1972. The oil fields were nationalized in 1982, and the National Petroleum Corporation was set up to implement public policy on crude-oil and natural-gas production. In late 1996, the Barbados National Oil Company signed an agreement with a US company to step up exploration activity, with the aim of making the country self-sufficient in energy. Since 2001, oil production has declined slightly. In 2017, the island's wells produced about 223,500 barrels of crude oil, and that number has remained steady for over a decade. Burning of fossil fuels accounts for 89.9 percent of electricity produced on the island of Barbados. However, renewable energy is also becoming more popular.

In the twenty-first century, Barbados has expanded its use of renewable energy. In 2017, renewable energy sources contributed to 3.8 percent of energy sales. In particular, the country has widely accepted solar energy. Its solar radiation levels are among the highest in the world. Solar energy has been commercially available since 1974, providing a substitute for natural gas and imported energy. Solar water heaters are also popularly used. To date, more than fifty thousand houses in Barbados, almost 50 percent, use solar energy to heat their water. A wind turbine at Lamberts in Saint Lucy also provides electricity to the Barbados Light and Power Company. In 2018, the government of Barbados received funding from the European Union and the IDB to expand further into wind energy, as well as harnessing thermal energy from the surrounding ocean.

Bagasse, a by-product of the sugar industry, is an important source of biomass fuel and is used primarily to meet the energy requirements of sugarcane processing.

One energy source that is not found in the country is hydroelectricity. Hydropower is a green energy solution in many countries around the world, but it is not used in Barbados. Why? Quite simply, Barbados doesn't have any rivers. It does, however, have access to the ocean. Some companies have been developing systems to harness the power of the ocean. In 2018, the government planned several studies with other environmental agencies to determine the feasibility of using ocean power, both wave and wind.

GETTING AROUND BARBADOS

A network of major highways, all beginning at Bridgetown, spans the island. Driving time from Bridgetown to the east coast has been greatly reduced with the completion of the trans-insular highway, the ABC Highway, completed in 1989. It cuts across the island. Public transportation is offered. There are government-operated buses, privately run minibuses, and individually owned minivan cabs. Minibuses are perhaps the most popular form of transportation,

Barbados's international airport, named after Sir Grantley Adams, can be found about 8 miles (13 km) outside of Bridgetown.

as they are usually better maintained than government buses and less crowded than minivans. Virtually any place on the island can be reached by public bus, as buses cover the entire extensive paved-road network on regular schedules. There is also a helicopter shuttle service that provides air-taxi services to a number of sites on the island, mainly on the west coast tourist belt.

Barbados's only international airport, the Grantley Adams International Airport, is 8 miles (13 km) east of Bridgetown. It is served by several international airlines, including Caribbean Airlines, British Airways, American Airlines, Virgin Atlantic, and Air Canada. Miami is about four hours away by air and New York City five hours.

The port of Bridgetown was dredged in 2002 to allow safe access for many of the largest British, continental European, and American cruise ships in the world. The number of cruise-ship passengers arriving in Barbados has been increasing steadily. From 2016 to 2017, passenger arrivals increased 12.9 percent, from 725,020 to 818,752.

A train service, now discontinued, operated from Bridgetown from 1881 to 1938, linking places such as Bath, Martin's Bay, Bathsheba, and Belleplaine. The journey to Bathsheba often took three to four hours, depending on the condition of the railroad, which was sometimes obstructed by landslides. Although the train doesn't operate anymore, the Barbados Hiking Association hosts a yearly train hike that allows tourists to walk the 25-mile (40 km) route.

INTERNET LINKS

https://vimeo.com/219516199
British clothing company Turnbull & Asser created a short film about the rarity and quality of West Indian Sea Island cotton, viewable on Vimeo.

https://www.visitbarbados.org
The official tourism site for Barbados provides travelers with tips for exploring the island.

http://www.windmillworld.com/world/barbados.htm
The Windmill World website has a gallery of pictures of some of the older windmill structures that can be found around Barbados and what has been done to preserve many of them.

ENVIRONMENT

Sargassum seaweed, the brown growth on the water's edge here, is a big threat to Barbados's many beaches.

5

BARBADOS'S COASTLINE, ITS CORAL reefs, and fishery are integral to the country. They ensure residents and visitors have food to eat, as well as provide people with employment and entertainment. However, the country's marine areas and coral reefs are not as healthy as they once were. This is due to climate change, domestic sewage, sediments from the construction industry and agriculture, and other pollutants that have seeped into the sea. Removal and infilling of mangrove swamps, such as Holetown Hole, have destroyed important nursery areas for fish. The most pressing environmental problem is the uncontrolled handling of solid wastes, which can contaminate the water supply. Despite the pollution issues, 99.7 percent of Barbados's population has safe water to drink.

SARGASSUM SEAWEED

The Sargasso Sea is the only sea in the world not surrounded by land but by ocean. Its borders are currents in the North Atlantic Ocean that move in a clockwise direction. Because of its unique geographical location, the sea is tranquil and clear to about 200 feet (61 m). Portuguese explorers were the first Europeans to happen upon this unique body of water. The sea is named for its floating mat of seaweed, sargassum, which is an important part of the ocean habitat. Sargassum is a breeding ground and home to shrimp, crabs, eels, turtles, and certain fish, and part of a yearly migratory route for humpback whales, tuna, and birds.

Unfortunately, the sargassum has begun to travel and reproduce outside of the sea of its origin, and this is creating big problems in coastal areas of the United States and the Caribbean, including Barbados. The seaweed grows in enormous quantities, and when it hits land, it creates impossible-to-control piles up to 23 feet (7 m) deep. This causes damage to beaches and suffocates other types of plant life and coral reefs. Sargassum that isn't removed rots and begins to stink. The fishing industry and tourist industry in Barbados have both been severely disrupted by sargassum. The Barbados government called for a state of emergency in June 2018 as workers struggled to remove the seaweed from seven beaches along the eastern and northern coasts. Scientists are working to understand this phenomenon, and many have pointed to climate change as the cause.

PROTECTING COASTAL ZONES

Barbados is one of the world's most densely populated countries. Most of the island's population and economic activities are located within a narrow coastal band. The coastal zone is extremely important to the economy of the island. Coastal development, climate change, and other factors, however, have damaged the coastline and the adjacent marine zone. The Coastal Zone Management Act was introduced in 1998 to coordinate and update the existing statutes relevant to coastal management and make provisions for the protection of coral and other marine reserves.

The government of Barbados is committed to ensuring that the island's coastal waters are maintained and protected from pollutants. The Marine Pollution Control Act of 1998 facilitates the prevention, reduction, and control of pollution of the marine environment from every possible source.

The Fisheries (Management) Regulations Act of 1998 is in place to protect the marine environment and to prevent overfishing. It covers issues such as permissible mesh size on nets and forbids the use of entangling nets. It also prohibits the capture of lobsters carrying eggs and the removal of eggs from lobsters, as well as the capture, possession, or sale of turtles, turtle eggs, and turtle parts. In addition, the act makes it illegal to land a tuna with a live weight of less than 7.05 pounds (3.2 kg), and it protects coral and aquatic flora from being harvested for ornamental purposes. Fines or a prison sentence of up to two years may be imposed if these or similar regulations are broken.

Leatherback sea turtles can be found laying eggs on Barbados beaches, but the species faces many dangers.

Barbados's main environmental agencies are the Ministry of Housing, Lands, and Rural Development, established in 1978, and the Barbados Water Authority, established in 1980. These agencies are responsible for addressing Barbados's primary environmental issues, which include coastal pollution from oil slicks and soil erosion, particularly in the northeast. In 1981, a marine reserve was created to protect the coastline. The Barbados Marine Trust is a nongovernmental organization, begun in 2000. It is dedicated to promoting environmentally and socially sustainable use of the marine areas of Barbados. One of their projects in the early 2000s was deploying thirty reef balls to a specific area of the ocean. These cement structures were designed to attract marine life to a region. They are strong and resistant to outside factors such as human meddling, physical obstacles, or chemical interference. They can be used up to eight years. There has been success in nurturing reef environments at the reef ball sites.

AT-RISK AND ENDANGERED SPECIES

There are a few endangered species in Barbados, including the Atlantic goliath grouper, the Eskimo curlew, the smalltooth sawfish, and elkhorn

Barbados is a nesting ground to a large population of hawksbill turtles and leatherback turtles, and on an island that is densely populated and almost completely developed, keeping those turtles safe is important. The job of the Barbados Sea Turtle Project is to monitor beaches for nesting turtles and collect data on their activities. Volunteers also protect and relocate nests that are in danger due to wave activity or predators. Hatchling sea turtles instinctually move toward the brightest horizon, which under normal conditions would be the ocean in moonlight. But the brightest horizons on the developed beachfronts of Barbados tend to be hotels and homes, leading hatchlings toward danger. The Barbados Sea Turtle Project works with homeowners and businesses to shut down light sources to help guide hatchlings toward the ocean instead. They also work to clean up garbage on beaches to keep larger turtles from ingesting litter or becoming tangled in discarded fishing equipment.

and staghorn coral. The Barbados raccoon, the Barbados giant rice rat, and the Caribbean monk seal have all become extinct. Hawksbill sea turtles are critically endangered globally, and the most serious threat to their existence is from humans.

The Barbados National Trust established a replanting program to save the Barbados mastic tree. The tree has been harvested as a source of timber since the arrival of the Europeans. It is indigenous to the Caribbean, but intensive harvesting and habitat destruction have made the tree extremely scarce. The sole remaining wild tree on the island was spotted in 1989, growing on the roadside where it was brushed by passing cars and polluted by exhaust fumes and where any road-widening scheme would mark its demise. Seeds from this one remaining tree have been collected and germinated, and the resulting plants—around thirty specimens—are being grown in protected public sites on the island, including at the Andromeda Botanic Gardens and Welchman Hall Gully. Other mastic saplings have been donated to the Inter-American Institute for Cooperation on Agriculture to be replanted.

Preserving coral is of particular importance. Coral is delicate, composed of tiny invertebrates called polyps. These polyps have tough exteriors made of limestone, and when they attach themselves to the ocean floor and begin to bud (reproduce by dividing themselves), over time, this becomes a colony. Over centuries—even thousands or millions of years—these colonies create a vast habitat that helps sustain about 25 percent of marine life. Coral is very sensitive to change. A change in temperature or increased pollution can cause coral to expel the zooxanthellae algae that give coral its many colors. This is called "coral bleaching." In Barbados, in 1998,

Coral bleaching is actually the loss of colorful zooxanthellae algae, which give coral its many colors.

massive swaths of coral were affected by this phenomenon, and again in 2005. Increases in temperature are due to climate change. Boats, swimmers, litter, and other kinds of pollution can also cause damage to the life-sustaining coral reefs surrounding Barbados. Luckily, work is being done to help protect and sustain the reefs. The Coral Lab at the Bellairs Research Institute began work in 2016 to grow, rehabilitate, and transplant coral on the reef and then monitor it to make sure it stays healthy.

WASTE AND POLLUTION

The protection and enhancement of the environment is essential for the maintenance of good health. It has been estimated that every person generates about 2 pounds (0.9 kg) of solid waste each day. This amounts to an estimated island total of 292 tons (265 metric tons) a day, or 106,580 tons (96,688 metric tons) of solid waste every year. Organic matter accounts for 33 percent, nonorganic matter 26 percent, paper 20 percent, and plastic 9 percent of all wastes. Barbados is very concerned about the threats that this amount of waste can pose to the environment and is working to increase the number of Barbadians who recycle regularly.

Currently, only a small percentage of waste is recycled, around 30 percent. The remaining waste is disposed of at landfill waste sites. These landfill sites must be carefully constructed and monitored to ensure that no pollutants leak into the surrounding ground. Unfortunately, some residents and businesses do not adhere to proper waste-disposal practices. Plastic is not biodegradable, so if thrown on the roadside or into a gully it is likely to eventually wash into the sea, where it not only will be unsightly but will also add to coastal pollution and be hazardous for marine life.

The Mangrove Pond landfill site has been used for many years. In the early 2010s, concern grew that the landfill was becoming too full. The government of Barbados elected to build another landfill, called Greenland, which would replace the overused Mangrove Pond landfill. However, after completion, the Greenland landfill was deemed unsuitable for use and was abandoned. The Mangrove Pond site is still used, and a new waste-to-energy initiative has been devised. Likewise, a recycling plant was built next to the landfill. However, the area still faces capacity issues.

BURNING AND ILLEGAL DUMPING

Dumping of garbage in gullies or at the roadside is illegal and dangerous because it can contaminate the water supply and lead to diseases such as dengue fever and leptospirosis. Garbage dumped indiscriminately can also be a hazard to birds, fish, and other wildlife. The Barbados Environmental Association has estimated that the majority of the island's gullies are affected by illegal dumping. Some of these gullies are literally overflowing with the dumping of residential, agricultural, and commercial refuse. Even the roadside vendors of coconuts have been known to dump piles of coconut husks on the roadside or in fields instead of disposing of them properly. Dead animals and livestock manure are also an issue. In addition to making areas of Barbados unsightly, this can lead to odor. Some residents attempt to remedy the situation by burning refuse, but this is also environmentally damaging. The government has implemented a public education program to raise awareness of the problems that illegal dumping can cause and thereby encourage people to dump garbage in a responsible manner in the allocated places or to call the Sanitation Service

Illegal dumping and burning are big issues in Barbados. This bin delivers an important reminder.

Authority to arrange collection of items such as large furniture, tree stumps, and major household appliances that are not collected by the solid-waste collection trucks.

SOIL EROSION AND LANDSLIDES

In the twentieth century, Barbados suffered from eight landslides. These hazards were limited to the Scotland District, a region on the central east coast that consists of Saint Andrew Parish, most of Saint Joseph Parish, and part of Saint John Parish. The area covers one-seventh of the island and is made up of alternating beds of weak sandstone and shale that is highly weathered. Heavy rainfall increases groundwater instability, which in turn causes slope movement. In 1901, there was a landslide in Boscobelle when heavy rain resulted in the movement of a 642-acre (260-hectare) piece of land, destroying approximately eighty homes. The Scotland District Conservation Scheme, established in 1957, was set up to address the issue of soil erosion, and as a result, several communities have been relocated to less susceptible areas of the island. Hurricane season is a particularly vulnerable time for landslide conditions.

SHIPS AND POLLUTION

Pollution from the growing number of cruise ships, oil tankers, and other vessels visiting the island poses an increasing threat to the health and prosperity of Barbados. Shipping can harm the environment as a result of accidents in which oil and other pollutants are released, or even as a result of irresponsible actions by the ships' captains or owners. Cruise ships, with thousands of people on board, generate a lot of waste on a daily basis. Apart from oil, wastes include dirty water from dishwashers and clothes washers, sewage, plastic, paper, glass, and toxic substances such as tributyltin (TBT), a key ingredient in antifouling marine paint, and chemicals from film processing. These may enter the sea with an accumulative impact on people, coral reefs and other wildlife, and the scenic beauty of the coastline that attracts tourists in the first place. There have been quantities of tar balls, the result of oil spills and discharge, found on the windward beaches of Barbados.

OZZY OZONE TAKES ON THE ENVIRONMENT

In 1997, Barbados sought to improve public awareness of the necessity to protect the ozone layer, and the character of Ozzy Ozone was born. A local artist, Guy O'Neal, created the printed cartoon series. Ozzy Ozone has been reproduced on posters, key rings, erasers, pencils, mouse pads, pens, stickers, rulers, and refrigerator magnets. Ozzy became so successful that soon the character left Barbados and went global as the spokes-cartoon for the United Nations Environmental Programme (UNEP).

THE WATER SUPPLY

Drinking water in Barbados is in short supply because of damage to water infrastructure as well as drought.

Droughts and water shortages affect both crop production and livestock in Barbados. Lack of water can cause death and disease in both plant and animal life, leading to food shortages. Barbados is one of the top ten most water-stressed countries in the world.

Climate change is leading to drought conditions not only in Barbados but in many parts of the Caribbean. When the economy suffers because of drought, it becomes more difficult to fix the water infrastructure, often leading to salinization of water supplies in certain parts of Barbados.

In the country, household and industrial waste contaminating the water supply is a real threat, and decreasing quantities of freshwater for agriculture and drinking are a major concern, with Barbados officially listed as a "water-scarce country." Tourism, which brings a large number of visitors to the island, creates more of a problem, as do tourist facilities such as golf courses that need plenty of water. Tourist resorts use more water than comparable residential areas, so the use of water needs to be carefully managed.

One solution for the water crisis is a reduction in greenhouse gas emissions. Barbados is also active in attempting to overcome the water shortage by using advanced technologies such as reverse osmosis to obtain freshwater from seawater.

INTERNATIONAL AGREEMENTS

Barbados is party to a number of international environmental agreements, including the Convention on Biological Diversity, the Convention on International Trade in Endangered Species, the United Nations Convention to Combat Desertification, the Law of the Sea Convention, the Basel Convention on Hazardous Waste, the Ramsar Convention on Wetlands, and the Kyoto Protocol. The Paris Agreement of 2015 also seeks to help curb climate change. This alliance of 196 nations, including Barbados, allows countries to set their own goals for lowering carbon emissions and maintaining ecosystems that support biodiversity. Barbados's action plan includes lowering greenhouse gas emissions by 44 percent by 2030.

INTERNET LINKS

http://www.barbadosseaturtles.org
Follow the latest Barbados Sea Turtle Project news on the organization's website.

http://www.sciencemag.org/news/2018/06/mysterious-masses-seaweed-assault-caribbean-islands
Science magazine's website has additional information about sargassum seaweed, including a map of the most affected areas.

https://www.youtube.com/watch?v=owvlobgqRqk
Ozzy Ozone's cartoons can be viewed on YouTube.

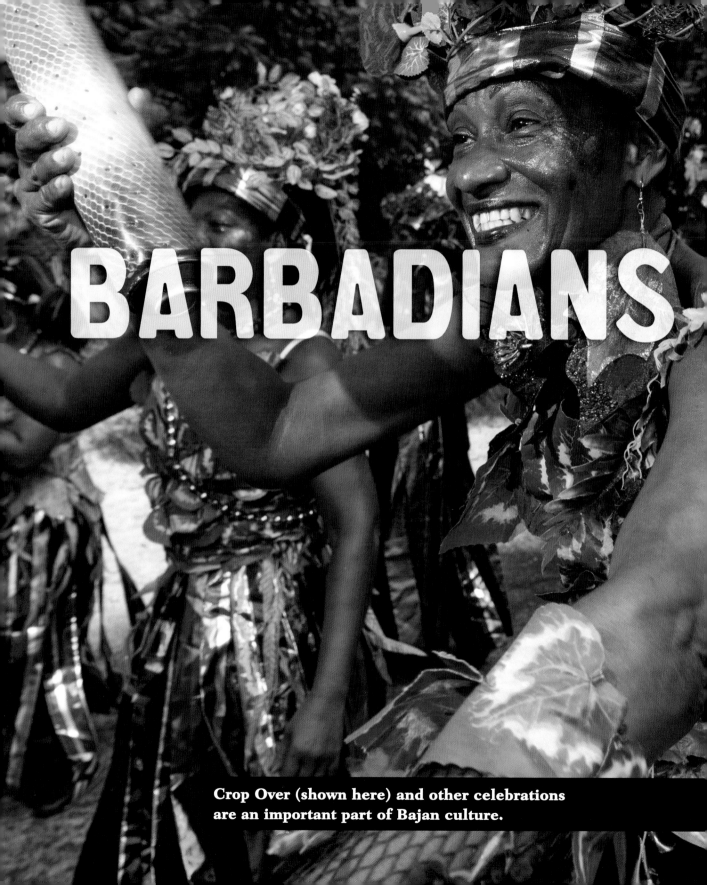

BARBADIANS

Crop Over (shown here) and other celebrations
are an important part of Bajan culture.

. . . .
"The people of
Barbados are this
little island's best-
kept asset."
—Totally Barbados

BARBADOS MIGHT BE A SMALL island, but it has many people living there. In fact, the population of over 292,300 lives on just 166 square miles (430 sq km) of land. This makes it one of the most densely populated countries in the world.

Barbadians come from many walks of life. More than 92.4 percent are direct descendants of slaves from Africa. Another 3.1 percent are mixed race, while 2.7 percent are white, and 1.3 percent are of full or partial Indian ancestry. (The remaining 0.5 percent are classified as "other" or "unspecified.") Barbadians are thus a multiethnic people, with Afro-Bajans, Anglo-Bajans of English or Scottish descent, Euro-Bajans, Bajan Jews, Bajan Muslims, Bajan Hindus, and even Arab-Bajans from Syria and Lebanon.

One-third of the population lives in the urban region that stretches along the sheltered west coast of the island from Speightstown in the north to Oistins in the south. The remainder lives in numerous villages and hamlets, ranging in size from one hundred to a few thousand people, scattered throughout the countryside. Many people live in the parish of Saint Michael, and eighty-nine thousand in the capital city of Bridgetown.

THE WEALTH GAP

As the original forest cover was replaced by fields of sugarcane, Barbados changed and the island became densely settled. The landed elite considered itself an aristocracy. Below this plantocracy in the social structure were hundreds of small-farm families, traditionally called the yeomanry. Below

them was a class of wage laborers, peasants, and unemployed vagrants made up of white indentured servants who had been displaced by black slavery.

Although intermarriages were few, interracial relationships between white planters and black slaves were common. The children from these unions often had lighter skin and were treated better than those with darker skin. This created a new class of Bajans.

In Barbados, a wide gap between the very wealthy and the very poor has existed for centuries. Although this gap has narrowed since the days of slavery, the contrast between the luxurious mansions of the wealthy and the small chattel houses of the poor remains significant, as does the difference in lifestyles.

The island's history and economic development have been dominated by about twenty families who still rank among Barbados's elite today. The great

Rights for lesbian, gay, bisexual, transgender, and queer (LGBTQ) people in Barbados are a slow work in progress. Certain laws make homosexual acts illegal and punishable by a life sentence, although the law has not been enforced in many years. The LGBTQ community is small but welcoming. Barbados Gays & Lesbians Against Discrimination (B-GLAD) and Equals Inc. are two organizations fighting for the rights of Barbados's LGBTQ residents. The first pride march took place in Bridgetown in July 2018.

wealth of these families was built on growing sugarcane on huge plantations. The island (which they called Bimshire) was their home, and unlike other West Indian planters, very few of these plantation owners were absentee landlords. Instead they assumed the role of lord of the manor and recreated patterns of English country life. Today many of their houses bear British names, and they continue to dominate the commercial and economic life of the island. Other millionaires and billionaires from all over the world have also made Barbados their home away from home.

REDLEGS

Before the slave trade brought Africans to Barbados to work on the sugar plantations, the island's labor force consisted of white indentured servants, many of whom were inmates of English jails and royalists who had been captured and imprisoned during the English Civil War. These people were sometimes referred to as "redlegs." This was because their legs would turn red from sunburn. Many of their descendants still live on the island.

The contracts of the indentured servants were sold to planters on arrival in Barbados, where the conditions of their servitude were often no better than slavery. When their indentures ended, some left the island. Those who remained lived in villages on the inhospitable eastern side of the island, where they survived by fishing and hunting turtles and crabs.

Sometimes planters, embarrassed to see them so destitute, provided schools, jobs, and even clubs for them. To keep the poor whites in the city from delinquency, the Young Men's Progressive Club (YMPC) was established in the 1920s. There they could play cricket, soccer, and indoor games, attend lectures, and benefit from cultural programs. The earliest Caribbean literary magazine, *Bim*, was started by Frank Collymore and Therold Barnes, early members of the YMPC and both descendants of poor whites.

INTERRACIAL COUPLES

In the past, white planters often had relationships with black mistresses or "outside" women, but accepting black or mixed-race individuals socially was another matter, and racial discrimination was practiced in commerce and in the civil service. Today, although attitudes are changing, Bajan whites and blacks tend to not marry one another. Most of the interracial couples seen on the island are foreigners.

AFRO-BARBADIANS

Slaves primarily from villages in West Africa were brought to Barbados from the seventeenth to nineteenth centuries, and their direct descendants who still live on the island are often referred to as Afro-Barbadian or Afro-Bajan.

Many Afro-Barbadians were sent overseas in World War II, and by the 1960s, politicians who had spent part of their life abroad were proud to be black and Bajan. Leaders such as Errol Barrow, who had been a World War II airman and trained in London as a lawyer and economist, and Sir Grantley Adams,

The following excerpt from Bruce St. John's Bumbatuk 1 *reveals the sense of unity and national pride that exists in Barbados today:*

All o'we is Bajan!
Bajan to de backbone ...
Bajan black, Bajan white,
Bajan hair curly, Bajan hair straight,
Yo' brother red, yo' sister brown
Yo' mother light-skin, yo' father cob skin ...

another London-trained lawyer, worked toward independence for Barbados. Sir Arleigh Winston Scott, an Afro-Barbadian who had trained as a doctor in the United States, in 1967 became the first native governor-general of Barbados.

Today, Afro-Barbadian heritage shines through during festivals and in music and dance styles of Barbados. Many insist on respect for their hard-won culture. African traditions and folklore have been resurrected, and schoolchildren are encouraged to read the African-inspired poetry of Edward Kamau Brathwaite and the writings of George Lamming, Bruce St. John, and others who have explored the meanings of being Bajan in literary forms.

THE NEW FACES OF BARBADOS

In the last century, there has been an influx of immigrants from India, Pakistan, and Lebanon, as well as from the United States, Canada, Great Britain, Germany, South America, and even China. Immigrants from India and their descendants make up 1.3 percent of the population. People move to Barbados for a number of reasons: business opportunities, a change of pace, or even just getting to experience life on one of the most laid-back islands in the Caribbean. A few (around 144 individuals in 2016) are refugees

Passing along stories and heritage from parent to child is an important part of Bajan culture.

from other countries. As immigrants move into Barbados, they often maintain their own sense of culture and identity, creating pockets of cultural diversity across the island.

BARBADOS FASHION

Most Barbadians are stylish but conservative in their dress, in part because of British influence. Women vendors in the marketplaces, for example, often favor old-fashioned, matronly dresses and tie their hair up in handkerchiefs. Office workers, on the other hand, are often seen in high heels and tailored dresses or skirts and blouses. Skimpy clothes are frowned on in towns and are usually seen only at beach areas.

Even in the most rural areas, schoolchildren, both boys and girls, wear uniforms of pressed shirts and ties, with girls wearing their hair neatly braided and tied with color-coded ribbons. For social events such as weddings and parties, Barbadians love to dress up, and they always wear their Sunday best for church meetings.

FAMOUS BARBADIANS

One of the world's top cricket players, Bajan national hero Sir Garfield Sobers, was knighted by Queen Elizabeth II during her visit to Barbados in 1975. Another cricket hero, Sir Frank Worrell, who appears on the Bds$5 bill, was captain of the hugely successful West Indian team that toured Australia in 1960 and 1961. Worrell is buried in a prominently marked grave at the Cave Hill campus of the University of the West Indies.

Calypso artist Anthony Carter, better known as the Mighty Gabby, is famous for his songs of cultural identity and political protest that speak for emerging black pride throughout the Caribbean. Red Plastic Bag (born Stedson Wiltshire), also known as RPB or just Bag, is another calypsonian. He combines the sounds of soca and reggae, and his biggest hit, "Ragga Ragga," has been recorded in seven languages.

Frank Collymore is regarded as the founder of the Barbadian literary movement. George Lamming is an internationally recognized novelist and scholar. Karen Lord is the award-winning author of *The Best of All Possible Worlds*, *Redemption in Indigo*, and *The Galaxy Game*.

To date, the most recognizable Barbadian is pop singer Rihanna. Born Robyn Rihanna Fenty in Saint Michael's Parish, Rihanna once served in the Barbados Cadets Corp. Fellow R&B artist Shontelle was even her drill sergeant. In 2016, Rihanna achieved her fourteenth number-one hit since the start of her career, surpassing Michael Jackson's thirteen. (Only Mariah Carey and the Beatles have more.) Rihanna is also a successful entrepreneur, launching Fenty Beauty in 2017. The company earned $72 million in just one month following the launch. Fenty Beauty caters to a wider variety of makeup consumers, offering forty different shades of foundation.

Rihanna is the most famous person to grow up in Barbados.

INTERNET LINKS

https://barbados.org/people/index.htm#.W283LC-ZOqA
Barbados.org has profiles of some famous Barbadians.

https://www.pinknews.co.uk/2018/07/24/barbados-first-pride-parade
This website shows pictures from Barbados's first pride march in 2018.

http://www.rihannanow.com
Learn more about Rihanna, her music, and her line of beauty products on her website.

LIFESTYLE

Barbadian families are close. Most often, women are the heads of the family.

BARBADOS'S BRITISH PAST HAS given it a mixture of African and British heritage today. The latter predominates in institutional ways, including the form of government, education, and legal framework, but African influences remain strong in family life and in music and dance.

Supportive networks of female relatives, such as sisters, mothers, and daughters, are especially strong. These networks sometimes include male relatives such as uncles, brothers, cousins, and grandfathers as well. Many households in Barbados are headed by women, and the family home remains a place to which Barbadians can return at any time in their lives.

WEDDINGS AND MARRIAGE

Many women enter into a number of unions before settling down to marriage. Couples may start with a "visiting union," where the woman lives with her parents and is visited by her male companion. Sometimes the couple moves in together and eventually marries, but often they remain casual and eventually separate.

In addition to home and children, which are the main concerns for most women, marriage is an ultimate goal, even if the women have to wait many years. The average marrying age in Barbados is thirty-four for men and thirty-two for women. Bajan weddings were once grand affairs with no expense spared. Although elaborate receptions are not

"Healthy activities and lifestyle choices in Barbados are on the rise and our 'no stress' policy is essential to any healthy balanced lifestyle."
        —Totally Barbados

as common because of the rising cost of living, weddings are still important celebrations for Barbadians.

Weddings are usually held in a church on a Saturday afternoon. The bride is usually dressed in white lace, satin, or chiffon, and she may have as many as eight bridesmaids. The groom and his best man put on stylish, dark suits with orchid boutonnieres.

After the ceremony, the wedding party drives in procession to the reception, where, amid speech-making, the couple is toasted, and an elaborately decorated cake is served. This is usually followed by much dancing and feasting until about 11 p.m.

FAMILY DYNAMICS

For many generations, couples usually led relatively separate lives, even engaging in different leisure activities. Fathers took an interest in their children's education, but most believed that their primary responsibility was to provide financial support, even if they no longer lived with the children's mother. Family life was centered around the mother, who performed all the

Mothers and their children are normally close in Barbados. This woman braids her daughter's hair.

child-rearing tasks. Her relationship with her children was usually close and lasting.

Mothers also took their responsibilities seriously. They were often strict disciplinarians, insisting on good manners and respect for elders. Children were taught to use appropriate greetings when passing people on the road or on entering shops. Three-generation households, especially those consisting of grandmother, mother, and children, were common in Barbados.

Women-led families and the instillation of moral and social values remain today, but with increasing opportunities for women to work outside of the home, traditions are changing. An economy becoming less dependent on agriculture and growing into the manufacturing and tourism sectors allows for more women to seek jobs outside the home. Many are finding employment in managerial and technical industries. Today, 65 percent of women work, compared to 77 percent of men.

As previously mentioned, couples are marrying later in life, and both usually continue working. Most rely on a relative, such as the grandmother, to help out with their children, although a fortunate few may be able to afford a housekeeper. Contraception, now generally accepted and easily available, limits the number of children. And relationships between men and women are improving, with men offering more emotional support and help with childrearing than in the past.

DEATH AND FUNERALS

Regardless of their religious affiliation, most Bajans consider funeral attendance important. Funerals start around 4 p.m. and follow a set ritual. The open coffin is placed near the entrance of the church. Close relatives stand on one side, while other mourners file past the body. Pamphlets detailing hymns to be sung and other procedures to be followed are handed out. The coffin is then closed and wheeled farther into the church for the service, which includes hymns, prayers, the officiating priest's address, and a eulogy by a close friend of the deceased. As the last hymn is sung, the coffin is turned around and wheeled feet first to the door. Pallbearers carry it to the cemetery or into a hearse, which leads a procession of vehicles to the cemetery.

Funerals are attended for a variety of reasons—the deceased might be a relative, a neighbor, a casual or job-related acquaintance, or a close friend. Ensuring that the funeral has a good turnout, especially if the death occurred in unusual circumstances, is important. The black clothes that were once required wear at funerals have been replaced by subdued or darker colors. Wearing bright colors to a funeral is considered a sign of disrespect. Nowadays, a get-together is usually held after the funeral, during which a variety of food and drink is served. There is no dancing or music, but loud talk and laughter may continue for several hours, serving to relieve temporarily the sadness of the bereaved.

Some Barbadians believe that the dead can convey messages to their kin through dreams. They hold wakes called nine-nights to ensure that the soul has a safe journey to the next world. They may also conduct ceremonies to communicate with the dead in the hope that the dead will rectify problems they may have caused while alive.

"The funeral is a ceremony of proven worth and value for those who mourn. It provides an opportunity for the survivors and others who share in the loss to express their love, respect, grief and appreciation for a life that has been lived."
–On Funeral Etiquette, Tudor's Funeral Home, Barbados

HOMES AND ARCHITECTURE

A high percentage of houses in Barbados are occupied by the owners. Almost all households have running water; only about 1 percent do not. In kitchens, 96 percent of homes have stoves, and 94 percent have refrigerators. Sixty-nine percent of homeowners enjoy the convenience of a washing machine. Modern houses are often built from concrete. Many new residential estates for the middle class have sprung up, where satellite dishes and solar panels on the roof are not unusual.

Chattel houses are a popular style of home in Barbados.

Modest chattel house—style homes continue to be popular today. Traditionally, this type of house was home to slaves. They were not allowed to own land, and therefore their homes were built to be moved easily. The foundations usually consist of stones, and the walls of the houses are weathered planks. Traditionally, each window has three wooden shutters called jalousies, two hinged at the sides and one hinged from above to allow for flexibility in adjusting to sun and wind. Some chattel houses look weather-beaten and neglected, while others have been given a fresh coat of brightly colored paint.

Barbados also has several plantation houses, most of which have been taken over by the Barbados National Trust. The lifestyle that created these grand homes no longer exists on the island, and the houses are now mainly of historical interest.

The planation Bush Hill House, once visited by George Washington, still stands today.

Walls of plantation homes were built thick, and roofs were designed to withstand winds in case of a hurricane. Saint Nicholas Abbey in the parish of Saint Peter is the oldest house on the island and one of only three remaining examples of Jacobean architecture in the Americas. The house is believed to have been built in the 1650s. The interior, filled with beautiful antiques and paintings, offers a glimpse of plantation life during those early years.

The Drax Hall Estate in the parish of Saint George is another fine example of Jacobean architecture. The plantation, one of the first to cultivate sugarcane on a large scale, is the only estate to have stayed in the same family since the seventeenth century. It is not open to tourists, as it is a private residence.

Sunbury Plantation House in the parish of Saint Philip is now a museum, with a unique collection of plantation artifacts and tools, such as antique plows and cane carts, on its grounds.

SCHOOLING

Barbadians have one of the highest literacy rates in the world, estimated at 99.7 percent. School attendance is compulsory for all children between the ages of five and sixteen, and all government schools, both elementary and secondary, are free.

Pupils between five and eleven years of age attend the more than ninety public and private primary schools in Barbados. Children under five years of age go to nursery schools, of which there are ten publicly available. Primary school pupils graduate to secondary school when they reach the age of eleven.

Education is important in Barbados. It helps with childhood development and learning and prepares individuals for a chosen career.

IRVING WILSON

Irving Wilson was a teacher in Barbados who dedicated many years of his career to helping special-needs students. He went on to found and serve as the first principal of the School for the Deaf and Blind, now the Irving Wilson School. He believed strongly in the idea that "disability is not inability." In 2014, he celebrated his ninety-sixth birthday. To commemorate the special occasion, he was honored with a performance at the school, which he attended with his daughter, son, and granddaughter. He died in 2015.

Regardless of their social and economic background, all children in elementary school receive low-cost meals supplied by the government.

The goal of nursery schools in Barbados is to help in personality development, offering both creative and science-based learning, reading, writing, and arts and crafts. Primary school students learn reading, writing, important problem-solving skills, health, music, art, languages, and more.

Students between the ages of eleven and eighteen are enrolled either in one of the twenty-two government-run secondary schools or in one of the nine private secondary schools.

The goal of secondary schooling is to help students prepare for future careers by giving them the necessary tools in literacy, public speaking, and mathematics.

Children with developmental delays, physical impairment, or other disabilities are educated both at special schools or often in specially equipped classrooms. Seven public primary schools in Barbados offer these types of classrooms. Hearing and vision-impaired students and some autistic learners attend the Irving Wilson School in Bridgetown. Programs have been developed to help students get the type of education best suited to their needs.

After the age of eighteen, upon completion of secondary school, students may choose to continue on to higher education. The Erdiston Teachers' College, opened in 1948, provides training for aspiring teachers. Samuel Jackman Prescod Institute of Technology provides training for the electrical, building, and engineering trades; commercial and agricultural studies; and human ecology,

which includes cosmetology and home economics. The Barbados Community College offers a wide range of academic, vocational, and technical programs, including fine arts, health sciences, liberal arts, and science.

The government also pays the tuition fees of all Barbadians at the Cave Hill campus of the University of the West Indies, but the student is responsible for a university registration fee each semester. The University of West Indies offers courses in arts, natural sciences, social sciences, and law, as well as advanced education for adults at the extramural center. The Cave Hill campus is linked to the university's two other main campuses, in Jamaica and Trinidad, via an online network that allows teleconferencing and distance teaching. In 2009, it began its first open campus, which provides opportunities for students outside the main campuses to access learning at forty physical sites situated in sixteen other Caribbean countries. Barbados also has several secretarial colleges, vocational colleges, and language institutes.

Codrington College (shown here) is a theology school in Barbados. It has trained many men who have passed through its doors over the years.

HEALTH CARE

Barbadians enjoy a high standard of health care. Several government polyclinics offer health services, including maternity and child care, family planning, health education, school health services, control of communicable diseases, and environmental health. The Winston Scott Polyclinic, the island's largest polyclinic, has facilities for X-rays, yellow-fever surveillance, bacteriological analysis, and food testing, as well as an eye clinic and a skin-disease center. Treatment and medication at these walk-in clinics are free for all Bajans. Drug benefits offer free medications to people with chronic illness and everyone over the age of sixty-five and under the age of sixteen.

Many Barbadians receive medical treatment at the Queen Elizabeth Hospital in Bridgetown.

Vaccines are also provided for free for many of the island's residents, although not all vaccines are covered by the government. The hepatitis B vaccine, for instance, is free to medical students and babies only. Visitors to the island often need to be vaccinated against hepatitis A and typhoid, which can spread through tainted foods. There is also a small risk of Zika virus (spread by mosquitos) on Barbados, since an outbreak there in 2016. Preventative measures have been taken to help people avoid infection by advising visitors and residents to use mosquito nets while sleeping and use insect repellent regularly.

TRADITIONAL MEDICINE

Although modern medicine has superseded traditional folk cures, many Bajans still turn to the indigenous plants and herbs originally used in teas and cures by the early migrants and to the bush medicine brought over from Africa by their ancestors.

The Rastafarian movement also prefers natural cures, further extending the range of Barbadian folk medicine. Coconut water, sold by Rastafarians on street corners, is regarded as a preventative and a cure for illnesses of the kidney and the bladder. Similarly, coconut oil can be rubbed on the head to break up a cold or into the scalp to loosen dandruff two days before washing the hair.

The pawpaw, as the papaya is known on the island, has many uses. It helps bowel movement and can help reduce hypertension, or high blood pressure, when eaten green, in two small, cooked slices. To prevent infection, many Bajans apply several thin slices over a cut and then bandage them into place for two or three days.

The cactus-like aloe plant also has many uses. To ease colds, irritated throats, and constipation, a small piece of the inner pith is swallowed with a pinch of salt. Aloe slices can be bandaged onto cuts to aid healing, and for sunburn one side of a piece of aloe is peeled and the cool inside is rubbed over the affected area. It is extremely soothing and can even stop the skin from peeling.

This aloe plant is located in the Flower Forest Botanical Gardens in Barbados.

A bitter green brew made from the circee bush is used to reduce fevers and relieve influenza symptoms. Wonder-of-the-world, when chewed with a pinch of salt, is believed to relieve mild attacks of asthma.

Many Barbadians also believe that planting and growing your own food is key to the healing process.

INTERNET LINKS

https://barbados.org/architec.htm#.W3Brxi-ZOqA
Barbados.org offers more information on types of architecture and home design.

https://www.barbadoschildrendirectory.com/primary-schools
Learn more about the education system in Barbados and see a complete list of schools on the Barbados Children Directory website.

RELIGION

People gather for Sunday worship at the Diamond Corner New Testament Church in Barbados.

BARBADOS'S OUTLOOK ON RELIGION has changed over the centuries. In the early days, despite an official policy of religious tolerance, many religious groups were treated badly. Catholics, Jews, and nonconformist Protestants were discriminated against and kept from all seats of political power. Today, some 66.4 percent of the population is Protestant. Leading Protestant denominations include Anglican, Pentecostal, and Adventist. Other Christian groups, such as Roman Catholics, have a presence too. In addition, there are followers of more than one hundred other religions, denominations, and sects in Barbados, such as Rastafarians, Jews, Muslims, and Hindus.

"Barbados is spiritually alive. it vibrates with enlightenment and vitality."

—Barbados.org

There are more than one hundred established religions on the island of Barbados, and most families attend some type of religious gathering at least once a week. Most Christians go to church. The Anglican churches established in the seventeenth century are some of the largest places of worship on the island, but some gatherings take place in halls or even houses.

THE ANGLICAN CHURCH

Today, Anglicanism is the largest Christian faith in Barbados. Over 23 percent of Barbadians identify as Anglican. This faith was first created in the 1500s, when King Henry VIII of England divorced his wife, Catherine of Aragon, and married Anne Boleyn. To do this, he separated from the Catholic Church and established his own, closely related religion, which the monarch led.

In early colonial Barbados, Anglican clergymen were an important element in the plantocracy that dominated public life and all civic organizations,

Easter kites line a wall here in Saint Philip's parish. Kite flying is a popular Easter activity in Barbados.

fashioning social ideologies based on white, Anglo-Saxon Anglicans. It was not until 1797 that Anglican ministers were allowed to offer slaves some religious training. Later, Anglican religious training became part of the preparation for emancipation.

Anglicanism endured centuries as the official religion in Barbados. Its parish churches once dominated rural life, but this is less true today. Anglicans in Barbados are adherents of the Church in the Province of the West Indies.

OTHER PROTESTANTS

The first Methodist missionaries arrived in Barbados in the late eighteenth century and initially struggled to spread their faith in the face of repression. In 1823, their church was destroyed, and proclamations threatening to abolish Methodism were posted in Bridgetown. Led by Sarah Ann Gill, however, the Methodists resisted. After the Emancipation Act was passed, Methodist ranks were swelled by the newly freed slaves. Today there are several Methodist churches on the island, and 4.2 percent of Barbadians practice the faith.

The Moravian Church is the oldest Protestant religion in the world. The church became known for supporting slaves under its leader Benjamin Brookshaw, and in 1816 its members were granted virtual immunity from the terror of the slave revolt. Today, at 1.2 percent of the population, Moravians in Barbados are predominantly black.

Similar to the other non-Anglican faiths, Catholicism was suppressed in Barbados before the nineteenth century. The first Catholic church in Barbados was built in 1848. Catholics are a small minority on the island, at 3.8 percent of the population.

Locals refer to the followers of the indigenous Apostolic Spiritual Baptist religion, founded by Bishop Granville Williams in 1957, as Tie-Heads. They wear colorful gowns of different hues symbolizing particular qualities, and all tie cloths around their heads. During services, lively music is accompanied by foot stomping, hand clapping, and dancing. Baptists make up 1.8 percent of Barbadians.

There is a small percentage of Muslims living on Barbados, around two thousand individuals. The first to arrive in 1913 was a silk merchant named Abdul Rohul Amin from West Bengal, India. (While the main religion of India is Hinduism, 14.2 percent of Indians practice Islam.) Over the years, more and more Bengalis arrived, some of them marrying locals and starting families whose descendants still live on the island today. These new citizens found a foothold in Barbados as traveling traders who helped to bring necessary goods to the poorer rural regions of Barbados.

The Barbados Muslim Association was founded in 1997, with the goal of representing those who practice Islam across Barbados. Today, there are five mosques on Barbados where its Muslim residents can gather. However, acceptance of Islam has been slow to take hold there. The wearing of the hijab by Muslim women is one issue facing challenges. In May 2018, a teacher named Nafiesa Nakhid was asked to remove her hijab since it violated school rules. Many Muslim women attempting to get a government identification card are asked to remove their headwraps for the photo. Nevertheless, some progress is being made. In 2016, many Barbadian women took part in World Hijab Day, wearing the religious headscarf to help highlight the struggle of Muslims.

THE RASTAFARIAN MOVEMENT

The Rastafarian movement began in Jamaica in the 1920s when Marcus Garvey advocated a back-to-Africa ideal and urged his followers to "look to Africa, when a black king shall be crowned, for the day of deliverance is at hand." Then in Ethiopia in 1930, Ras Tafari, who claimed to be a direct descendant of the biblical King David and the 225th in an unbroken line of Ethiopian kings from the time of Solomon and Sheba, was crowned Emperor Haile Selassie I, "King of Kings, Lord of Lords, and the Conquering Lion of the Tribe of Judah." This last title inspired the dreadlocks and the strutting walk by which Rastafarians became identified.

The Rastafarian movement began in Jamaica and spread to Barbados.

Introduced in Barbados in 1975, the movement spread quickly and for a time attracted undesirable elements, such as criminals and rebellious youths who used it as an excuse to smoke marijuana, which is considered a sacrament among Rastafarians. This made the movement unpopular with more conservative Barbadians. In due course, however, the fad died down, and some of the remaining Rastafarians have made names for themselves in sports and the arts. One percent of Barbadians are practicing Rastafarians today.

SUPERSTITION AND FOLKTALES

The lack of Christian missionaries in the early days enabled slaves to retain African folk beliefs and superstitions, some of which still exist. A few are listed here:

Obeah practitioners often practice their craft on the streets for passersby.

OBEAH, similar to the voodoo practices of Haiti, is a form of witchcraft believed to have originated from a West African religion called Obi. The practice of obeah was brought to the Caribbean by slaves, and practitioners continue to pass down its teachings through word of mouth today. The wider use of obeah is mostly shrouded in secrecy, but those who practice it claim it can be used for healing, to ward off evil, or to bring luck through spells and potions. Come-to-me sauce is an obeah potion believed to make the woman who administers it irresistibly attractive to her victim. Stay-at-home sauce is said to discourage husbands from straying. During the era of slavery, obeah made white slave owners nervous because of harmful spells and poison making. To allay fears, laws were passed in the early nineteenth century that forbade the possession of poisons or any potentially poisonous substance.

DUPPIES (DOO-PEES), or spirits of the dead, are supposed to roam the earth at night. To prevent them from entering homes, people hang herbs in the windows and doorways and scatter sand around the house. This forces the duppy to stop and count each grain, which keeps them busy until daylight. Sprinkling a few drops from a new rum bottle on the ground for the spirits remains a Barbadian tradition. Duppy dust—grave dirt or pulverized human bones—is supposed to be fatal when thrown on a victim or put in his or her food.

CONRADS (KON-RADS), or avenging ghosts, are said to take possession of their victims' bodies and shout nasty things in strange voices.

BACCOOS (BAH-KOOS), bestowers of good or evil depending on the amount of attention they get, are tiny men said to often live in bottles.

CHURCHES AND OTHER PLACES OF WORSHIP

Saint Michael's Anglican Cathedral in Bridgetown was completed in 1789. An earlier version of the church, built in the 1600s, was leveled by the hurricane of 1780. The current cathedral seats 1,600 people. It also has the largest pipe organ in the Caribbean. Many island notables are buried in the adjacent churchyard, including Sir Grantley Adams, first premier of Barbados and head of the West Indies Federation from 1958 to 1962, and his son, Tom, who was prime minister from 1976 to 1985.

Saint Michael's Cathedral in Bridgetown was first built in 1628 and rebuilt several times to keep the structure standing through the centuries.

The original Barbados Synagogue in Bridgetown was built in 1654 by Jews from Recife, Brazil. Persecuted by the Dutch, they settled in Barbados and, being skilled in the sugar industry, quickly introduced the crop and passed on their skills to local landowners. The synagogue, destroyed by a hurricane in 1831, was rebuilt in 1833 but abandoned in 1929. The distinctive white building has been restored in the past several years. An official Synagogue Historic District opened in April 2017 to allow people to visit the area's historical buildings.

Saint James Parish Church, just north of the Holetown town center, is the site of the region's oldest church. The original building, built in 1660, was replaced by a more substantial structure in the mid-nineteenth century, but a few vestiges of the original remain, including a bell inscribed with the name of King William cast in the late 1600s.

Other places of Christian worship include the Emmanuel Baptist Church, the First Church of Christian Scientists, and the Roman Catholic Saint Patrick's Cathedral (all in Saint Michael), and the Anglican Saint Lawrence, the Methodist Hawthorne Memorial, the Bethlehem Moravian, and the Roman Catholic Saint Dominic's (all in Christ Church). There are five mosques spread across Barbados where Muslims gather for congregational prayers, the largest of which is the Jumma Masjid in Bridgetown.

INTERNET LINKS

http://anglican.bb/Content/?documents
Learn more about the Anglican Church of Barbados on the organization's website.

https://scholar.library.miami.edu/slaves/Religion/religion.html
Read more about obeah on the University of Miami website.

https://synagoguehistoricdistrict.com
The Synagogue Historic District has its own website where readers can see pictures of the area and plan a visit.

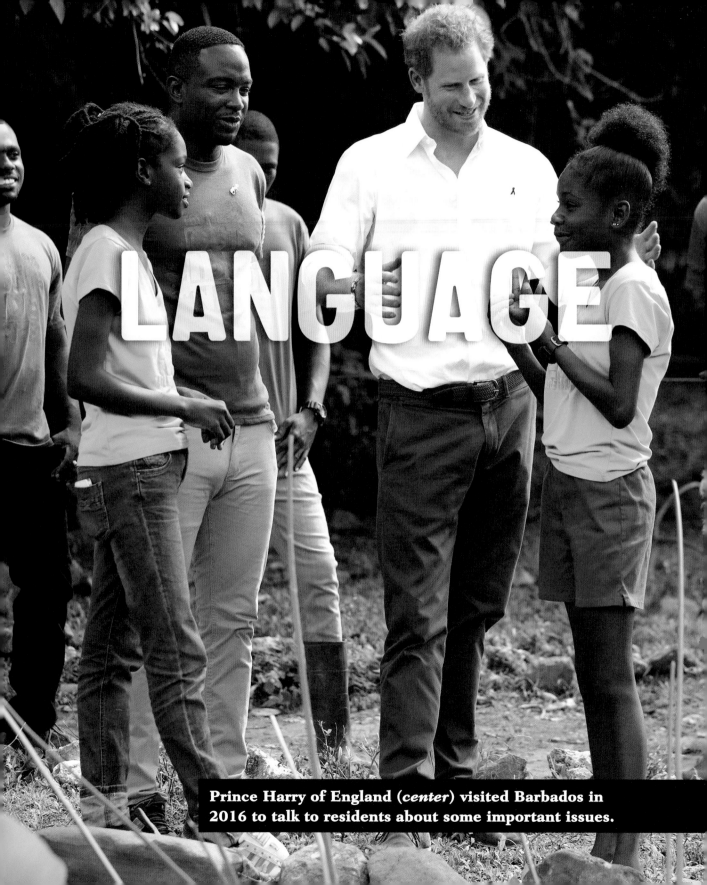

LANGUAGE

Prince Harry of England (*center*) visited Barbados in 2016 to talk to residents about some important issues.

THE OFFICIAL LANGUAGE OF Barbados is English, but many Bajans speak a dialect of the English language derived from their West African slave ancestors mixed with British English, resulting in the colorful and expressive dialect, or patois, called Bajan. Speech is fast paced, and many colorful turns of phrase are incorporated, which can make it hard to understand for some nonnative speakers. Bajan, like other Caribbean dialects, was long dismissed as the language of the illiterate, restricted to the kitchen and the backyard. However, growing pride in black heritage and the emergence of Barbadian writers, poets, and linguists has proved that Bajan has a beauty of its own.

English's history developed gradually in Barbados. Originally, African expressions were translated literally into English but pronounced with African intonations. The English influence slowly became stronger,

"Bajan dialect is a unique language of Barbados. Its origin dates back to the times when slaves were brought to Barbados and forced to speak English."
—Barbados Pocket Guide

boy, girl . . . . *commonly used by islanders when addressing adults as well as children*

cheese on bread . . . . *wow*

go so, swing so . . . . *used in giving directions (combined with hand movements that must be watched because they are a visual reference to the direction!)*

licking ya mout . . . . *talking too much*

limin' (also lime, lime about) . . . *hanging out; relaxing*

no problem . . . . *all-purpose response to any request*

one time . . . . *immediately; right away*

study . . . . *take time to consider; think about*

wine . . . . *dance movement of winding the hips, essential to carnival dancing*

workin' up . . . . *dancing in general*

These two Speightstown residents enjoy a conversation on a pleasant day in Barbados.

however. Today, in addition to English, Barbadians often learn other languages in order to communicate with tourists and other visitors to the island. French and Spanish are frequently taught in schools.

BAJAN AND ENGLISH

The following poem by Bruce St. John serves as an example of the Bajan language:

BAJAN	ENGLISH
We' language limit?	Is our language limited?
Who language en limit?	Whose language isn't limited?
Evah language.	Every language
Like a big pot o' Bajan soup	Like a big pot of Bajan soup
Piece o' yam, piece o' potato	Piece of yam, piece of potato
T'ree dumplin', two eddoe.	Three dumplings, two eddoes
One beet, two carrot.	One beet, two carrots

Piece o' pigtail, piece o' beef	Piece of pigtail, piece of beef
Pinch o' salt, dus' o' pepper	Pinch of salt, dusting of pepper
An' don' fuget okra	And don't forget okra
To add to de flavor	To add to the flavor
Boil up, cook up, eat up	Boil it, cook it all together, eat it up
An' yuh still wan' rice	And you still want rice

From this comparison, the following can be deduced:

• In Bajan the same form of pronoun can be used as subject, object, or possessive: "we know," "tell we" (tell us), and "we language" (our language).

• A statement becomes a question only by the use of a different intonation.

• Endings such as -ed are left out, and in general, words often have the last letter unpronounced, and no s needs to be added to indicate plurality.

There is no th sound in Bajan, and it can be replaced by any of the following: f, v, t, d, z, or k:

Breathe becomes	breav
With	wit, wid, or wif
Clothe.	cloze or clove
Think	t'ink
The	de
Strengthen.	strengken or strengfen

Bajans use the present tense even for past actions and express "habitual" actions by saying something "does" happen. Instead of using the word "very," Bajans say something is "pretty, pretty, pretty" or "real p-r-e-t-t-y," with great emphasis placed on the word pretty.

STORYTELLING AND MYTHS

Bajans love to entertain one another with ghost stories, and myths and legends from African sources are part of everyday conversation. Folktales and songs combine legend, history, religion, and local events. They can be educational, as they often contain a moral, or purely entertaining, or sometimes both. The West

THE NATIONAL ANTHEM OF BARBADOS

The Barbados national anthem is important to the country's citizens since their fight for independence was such a difficult and lengthy struggle. The music was composed by C. Van Roland Edwards, who had no formal training but had been writing music since his childhood. The lyrics were written by Irving Burgie, an American composer whose mother was from Barbados. Burgie's lyrics are below:

> In plenty and in time of need
> When this fair land was young
> Our brave forefathers sowed the seed
> From which our pride is sprung
> A pride that makes no wanton boast
> Of what it has withstood
> That binds our hands from coast to coast
> The Pride of Nationhood
> We loyal sons and daughters all
> Do hereby make it known
> These fields and hills beyond recall
> Are now our very own
> We write our name on history's page
> With expectations great
> Strict guardians of our heritage
> Firm craftsmen of our fate.
> The Lord has been the people's guide
> For past three hundred years
> With him still on the people's side
> We have no doubts or fears
> Upward and onward we shall go
> Inspired, exulting, free
> And greater will our nation grow
> In strength and unity.

African "Anancy" folktales inspired the phrase "nancy story," implying a tall tale or a lie. A mother might say to her children, "Don't give me no nancy story!"

The following is a Bajan folktale: A sick man visits a metaphysician in Bridgetown. The practitioner explains that pain and illness exist only in the mind, and all the sick person has to do to get well is to "affirm and believe" that the pain has gone. The sick man follows the practitioner's advice and recovers his health. When the practitioner asks for his fees, his patient tells him, "Wha' fees? All you have to do is affirm and believe dat you have receive de fees, and you have dem."

Greetings are important to Barbadians. This man tries out a friendly salute.

GREETINGS AND BODY LANGUAGE

Barbadians consider it impolite not to greet someone with "good morning," "good afternoon," or "good evening" when passing him or her on the road or entering a shop. Handshakes and smiles are exchanged on meeting. Sometimes acquaintances will embrace one another. Bajans often wave their hands to greet a passing friend, while conversing to emphasize a point, or merely to call a passing taxi or bus. Folded arms indicate that complete attention is being given to the matter under discussion, but standing with hands on hips usually shows defiance. Puckered lips producing a *chupse* sound express disgust. During a discussion, a Barbadian might say "For true?" which is an equivalent of the American phrase "For real?" "Kawblema!" is a Bajan way of saying "Oh my goodness!" To say goodbye, Barbadians say "Goodbye" or "See ya!"

LIBRARIES

In the early part of the eighteenth century, it was said that "everything was imported into Barbados except books." A literary society was established in 1777 and a library association in 1814, but both were private organizations for members only.

"When a noisy cricket enters the house it indicates that money is coming to the house. Therefore, you must not kill, or evict, the insect—let it be and good fortune will come to you and your home."
-On Bajan Beliefs, Totally Barbados

The public library in Bridgetown is one of eight that can be found around the island.

In 1847, three years before the first Public Libraries Act was passed in Britain, an act was passed in Barbados establishing a public library and museum on the island. However, the library was considered to be "miserably deficient in every branch of literature" by Greville John Chester, an English author and clergyman who spent some months on the island in 1867 and 1868. The National Library Service headquarters on Bridgetown's Coleridge Street, paid for by the Scottish-American philanthropist Andrew Carnegie on condition that it should always be maintained as a free library, was opened in 1906. Today, the headquarters in Bridgetown is joined by seven additional library branches spread across the island. Both locals and visitors can sign up for membership.

STAYING IN TOUCH

Barbados is one of the most wired countries in the world when it comes to telephone infrastructure, telecommunications, and the internet. The island is on its way to providing universal Wi-Fi access. The main internet service providers

These payphones provided by Flow stand at the ready in Christ Church parish.

are Flow, Sunbeach Communications, and TeleBarbados. The 2016 CIA World Factbook reports that internet usage was at 79.5 percent of the population, a little ahead of the United States, which stood at 76.2 percent of the population. In 2016, Barbados had 332,208 cell phones, or more phones than the total population. The two mobile service providers are Flow and Digicel.

The Caribbean Broadcasting Corporation was founded in 1963 by an act of Parliament and today operates three radio stations in addition to the CBC television channel. Daily newspapers include the *Barbados Advocate* (established in 1895) and the *Daily Nation*. Regional and international publications are also readily available. Online news resources include the online *Barbados Advocate*, *Loop News*, and *Barbados Today*. The Totally Barbados website has a podcast so listeners can learn more about the country.

TRADITIONAL PROVERBS

Proverbs expressing folk values are constantly used in Bajan homes. Their commonsense wisdom is intended to instruct or admonish people in matters that occur frequently:

If greedy wait, hot will cool.	*Patience will get you what you want.*
One bellyful don' fattan a hog.	*Sustained effort is needed to achieve good results.*
Hungry mek cat eat salt.	*Necessity makes people do unusual things.*
De sea en' got no back door.	*The sea is not a safe place.*
Mek-sure better than cock-sure. . . .	*Making sure is better than taking things for granted.*
Every skin teet' en' a laugh.	*Friendly smiles may not be genuine.*
Hansome don' put in pot.	*Physical beauty does not provide practical benefits.*

INTERNET LINKS

http://www.barbadospocketguide.com/our-island-barbados/about-barbados/bajan-dialect.html
The Barbados Pocket Guide has a long, alphabetized list of popular Bajan phrases and words.

https://www.totallybarbados.com/articles/barbados-podcasts
Listen to the Totally Barbados podcast on the organization's website.

https://www.youtube.com/watch?v=3BhrdeMturw
YouTuber ShaLee demonstrates some English and Bajan phrases.

ARTS

The creation of pottery and dinnerware is an art in Barbados.

10

B ARBADIANS HAVE A LONG cultural heritage, and many are proud of it. That pride is particularly apparent in their music, especially in the performance of calypso, a type of rhythmic, traditional music that was once a way of communicating and storytelling for Barbadian slaves. Calypso is still widely popular in Barbados today.

The songs of the island's most famous folk and calypso musician, the Mighty Gabby, are infused with a deep love for his homeland. Popstar Rihanna has never shied away from showing pride for her homeland. Her *Anti* album from 2016 gave fans a taste of her roots with some Caribbean rhythms. Barbados also has a rich tradition of arts and crafts, literature, and architecture. The melding of African and British cultures in Barbados has created a distinctive and energetic culture with fine and colorful music, literature, art, crafts, and history. The vibrant art community explores many media, blending Afro-Caribbean and Western influences to create original work in all fields of the arts and crafts.

TRADITIONAL AND NEW MUSIC

Caribbean music has its roots in African folk music and drumming, with some Spanish, French, and English influences. Reggae and calypso are the two types of music heard most often, with their catchy, singable tunes blaring in minibuses and out of restaurants and beach bars. Soca,

This club in Barbados is a great place to hear some calypso beats.

which blends soul with calypso, is dance music with bold rhythms. Heavy on the bass sounds, soca is heard most frequently during carnivals. The spouge style of music, originating in the 1960s, is a blend of ska (from Jamaica) and Trinidadian calypso with some other types of music thrown in. Less traditional types of music are also finding a foothold in Barbados. Rap and hip-hop have taken off, and music producer Strat Carter seeks to bring Barbadian hip-hop artists to the world.

A HISTORY OF CALYPSO

African slaves brought their songs to the West Indies beginning in the early 1600s. Plantation owners thought that beating drums and other loud instruments could encourage their slaves to revolt, so all such instruments were banned. But music remained a vital part of the Africans' daily lives and could not be suppressed. The slaves sang while they worked, celebrated holidays with songs, and sang at funerals. This music, indigenous to Barbados, could only be performed in private, out of earshot of the plantation owners. After the slaves were emancipated in 1838, their music survived only by becoming folk music.

Calypso, which originated in Trinidad, began influencing Barbadian folk music in the early twentieth century. The songs from Trinidad increased the range of both melodies and lyrics, which changed from mere gossip and scandal to include satire and social commentary. Calypso was not taken seriously, however, and early singers were regarded as comics rather than serious performers. Talented Barbadian performers such as the Mighty Charmer and the Mighty Sugar were forced to move to Trinidad for recognition and to make their records. Eventually, in the 1960s and 1970s, a group of white middle-class Barbadians called the Merrymen created a series of hits by combining folk and country music with Bajan calypso.

Contemporary calypso features biting social commentary, political satire, and sexual innuendo. Calypso competitions are now a major part of carnival festivities, with singers competing for the title of "king."

THE KING OF CALYPSO

The Mighty Gabby, whose real name is Anthony Carter, began singing at the age of six and placed third in his first calypso competition in his teens. He spent a few years in New York, perfecting his writing and performing skills, and on his return to Barbados he became the Barbadian equivalent of Jamaica's Bob Marley. He has also won recognition as Folk Singer of the Year, and his music speaks for the thousands of Barbadians who see their culture as being under threat from foreign influence.

The Mighty Gabby also advocates for countries outside of the Caribbean. In 2017, he released a song called "Free Palestine" in protest of Barbados, Haiti, and the Bahamas refusing to vote for a 2012 UN resolution that would upgrade Palestine to a nonmember observer state. (The resolution passed.) The lyrics of the song are below:

> Barbados, Haiti and Bahamas
> Refuse to behave the way they should
> They wouldn't join the United Nations
> In recognizing Palestine nationhood
> That's why I say:
> Free Palestine, Free Palestine
> Let the wall come down, stop the occupation
> Free Palestine, Free Palestine
> Let the wall come down, bring peace to the region

TUK MUSIC

The *boom-a-tuk, boom-a-tuk* sound given out by the big log drum gives these bands their name. For more than one hundred years, tuk (also known as tuck or took) music has been played at picnics and excursions and on public holidays. It is lively, with an intricate, fast beat suggestive of English military bands. Tuk bands travel from village to village playing popular tunes and

encouraging the villagers to contribute their own compositions. People dress up in unusual clothes, and everyone joins in the dancing and fun. Traditional dancers such as the tiltman, who performs on very tall stilts, usually accompany tuk bands and solicit contributions from the audience.

MUSICAL INSTRUMENTS

Originally from Trinidad, the distinctive, melodious sounds of the steel drum (or steel pan) have spread throughout the Caribbean, including Barbados. It was created by musicians who took discarded oil drums and hammered out the steel bottom, tuning different sections to specific pitches. Drummers now play together in bands.

Other musical instruments used in both traditional and more modern Barbadian music styles include the xylophone, cymbals, bongo, acoustic guitar, banjo, and bow fiddle. Often, instruments used in folk music were made from "found" items, like bamboo, conch shells, water-filled bottles, and more.

Dance is taught in schools in Barbados. Here, dancers take part in a Bridgetown festival.

DANCE STYLES

It is said that most Bajans can dance before they can walk. Many primary schools teach dance as part of the curriculum. When music fills the air, toddlers stand and sway to the rhythm of calypso. Early planters quickly realized that their slaves worked better when they were allowed to enjoy their own form of dancing and music once or twice a week. The dancers shout, clap their hands, and chant, twisting and turning energetically.

In recent years, after formal ballet became available to a larger number of Barbadians, modern dance techniques have developed, and folktales have inspired performances by groups such as the Barbados Dance Theater. Jazz dance, tap, ballroom dance, and contemporary dance styles have all become a part of dance culture in Barbados.

HOLDERS SEASON

The Holders House is a seventeenth-century plantation that has been converted to a bed and breakfast. On site, there is a theater where, every year, the Holders Season music and theater festival takes place. Musicians from all over the world, as well as local talent, arrive to play this festival. There are performances by Broadway stars, stand-up comedians, and opera singers. Renowned opera star Luciano Pavarotti performed at Holders in 1997.

THE BARBADOS LANDSHIP

The landship movement developed from early friendly societies—institutions that, for a small weekly payment, provided insurance for the sick as well as death benefits. Landships provided the working class with a social organization that satisfied their need for cultural expression as well as assistance for workers in times of need. The Barbados Landship was a land-based organization similar to and modeled on the British navy. Its members were ranked and defined in accordance with the hierarchy of the British navy. Meetings and parades displayed naval-style drills, uniforms, and discipline.

Many communities developed their own landships in the 1920s. These competed in displays of discipline, uniform, drill, and other naval rituals. Today there are a half-dozen landships, and no big occasion in Barbados, from a state funeral to the Crop Over festivities, is complete without landship participation. The Barbados Landship organization took part in Barbados independence celebrations in 1966 and continues to hold a place in Barbados today.

THEATER IN BARBADOS

Plantation improvisations called tea meetings in the 1600s provided entertainment in the form of enslaved Africans reciting passages and spontaneous speeches or performing slapstick skits for their own entertainment. Troupes of traveling actors would also give spontaneous open-air performances when their ships came into port. The first mention of theater in Barbados,

Dinner shows give travelers the opportunity to learn more about Barbadian culture while enjoying some of the island's cuisine. Many party and tour cruises around the island offer dinner with entertainment. Harbour Lights Barbados is a beachfront nightclub with a twice weekly dinner show that gives visitors a taste of the Crop Over festival, with bands, dancers, stilt-walkers, and fire-eaters.

The chance to see a live performance like this one and have dinner is a popular activity for tourists in Barbados.

however, appeared in George Washington's diary when he noted that he attended a presentation of *The Tragedy of George Barnwell* in 1751.

By 1783, a theater called Patagonian, which presented plays including those by William Shakespeare, was facing competition from a rival theater called the New Theater, whose comedies and pantomimes drew large crowds. These audiences were made up exclusively of the white planter class. It was not until after World War II that nonwhites such as the Green Room Players began to stage productions of local and international plays.

Stage One Theater Productions, established in 1979, concentrates on works about the Caribbean way of life. It also holds a yearly Youth on Stage theater arts workshop for children and teens to perform on stage.

ARCHITECTURE STYLES

Architecture in Barbados is a blend of British tradition and tropical design, elegance, and simplicity. There are grand Georgian, Jacobean, and Victorian buildings on the one hand and basic wooden houses of the early settlers and slaves on the other. The wealth of the large sugar plantations resulted in the construction of great houses—solid structures built from natural coral limestone and furnished with mahogany furniture.

Speightstown retains its early architecture. Bridgetown's colonial buildings on Broad Street exemplify the grandeur and architectural flourishes of the turn of the century, but over the years they have been increasingly surrounded by more modern structures. The public buildings with neo-Gothic facades, erected in the nineteenth century on the northern side of National Heroes Square, accommodate the Houses of Parliament.

Some of Barbados's most distinctive buildings are chattel houses. These simple, rectangular wooden homes—built on cement or stone blocks so that they could be moved—are often painted in combinations of vivid colors such as turquoise, lime, pink, and yellow. They are a favorite subject for culture-preserving painters such as Fielding Babb, Adrian Compton, the twin Stewart brothers, the twin Cumberbatch sisters, and Oscar Walkes.

Some examples of chattel houses can be seen at the Tyrol Cot Heritage Village in Bridgetown. The village is associated with Tyrol Cot Great House, a mansion constructed in 1854 by local builder William Farnum. Blending Palladian and tropical design, Tyrol Cot was the home of Sir Grantley Adams for sixty years. It is filled with his collection of antique furniture and memorabilia.

Meanwhile, the chattel houses of Tyrol Cot Heritage Village display the work of craftsmen and artists who work on-site. The houses are built of traditional materials and incorporate many carefully reproduced details, such as gingerbread trim, verandah latticework, and wooden shutters. The Barbados National Trust, which runs the village, works to maintain and preserve historic and architecturally significant locations across Barbados.

Tyrol Cot, the home of Sir Grantley Adams, is a popular destination for those seeking a piece of Barbadian history.

ARTISTS AND CRAFTSPEOPLE

It is difficult to distinguish between arts and crafts in Barbados. For centuries, artists and craftsmen have turned functional things into works of art by decorating everyday objects. Slaves did not have time to develop their art in traditional forms, so their art was often something practical rather than just decorative. This tradition survives today. For example, calabash pots, originally used to carry water, are often carved, decorated, and turned into handbags.

The Temple Yard Rastafarian market has a host of unique artwork on display. Community craftsmen produce the items, which are usually made from leather, clay, wood, and straw. It is a popular place for tourists to visit as well.

The island's chief showcase for handicrafts is Pelican Craft Centre near Bridgetown Harbour. It has galleries and workshops where craftsmen can display their products, including coconut-shell accessories, straw fans, bottle baskets, and mahogany objects such as key rings, jewelry boxes, coaster sets, and letterboxes. Pottery, wall hangings, woven baskets, mats, rugs, and shell and coral jewelry are also featured. For more functional pieces, Earthworks Pottery in Saint Thomas Parish makes collectible pottery pieces for homes, restaurants, and other businesses.

THE POTTERY OF CHALKY MOUNT

Chalky Mount, in Saint Andrew Parish, refers to both the village and the range of hills in which it is nestled. Both are famous for the natural clay deposits dotting the region and the pottery made from them. For centuries, these deposits have been the source of material for making household items such as lamps, candle stands, cups, plates, and bowls, as well as the clay pots used as stoves

Chalky Mount is famous for its natural clay deposits, used in pottery making.

FIELDING BABB

One of the most popular fine artists on Barbados, Fielding Babb was born before art was really taught in schools, and before artists were able to make ends meet with their work. He was discovered by artist Charlie Best at the age of twelve.

Babb started out as a watercolorist, but he eventually took up working with oils. Creating a three-dimensional effect by laying oil paints with a palette knife became Babb's trademark style. He wanted his work to reflect the life and history of Barbados. He painted historical buildings and people going about their daily tasks.

Babb's works can still be seen in galleries across Barbados.

in many homes and the jugs called monkeys designed to cool beverages. The potter's craft has been handed down in families from generation to generation. Courtney Devonish, originally from Chalky Mount, has a gallery and workshop on the island of Anguilla. Trained in Italy, he is able to create classic European styles as well as traditional island pottery.

MURALS AND STREET ART

Local communities and schoolchildren are encouraged by the National Cultural Foundation to express their creativity. Colorful representations of present-day Bajan daily life can be found on the walls of schools, community centers, and post offices. The Speightstown mural, depicting historical images of Amerindian inhabitants and local wildlife, is impressive at 80 feet (24 m) wide and 20 feet (6 m) tall. The South Coast Boardwalk mural, a depiction of local sea creatures, was made from broken pieces of pottery.

Graffiti or street art, which is sometimes controversial because these artists often don't ask for permission, can also be spotted frequently on Barbados.

NOVELS AND POETRY

Barbados has produced several respected novelists and poets who blended folk beliefs with their own experiences, creating a rich literary tradition. In the

1940s, the British Broadcasting Corporation radio program *Caribbean Voices* and the Barbadian magazine *Bim*, edited by Frank Collymore, brought to public notice writers such as George Lamming, Oliver Jackman, Derek Walcott, Monica Skeete, and others who later authored highly acclaimed novels and poetry.

Many early Bajan novels dealt with childhood, coming of age, and the search for self in a world of color and race, bondage, and freedom. George Lamming's *In the Castle of My Skin*, *The Emigrants*, and *Season of Adventure*, in which a mixed-race woman searches for the meaning and value of her life when voodoo drums send her into a frenzy, have become classics. Geoffrey Drayton's *Christopher* deals with a white Bajan boy growing up in a black society, while Austin Clarke's *Amongst Thistles and Thorns* is the reverse—a black Bajan boy coming to terms with a white society. Novelist Karen Lord won the Frank Collymore Literary Endowment Award in both 2008 and 2009 for her first and second novels, *The Redemption in Indigo* and *The Best of All Possible Worlds*. Both were published and have won numerous awards.

INTERNET LINKS

http://barbadosnationaltrust.org/project/tyrolcot
See pictures and learn more about Tyrol Cot on the Barbados National Trust website.

http://secretbarbados.com/project/chalky-mount
Watch Chalky Mount artist John Springer make a soup bowl in under a minute on the Secret Barbados site.

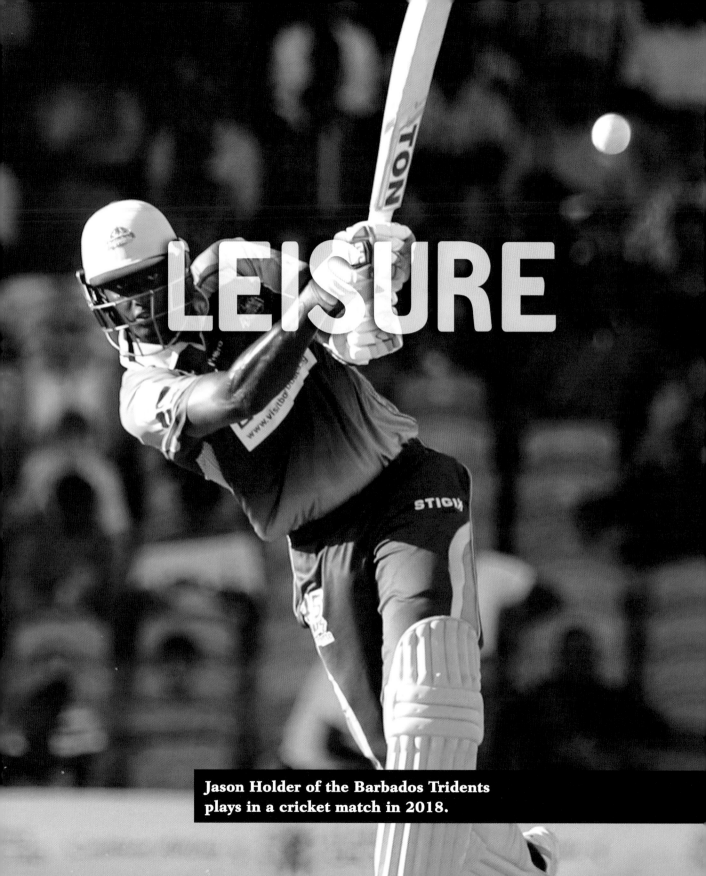

LEISURE

Jason Holder of the Barbados Tridents
plays in a cricket match in 2018.

11

BARBADOS IS A TROPICAL PARADISE with much to offer visitors and residents alike. All year round, people enjoy a great variety of sports and other leisure activities. Barbadians love to play, relax, and entertain themselves, and if they cannot afford the costly equipment required for some sports, there are plenty of other pursuits that can be enjoyed inexpensively. The most popular sport in Barbados is cricket. The people of Barbados have a reputation for being all about sports, and the island is known to provide world-class facilities and a broad range of activities on land and sea. Cricket, hiking, walking, running, dominoes, tennis, diving, surfing, windsurfing, snorkeling— all kinds of sports, recreation, and leisure pursuits are popular in Barbados.

"To say that cricket in Barbados is a passion would be an understatement. Bajans eat, drink and sleep cricket."
—VisitBarbados.org

CRICKET, YESTERDAY AND TODAY

Cricket was introduced about two hundred years ago by the British military, who regularly held cricket matches at the Garrison Savannah, now a well-known horse-racing track. The game soon became popular with white planters and merchants, who set up their own clubs and organized matches. Cricket was considered to be character building and to reflect the nobler values of British culture.

Early on, the clubs—such as the Wanderers (formed in 1877 by members of the mercantile community) and the Pickwick (formed in 1882 by members of the plantocracy)—were strictly white. Black and mixed-race professionals formed their own club, Spartan, in 1893. Their members turned away Herman Griffith, a public health inspector, because he was considered to be socially beneath them. Griffith's supporters broke away and formed the Empire Club, and Griffith became one of the great players of the game and the first black captain of a Barbados team. These four clubs are still active, but their conditions of membership no longer include race or social standing.

Early cricket was centered around Bridgetown and confined to a comparatively small portion of the population. Nevertheless, artisans and other workers soon formed their own clubs. Recognizing the game's potential for building community spirit, plantation employers encouraged their workers to play cricket by providing them with land for a pitch and supplying them with secondhand equipment no longer needed by their own clubs. These teams arranged their own competitions, and rivalry was intense.

When the Barbados Cricket League was formed, it brought the different groups of cricketers together. The white plantation owners and business executives found camaraderie with and respect for the black civil servants and lawyers they played against. Cricket can thus be said to have helped pave the way to independence.

When Barbados became independent in 1966, it challenged the rest of the world to a showcase cricket match. It remains one of the international capitals of cricket and always contributes a large contingent to the West Indies team.

Test cricket is played at international levels between January and April in Kensington Oval, which is filled mostly to its twenty-eight-thousand-spectator capacity. This venue was renovated between 2005 and 2006 to help accommodate spectators to the 2007 Cricket World Cup. The Cricket Association and the Cricket League have matches on Saturday afternoons and sometimes on Sundays during a season lasting from early June to mid-September.

Friendly matches are played on beaches, open pastures, and village fields year-round. Young boys who dream of making a name for themselves know that mastering cricket could mean more to their future than any other skill. As a result, they play cricket anywhere, anytime.

SOFTBALL CRICKET

Using tennis balls and slim mahogany bats instead of leather balls and regulation willow bats from England, this modified form of cricket has traditionally been played on Sunday mornings. Many softball teams compete for places on the Barbados teams that regularly tour the United States and Canada. In recent years, softball cricket has not been as popular in Barbados. However, efforts are being made to bring it back to the top of the island's sporting world.

WALKING, HIKING, AND RUNNING

Long-distance running is a popular activity in Barbados. All over the island, men and women walking briskly or running have become a common sight. An annual Run Barbados Marathon Weekend is held on the first weekend in December. The marathon, half marathon, 10K, and 5K take participants over paved roads along the coast and in and around Bridgetown. Each event attracts male and female competitors from around the world. Hikes across the island are also popular with tourists, including the Colin Hudson Great Train Hike, which follows the long-abandoned railway track that runs from Bridgetown to Belleplaine on the east coast.

DOMINOES AND BACKGAMMON

Dominoes, played with such enthusiasm that the slap of the dominoes on the table can be startling, is the national table game. Dominoes are so popular in

Tile games like dominoes originated in China as early as the tenth century CE. In the mid-1700s, the style of dominoes more familiar to westerners arrived in France and Italy, where it possibly got the name "dominoes" from the black-and-white domino masks worn during carnivals in Venice, Italy. The game was introduced to Britain by French prisoners, and then arrived in Barbados via British colonists. Today there are over eighty games to be played with dominoes, including the more traditional blocking-style games (popular in Barbados), types of solitaire to be played with dominoes, and scoring games. Some games include Chickenfoot, Super Train, Moon, and Fishing. The art of setting up dominoes and knocking them over is known as "toppling."

"Dominoes is incredibly popular in Barbados! In rum shops and fishing villages you'll often hear the sound of people 'slamming a dom' while discussing the day's events and local politics."
–Barbados.org

Barbados that there is a National Dominoes Association that regulates domino competitions each year. Top dominoes players come from all over the world to participate in dominoes competitions and festivals. Less iconic, but still popular with the locals, is backgammon, played frequently at rum shops across the island.

WATER ACTIVITIES

Constant sunshine and steady breezes on the southern coast produce ideal conditions for windsurfing. At the Soup Bowl, a bay near Bathsheba, waves from the Atlantic Ocean and clean, shark-free waters create equally ideal conditions for surfers.

Yachting is another popular sport. Coral reefs and sunken wrecks in clear water surrounding the island also provide scuba-diving enthusiasts with excellent diving sites.

PARKS AND WILDLIFE RESERVES

Several national parks and wildlife reserves on the island have become popular recreation areas for both Barbadians and visitors. Perhaps the best known, Farley Hill National Park consists of several acres of tropical trees and plants on a cliff up to 899 feet (274 m) above sea level, overlooking the Scotland District. Bought by the Barbados government and declared a national park, it was officially opened by Queen Elizabeth II on February 15, 1966, just several months before the island's independence.

The Barbados Wildlife Reserve is a 4-acre (1.6 ha) forest where animals like the green monkey can be studied and conserved. The brick paths of the reserve were constructed from bricks that were once used in the construction of sugar factories, and buildings were built from coral rock. Other animals that live at the Barbados Wildlife Reserve include the mara (a rodent), iguanas and other lizards, parrots, tortoises, and snakes.

Visitors to Barbados's parks and wildlife reserves can hike on the nature trails, check out some beautiful views of the island, picnic, play cricket, or go exploring on a bicycle. Playgrounds give children a chance to learn and use their imaginations while having fun.

While most of Barbados has been developed, Farley Hill National Park offers a glimpse of its natural state.

INTERNET LINKS

https://www.barbadoswildlifereserve.com
The website for the Barbados Wildlife Reserve has pictures of some of the animal species, as well as information for visitors.

http://www.bcacricket.org/2010/index.php/
The Barbados Cricket Association has a website dedicated to the latest cricket news on Barbados.

http://www.domino-games.com/domino-rules
Domino-Games.com is a good resource for learning more about dominoes and how to play a variety of games.

FESTIVALS

Glitter, feathers, and jewels adorn this
Crop Over reveler in 2013.

12

RELIGIOUS HOLIDAYS, SUCH AS Christmas and Easter, are some of the major celebrations in Barbados, but many other festivals occur throughout the year. These events include the Barbados Reggae Festival in April, the Holetown Festival every February, the Oistins Fish Festival over Easter weekend, Crop Over from late June to early August, and the National Independence Festival of Creative Arts (NIFCA) in November. A number of sports festivals, such as the Mount Gay Rum Round Barbados Race Series in January and the Barbados International Hockey Festival in August, as well as several cricket festivals, are also held throughout the year.

BARBADOS REGGAE FESTIVAL

This weeklong music festival takes place in April and showcases some of the biggest names in reggae music, as well as local and up-and-coming talent.

"Every August, hundreds of thousands of people from around the globe make their way to the picturesque island of Barbados to take part in … activities from amazing concerts and breakfast fêtes where popular DJs play the best in calypso and soca, to dusk-to-dawn parties where revelers get covered in paint and mud for the fun of it—all of which leads up to the main event: Grand Kadooment Day."

—Shammara Lawrence, *Teen Vogue*

Barbados enjoys a variety of festivals throughout the year, from carnivals to street fairs, culinary feasts to sports celebrations and cultural events. The combination of British, African, American, and Amerindian elements ensures that the festivals are an exhilarating, colorful, and dramatic demonstration of the living culture of the Bajan people.

These musicians parade on the streets of Holetown for the city's annual festival.

People travel from all over the world to attend this festival and to enjoy the beach dance parties, cruises, and events.

FESTIVAL IN HOLETOWN

The site of the landing of the first permanent settlers on February 17, 1627, is the setting for a week of continuous entertainment each year at the highly anticipated Holetown Festival. Medieval songs are sung in churches, whereas more modern beats can be heard in the fairgrounds. Jazz, gospel, brass, and folk concerts are held by the light of the moon on the beach where the first eighty settlers landed nearly four hundred years ago.

THE FISH FESTIVAL

Held over the Easter weekend, the Oistins Fish Festival pays tribute to the island's fishing folk, who hold competitions over several days to demonstrate their skills in fishing, fish deboning, boat racing, and even crab racing. Spectators throng the beaches, marketplaces, and rum shops that line the roadsides and dance to steel drum bands.

CROP OVER

The origins of the Crop Over festival can be traced back to the 1780s, when plantation managers used to hold a "dinner and sober dance" to celebrate the

As the country's first prime minister, Errol Barrow is often considered the "father of independence" in Barbados. Therefore, the day honoring his memory is an important one. Barrow's work beyond the fight for independence extended to healing the infrastructure of Barbados and building up the country's tourism and manufacturing industries. He also advocated for free education and meals for all Barbadian children and introduced national health insurance and social security.

On the holiday dedicated to Barrow's memory, Barbadians head outdoors for some cricket and attend some special events like the annual church service and lunch. The Errol Barrow Day Scenic Bus Ride takes people around the island to visit some important historical sites starting in Independence Square. Then there's an after party on the beach!

end of the sugarcane season, or Crop Over. Before emancipation, planters had to support their slaves year-round, but after 1838, Crop Over meant both less work and lower wages for many workers. For a final end-of-harvest celebration, farmworkers would use refuse from sugarcane plants to create a stuffed figure of a man they called Mr. Harding, who symbolized the period of time between sugar crops, when employment and money were scarce. Workers would parade around the plantation yards in their carts, their animals decorated with flamboyant frangipani and other flowers, and introduce Mr. Harding to the plantation manager. Then they would adjourn for dancing and food, with salted meat and rum contributed by the manager.

As the sugar industry in Barbados declined, so too did the Crop Over festival, and in the 1940s the festival was abandoned completely. It was revived in 1974, however, to pay tribute to the vital role of sugar in Barbados's history, and other elements of Barbadian culture were introduced to make the festival that exists today.

Perhaps the most elaborate and important festival in the country, Crop Over lasts for five weeks, from mid-June to August. The Ceremonial Delivery of the Last Canes opens the festivities and is followed over the next few weeks by attractions such as a decorated cart parade and a calypso competition. The Cohobblopot variety show blends drama, dance, and music, with the

Food is an important part of Christmas celebrations in Barbados. Traditional dishes like jug jug (a combination of peas, corn flour, and herbs), baked ham, and great cake take center stage. Great cake is made from dried fruits like cherries, raisins, and currants, spices, and a healthy dose of rum and port wine. Christmas season is filled with parties for family and friends. Queens Park in Bridgetown holds a Christmas event every year where Barbadians dress in their finest and meet up to enjoy the colorful fashions. Bridgetown is lit up with red and green lights, so many Barbadians enjoy driving around to look at decorations. Music is also a big part of the occasion. Country singer Dolly Parton and famed singer/songwriter Kenny Rogers's The Christmas Album *gets many Barbadians in the Christmas spirit, in addition to many local favorites.*

Rihanna makes an appearance at Crop Over in 2017.

crowning of the king and queen of the costumed bands. The massive Bridgetown Market street fair offers selections of Bajan cooking and local arts and crafts. The king of calypso is crowned at the Pic-o-de-Crop Show.

Crop Over ends with Grand Kadooment Day, a nationally celebrated holiday in early August. The grand finale is often the most attended and most celebrated part of the entire event. Around fifteen thousand Barbadians and visitors parade through the streets. Revelers dress up in spectacular costumes and dance along the streets in a huge carnival parade to the most popular calypso and soca sounds. At the end of the route, a lively party takes place with more music, color, fun, and food. Rihanna is often in attendance at the festival, and her participation and elaborate, colorful costumes have recently shone a new light on the fashion spectacular that is Crop Over. In recent years, the event has been covered by international fashion magazines, with costumes becoming more and more elaborate every year.

THE CREATIVE ARTS FESTIVAL

Bajans of all ages match their talents in music, singing, dancing, acting, and writing during the festival. There is a Literary Arts Gala and a cook-off for

New Year's Day . . . . . . *January 1*
Errol Barrow Day . . . . . *January 21*
Good Friday and Easter. . *late March/
early April*
National Heroes Day . . . *April 28*
May Day . . . . *May 1*
Whit Monday . . . . *seventh Monday
after Easter*

Emancipation Day . . . . *August 1*
Kadooment Day . . . . . . *first Monday
in August*
Independence Day. . . . . *November 30*
Christmas Day. . . . . . . *December 25*
Boxing Day. . . . . *December 26*

professional chefs. Performances by the finalists are held on Independence Day, November 30. Submissions come from schools, community groups, and even local prisons, since creativity is seen by many Barbadians as a path to rehabilitation. The festival isn't limited to offering up prizes for the most talented. It seeks to nurture the careers of local artists and performers in order to help the arts scene in Barbados thrive.

These two performers bring their musical talents to Crop Over in hopes of winning a prize.

INTERNET LINKS

https://www.thebarbadosreggaefestival.com
Learn more about the Barbados Reggae Festival, see videos of previous performances, and even plan a trip for next year.

**https://www.harpersbazaar.com/uk/fashion/style-files/news/
g38185/rihanna-barbados-carnival-outfits**
See some of Rihanna's most iconic Crop Over costumes on the Harper's Bazaar website.

**https://www.totallybarbados.com/articles/about-barbados/people/
barbados-national-heroes/errol-walton-barrow**
Read more about the "father of independence" Errol Barrow and see a list of his achievements.

FOOD

Fried fish at the Oistins fish market is a treat for tourists and locals alike.

13

BARBADIAN CUISINE IS THE culmination of a number of cultures, including American, British, African, West Indian, and Chinese. Seafood is the main source of protein, and the surrounding sea offers a wide variety of fish, including sea urchins and flying fish. Exotic fruits such as papayas, bananas, pineapples, and kiwis grow easily, as well as vegetables such as onions, celery, and potatoes.

Meals most often include a protein like fish or chicken, usually marinated in a combination of spices. This is typically served with a side dish like sweet potato, plantain, rice and peas, or a combination of vegetables and a salad.

Barbados offers an enormous variety of gastronomic delights, including spicy Bajan and other Caribbean specialties. Some of these dishes borrow heavily from African, Indian, and even Chinese sources.

SALT FISH AND *COU-COU*

African-inspired *cou-cou* (koo-koo) is considered the Bajan national dish. A mixture of cornmeal and okra is stirred vigorously to prevent lumps, packed into a bowl, and then turned out onto a plate. A depression is made in the center, and a sauce is ladled into this and around the mound. *Cou-cou*

Fried fish (*right*) is often accompanied by a number of tasty side dishes.

is traditionally served with salt fish. Originally imported to feed the slaves because it was an inexpensive source of protein, salt fish is now regarded as a delicacy.

SEAFOOD

Virtually a national symbol, flying fish is perhaps the most popular Bajan delicacy. Caught between December and June, it is frozen or dried for use during the rest of the year. It can be prepared in many ways, from salt bread sandwiches called cutters to gourmet dishes. Fresh from the surrounding waters come other seafood, such as lobster, shrimp, dorado (mahi-mahi), turtle, red snapper, tuna, kingfish, and mackerel. Unique are the crane chubb and sea eggs (white sea urchins' roe, which are deviled, breaded, or prepared to taste).

STEWED PORK

Barbadians love pork, and every bit of the pig is used in some way or another. Traditionally cooked midweek when fresh or more-expensive food runs out, stew food is made from finely chopped pig's tail, snout, head, and trotters (pig's feet). It is cooked with green vegetables, such as okra, squash, cabbage, or spinach, and served with ground provisions—root vegetables such as yams, sweet potatoes, and cassava—as well as breadfruit.

PUDDING

Pudding, which resembles a long dark sausage, is made from grated, well-seasoned sweet potato stuffed into a cleaned pig's intestine and steamed. The sausage is then cut into slices and served with a mixture made from pork—

including the head and the trotters—cooked, sliced, and soused (pickled) with lime juice, onion, hot pepper, salt, chopped cucumber, and parsley. This dish is a traditional Saturday night meal for family get-togethers. Leftovers are usually fried and served for breakfast the following day.

PRODUCE

Barbados's tropical climate yields fruits such as mangoes, papayas, bananas, guavas, avocados, and coconuts in abundance. Other fruits eaten include Barbados cherries and soursops—large green fruits with a slightly acidic, pulpy texture that are often made into a refreshing drink. Breadfruit is a staple in the Bajan diet. The size of a melon, breadfruit has white starchy and slightly spongy flesh that can be cooked in stews, fried, boiled, or pickled.

Also abundant are vegetables and fruits such as yams, eggplants, okras, pumpkins, plantains (resembling large bananas, these starchy fruits are usually fried or grilled and eaten as an accompaniment to other dishes), squashes, and christophenes, a common Caribbean vegetable shaped like a large pear that can be eaten raw in salads, used in soups, or cooked like squash.

OTHER POPULAR DISHES

Some other popular Bajan dishes include:
- *jug-jug* (jugg-jugg), a mixture of Guinea corn, green peas, and salted meat.
- pepperpot, a spicy stew made with a variety of meats.
- *roti* (ROW-tee), a curry filling of meat or chicken and potatoes wrapped in a tortilla-like flatbread.
- *conkies* (kon-kees), a mixture of cornmeal, coconut, pumpkin, raisins, sweet potatoes, and spices, steamed in a plantain leaf.
- macaroni pie, baked macaroni and cheese, often made with onion and a combination of ketchup and mustard

BUFFETS ON SUNDAY

The Bajan custom of entertaining family and friends on the weekend is still popular, and Sunday buffets in particular provide a good excuse for festive parties with plentiful food, drink, and music.

BAXTERS ROAD

In Bridgetown, Baxters Road is a popular place every night. Its shops and restaurants open their doors, and music and wonderful aromas fill the air. At one end, vendors stand over buckpots, or old cast-iron pots, deep-frying fish, chicken, or pork Bajan-style over bright coal fires. Locals and visitors mingle, eating and drinking until the early hours of the morning.

THE FAMOUS OISTINS FISH FRY

The coastal town of Oistins is considered the place to be on Friday and Saturday nights, in part because of its famous fish fry. This is a market on the beach where freshly caught fish and other seafood are cooked according to local recipes. There are numerous vendors to choose from, and music fills the air, making for a memorable evening out. Bajans and visitors eat their fill and dance the night away.

BARBADIAN DESSERTS

After a meal, Barbadians enjoy a number of different desserts, including local fruits, and sweet breads made from dried fruits and coconut. Cassava pone, which is a dense cake made from cassava, is also popular. British and American influences are also evident in cakes, bread pudding, pies, ice cream, and custard.

HUCKSTERS AND HAWKERS

In Barbados, street vendors often sell treats and produce to locals and visitors. But hucksters and hawkers are not to be confused! Hawkers sell fresh produce, sometimes from a small van, or the back of a bicycle, or just a regular spot on a street corner. They usually sell Wednesdays to Saturdays and spend Monday or Tuesday obtaining their particular produce from farms or plantations, often harvesting it themselves. Hawking is most profitable in the largest towns,

This man's colorful stand sells fruit and vegetables.

where there is passing trade, so hawkers are found mostly in Bridgetown, Oistins, and Speightstown. Hucksters, usually women, are street vendors who make and sell candy, chips, corn curls, nuts, and popcorn outside schools and at events or festivals. Sometimes they bake and sell traditional peanut cakes or chocolate fudge. These are normally sold out of cabinets to protect them from flies.

RUM AND OTHER DRINKS

Rum is the social drink of Barbados. It is drunk at weddings, births, christenings, wakes, and funerals, as well as on any other occasion that is a reason for celebrating. It may be drunk straight from a bottle passed from hand to hand, with ice, or diluted with fruit juices in the form of rum punches.

When it was first made in the 1640s, by distilling the juice extracted from molasses (the thick liquid residue left after most of the sugar has been taken out of the sugarcane juice), rum was not as refined as it is today. Then, it was called rumbullion because it was so potent. Planters sold their rum to ships for consumption by the crews and resale overseas, and to the taverns that sprang up all over the island and later became rum shops. Rum was in great demand and helped to make the planters prosperous. Mount Gay Rum claims to be the oldest in the Caribbean, and possibly all over the world.

There are nearly one thousand rum shops on the island today. They have become much more than shops selling rum. Functioning more like village stores selling groceries and fuel, they are informal community centers where men meet to exchange "gup and gossip," discuss politics, or simply hang out. Women rarely frequent rum shops and then only with a male escort.

The island beer, Banks, is popular with both locals and visitors. Other popular drinks include coconut water, fresh lemonade, and punches made from the juices of fruits such as mangoes, guavas, soursops, passion fruits, and tamarinds.

Maubey (maw-bee) is made by boiling bits of the bitter bark of the soldierwood (*Colubrina elliptica*) with spices. It is then strained and sweetened. Sorrel, the local Christmas drink, is prepared from the fresh or dried red sepals of the sorrel plant, which are boiled or infused in hot water with spices and rum added. Falernum (fal-er-nerm) is a local liqueur made with lime juice, granulated sugar, rum, and water that has been flavored with almond extract.

Coffee also has its fans in Barbados. Wyndhams is a coffee roaster in Barbados that imports beans from Ethiopia. Wyndhams is famous for its coffee blends with names like Duppies, Soup Bowl, and Dawl Patrol. There's no Starbucks on Barbados, just small, locally owned coffee shops around the island. Tea is also popular on Barbados because of its past links to Great Britain. In Bridgetown, people can have high tea at Chatters Tea Room or at other tea shops. It is an elaborate affair in which participants eat small sandwiches, scones, and cookies, and of course drink tea. Vendors also sell coconut water along roadsides.

INTERNET LINKS

https://barbados.org/barbados-recipes.htm#.W3c79y2ZOqA
Find links to Barbadian recipes on Barbados.org.

**https://www.buzzfeed.com/kelciewillis/things-all-people
-from-barbados-know-to-be-true?utm_term=.apQJepyq5W#
.kpdVW1AaDR**
Buzzfeed breaks down the most essential foods to try in Barbados and includes links to recipes.

COU-COU

This dish, usually served with flying fish, is the national dish of Barbados.

1½ cups cornmeal
5—6 medium-sized okra pods (sliced
  into bite-sized pieces)
1 small onion (chopped)
3 tbsp. butter
Water
Salt

Pour cornmeal into a bowl and add enough water to completely cover it.

In medium-sized saucepan, mix okra, onion, and salt and add enough water to boil. Bring to a medium boil until okra begins to soften.

Strain okra, reserving the water in a separate bowl.

Pour a quarter of the okra water back into the saucepan and add the saturated cornmeal. Cook over medium heat, stirring constantly.

Add more okra water gradually, until the *cou-cou* begins to simmer. Add okra and continue to cook and stir over low heat for another few minutes.

Remove from heat and stir in butter.

Enjoy with gravy and salt fish!

BAJAN SWEET BREAD

This dessert-like bread is filled with fruits like coconut and raisins (or dried cherries or apricots if the baker prefers) and is often buttered and served with hot tea.

2½ cups grated coconut
½ cup melted butter
4 cups all-purpose flour
1 tbsp. baking powder
1 tsp. salt
¾ cups granulated sugar
1 cup raisins or other dried fruit
   (cherries, apricots, figs, etc.)
1 egg, beaten
1¼ cups evaporated milk
1 tsp. almond extract

Sift together flour, baking powder, and salt into large mixing bowl.

Mix together in separate bowl melted butter, coconut, three-quarters of the sugar, raisins or other dried fruit, egg, milk, and almond extract until it makes a paste.

Add wet ingredients to dry and mix well until stiff dough is formed.

Pour into well-greased loaf pans.

Sprinkle each with remaining sugar.

Bake at 350°F (177°C) for 1 hour, until toothpick inserted in center comes out clean.

Cool in pans before removing gently.

Slice and serve with butter.

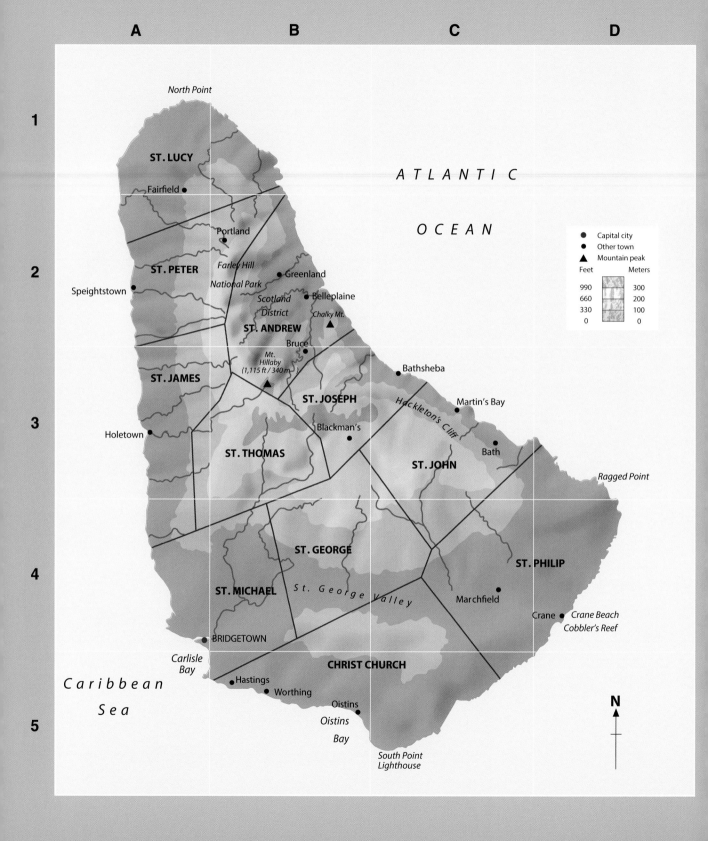

MAP OF BARBADOS

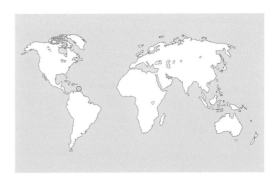

ECONOMIC BARBADOS

Services
 Airport

Port

Agriculture
 Fishing

Fish processing

Sugar processing

Natural Resources
 Oil fields

Manufacturing
Cement

 Pottery

 Rum

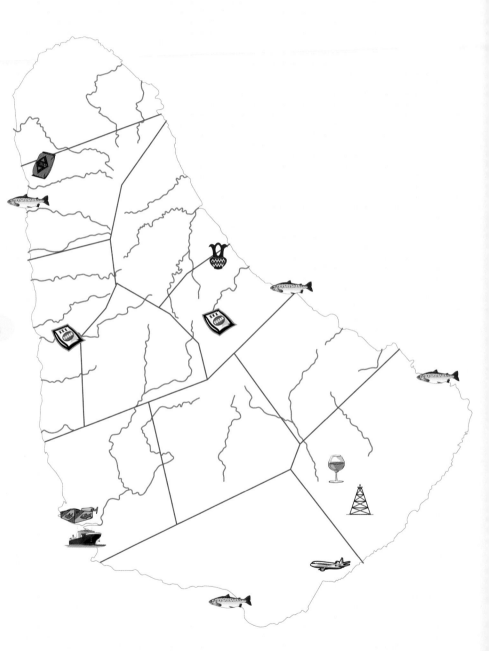

ABOUT THE ECONOMY

OVERVIEW

Throughout history, the Barbadian economy was based on sugarcane cultivation and related activities. Tourism has become one of the most important industries and a top revenue earner for Barbados. Informatics and offshore financing are also major foreign-exchange earners, with Barbados benefiting from a highly educated workforce and having the same time zone as the financial centers of the eastern United States. In the last several years, the economy of Barbados has begun to struggle because of massive government debt, 175 percent of the country's GDP. The tourism industry has also taken a hit because of increased concern about hurricanes, as well as the sargassum seaweed onslaught rendering many beaches unusable. Plans to improve the economy and reduce debt are in progress.

GROSS DOMESTIC PRODUCT (GDP)

$5.244 billion (2017 estimate)

CURRENCY

The Barbados dollar
1 dollar = 100 cents
US$1 = Bds$2

GDP PER CAPITA

$18,700 (2017 estimate)

GROWTH RATE

0.9 percent (2017 estimate)

MAIN EXPORTS

Manufactures, sugar and molasses, rum, foodstuffs and beverages, chemicals, electronic/electrical components

MAIN IMPORTS

Consumer goods, machinery, foodstuffs, construction materials, chemicals, fuel, electrical components

LABOR FORCE

144,000 (2017 estimate)

TOURISM

663,441 visitors (2017 estimate)

MAIN TRADE PARTNERS

United States, Trinidad and Tobago, Guyana, Jamaica, China, St. Lucia, United Kingdom

AGRICULTURAL PRODUCTS

Sugarcane, vegetables, cotton

NATURAL RESOURCES

Petroleum, fish, natural gas

CULTURAL BARBADOS

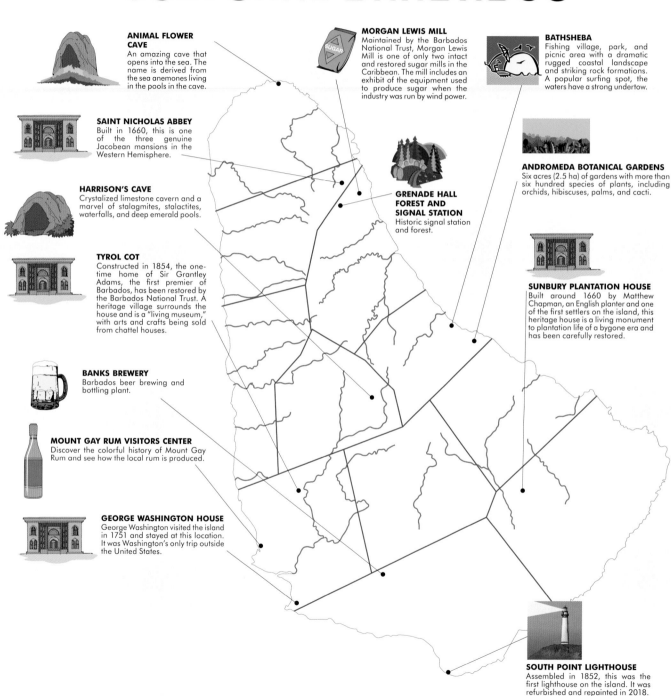

ANIMAL FLOWER CAVE
An amazing cave that opens into the sea. The name is derived from the sea anemones living in the pools in the cave.

SAINT NICHOLAS ABBEY
Built in 1660, this is one of the three genuine Jacobean mansions in the Western Hemisphere.

HARRISON'S CAVE
Crystalized limestone cavern and a marvel of stalagmites, stalactites, waterfalls, and deep emerald pools.

TYROL COT
Constructed in 1854, the one-time home of Sir Grantley Adams, the first premier of Barbados, has been restored by the Barbados National Trust. A heritage village surrounds the house and is a "living museum," with arts and crafts being sold from chattel houses.

BANKS BREWERY
Barbados beer brewing and bottling plant.

MOUNT GAY RUM VISITORS CENTER
Discover the colorful history of Mount Gay Rum and see how the local rum is produced.

GEORGE WASHINGTON HOUSE
George Washington visited the island in 1751 and stayed at this location. It was Washington's only trip outside the United States.

MORGAN LEWIS MILL
Maintained by the Barbados National Trust, Morgan Lewis Mill is one of only two intact and restored sugar mills in the Caribbean. The mill includes an exhibit of the equipment used to produce sugar when the industry was run by wind power.

GRENADE HALL FOREST AND SIGNAL STATION
Historic signal station and forest.

BATHSHEBA
Fishing village, park, and picnic area with a dramatic rugged coastal landscape and striking rock formations. A popular surfing spot, the waters have a strong undertow.

ANDROMEDA BOTANICAL GARDENS
Six acres (2.5 ha) of gardens with more than six hundred species of plants, including orchids, hibiscuses, palms, and cacti.

SUNBURY PLANTATION HOUSE
Built around 1660 by Matthew Chapman, an English planter and one of the first settlers on the island, this heritage house is a living monument to plantation life of a bygone era and has been carefully restored.

SOUTH POINT LIGHTHOUSE
Assembled in 1852, this was the first lighthouse on the island. It was refurbished and repainted in 2018.

ABOUT THE CULTURE

OFFICIAL NAME
Barbados

CAPITAL
Bridgetown

AREA
166 square miles (430 sq km)

POPULATION
292,336 (2017 estimate)

PARISHES
Barbados is divided into eleven administrative parishes: Christ Church, Saint Andrew, Saint George, Saint James, Saint John, Saint Joseph, Saint Lucy, Saint Michael, Saint Peter, Saint Philip, Saint Thomas

MAJOR CITIES
Bridgetown, Speightstown, Oistins, Holetown

OFFICIAL LANGUAGE
English

MAJOR RELIGIONS
Protestant, 66.4 percent (Anglican, 23.9 percent; Pentecostal, 19.5 percent; Adventist, 5.9 percent; Methodist, 4.2 percent; Wesleyan, 3.4 percent; Nazarene, 3.2 percent; others, 6.3 percent); Roman Catholic, 3.8 percent; other Christian, 5.4 percent; none or unspecified, 21.8 percent; Rastafarian, 1 percent; other, 1.5 percent (2010 estimate)

BIRTHRATE
11.7 births per 1,000 population (2017 estimate)

DEATH RATE
8.6 deaths per 1,000 population (2017 estimate)

INFANT MORTALITY RATE
10.2 deaths per 1,000 live births

LIFE EXPECTANCY
Total population: 75.5 years
Male: 73.2 years
Female: 77.9 years (2017 estimate)

MAIN POLITICAL PARTIES
Bajan Free Party
Barbados Integrity Movement
Barbados Labour Party
Democratic Labour Party
People's Democratic Congress
People's Empowerment Party
Solutions Barbados
United Progressive Party

TIMELINE

IN BARBADOS	IN THE WORLD
1623 BCE	
First settlement at Port Saint Charles.	**116–117 CE**
500 CE	The Roman Empire reaches its greatest
The Barrancoid Indians arrive from Trinidad, but	extent, under Emperor Trajan (98–117).
by 600 CE there is no record of them in Barbados.	
800	
The Arawak Indians arrive in Barbados.	
1200	
The Carib Indians conquer the Arawak	**1206–1368**
Indians; the Carib Indians disappear by 1500.	Genghis Khan unifies the Mongols and starts
	conquest of the world. At its height, the Mongol
	Empire under Kublai Khan stretches from China
	to Persia and parts of Europe and Russia.
	1530
1625	Beginning of transatlantic slave trade
Captain John Powell lands on Barbados and	organized by the Portuguese in Africa.
claims the island for King James I of England.	
1627	
English settlers establish a colony and develop	
sugar plantations using slaves brought from Africa.	
1663	
Barbados is made an English crown possession.	**1789–1799**
1816	The French Revolution.
Bussa's Rebellion.	
1834	
Slavery is abolished.	**1914**
1937	World War I begins.
Riots break out because of poor economic	**1939**
conditions; British Royal Commission is sent	World War II begins.
to investigate; Grantley Adams establishes	**1945**
the Barbados Labour Party (BLP).	The United States drops atomic bombs on
1951	Hiroshima and Nagasaki. World War II ends.
Universal adult suffrage is introduced,	
and the BLP wins general elections.	
1954	
Ministerial government is set up	
with Grantley Adams as premier.	

IN BARBADOS	IN THE WORLD
1955 Democratic Labour Party (DLP) is formed.	
1958 Barbados becomes a member of British-sponsored Federation of the West Indies.	
1966 Barbados becomes independent.	**1966** The Chinese Cultural Revolution.
1967 Barbados joins the United Nations.	
1983 Barbados supports and provides a base for the US invasion of Grenada.	**1986** Nuclear power disaster at Chernobyl in Ukraine
	1991 Breakup of the Soviet Union.
1999 The BLP wins a landslide election, with 26 of 28 seats in the House of Assembly.	**1997** Hong Kong is returned to China.
2003 The BLP wins general elections; Owen Arthur returns for a third term.	**2001** Terrorists crash planes into New York, Washington, DC, and Pennsylvania.
2004 Sea border disagreement with Trinidad and Tobago.	
2008 Parliamentary elections won by opposition DLP; David Thompson becomes prime minister.	
2011 The first wave of sargassum seaweed makes its way into the Caribbean.	**2012** The *Costa Concordia* cruise ship runs aground off the coast of Italy.
2016 Barbados makes its twelfth appearance at the Summer Olympics in Rio de Janeiro, Brazil.	**2015** ISIS stages an attack in Paris.
	2017 Hurricane Maria strikes.
2018 Barbados elects its first female prime minister, Mia Mottley.	**2018** US president Donald Trump places tariffs on goods imported from Europe, Canada, Mexico, and China, setting off a trade war.

GLOSSARY

Arawaks
Early inhabitants of Barbados, who originally came from South America.

baccoo (bah-KOO)
Tiny spirit believed to bestow good or evil, depending on the amount of attention he receives.

Caribs
An aggressive tribe that settled in the Caribbean islands, including Barbados, displacing the Arawaks.

cash crop
A crop that is grown and sold for profit, as opposed to for use by the farmer.

cassareep (ka-sa-REEP)
An original Arawak flavoring made from grated, ground cassava still used in cooking today.

chattel houses
Movable dwellings.

conkies (kon-kees).
A mixture of cornmeal, coconut, pumpkin, raisins, sweet potatoes, and spices, steamed in a plantain leaf.

conrad (KON-rad)
Avenging ghost.

duppy (DOO-pee)
Spirit of the dead who roams at night.

freehold
Complete ownership of property.

indentured servant
A servant who signs a contract to work in exchange for food, shelter, and other necessities; when the contract ends, they are freed from servitude.

infrastructure
The system of publicly available utilities and facilities that allow a country to function, including railroads, bridges, sewer networks, and water.

jug-jug (jugg-jugg)
Dish of corn, green peas, and salted meat.

obeah
A form of witchcraft.

parish
Unit of local administration.

plantocracy
Wealthy planter class.

soca
A form of dance music with bold rhythms and heavy bass sounds frequently played during carnivals.

suffrage
The right to vote.

FOR FURTHER INFORMATION

BOOKS

Corbin, Margaret. *Bajan Cooking: Authentic Cooking from the Island of Barbados*. Charleston, SC: CreateSpace, 2017.

Jackson, Naomi. *The Star Side of Bird Hill*. New York: Penguin, 2016.

Ligon, Richard. *A True and Exact History of the Island of Barbados*. Edited by Karen Ordahl Kupperman. Indianapolis, IN: Hackett, 2011.

Stuart, Andrea. *Sugar in the Blood: A Family's Story of Slavery and Empire*. New York: Vintage, 2013.

FILMS

A Caribbean Dream. A retelling of *A Midsummer Night's Dream* set in modern Barbados. Caribbean Film Production, 2017.

Island in the Sun. Film starring Harry Belafonte. Irving Burgie wrote two songs for the film: "Lead Man Holler" and the title song. It was filmed partially in Barbados. Darryl F. Zanuck Productions, 1957.

MUSIC

King, John, and various artists. *Soundtrip Barbados*. Reise-Know-How Sound GmbH & Co., 2009.

Hypasounds. *Get Up and Move*. BoomMuzik/VPAL Music, 2016.

The Merrymen. *Beautiful Barbados*. CRS Music and Media, 2004.

Rihanna. *Anti*. Westbury Road/Roc Nation, 2016.

Rihanna. *Good Girl Gone Bad*. Def Jam Recordings, 2007.

BIBLIOGRAPHY

Barbados Integrated Government. https://www.gov.bb.

Beckles, Hilary. *A History of Barbados*. 2nd ed. Cambridge, UK: Cambridge University Press, 2007.

———. *The First Black Slave Society: Britain's Barbarity Time in Barbados, 1636—1876*. Kingston, Jamaica: University of the West Indies Press, 2016.

Broberg, Merle. *Places and Peoples of the World: Barbados*. New York: Chelsea House, 1989.

CIA World Factbook, Barbados. https://www.cia.gov/library/publications/resources/the-world-factbook/geos/bb.html.

Corbin, Margaret. *Bajan Cooking: Authentic Cooking from the Island of Barbados*. Charleston, SC: CreateSpace, 2017.

Forde, G. Addington, Sean Carrington, Henry Fraser, and John Gilmore. *The A to Z of Barbadian Heritage*. Bridgetown, Barbados: Heinemann Caribbean, 1990.

Handler, Jerome S. *Plantation Slavery in Barbados*. Cambridge, MA: Harvard University Press, 1978.

Irving Burgie website. http://www.irvingburgie.com.

Lamming, George. *In the Castle of My Skin*. London, UK: Schocken, 1983.

Ligon, Richard. *A True and Exact History of the Island of Barbados*. Edited by Karen Ordahl Kupperman. Indianapolis, IN: Hackett, 2011.

Puckrein, G. A. *Little England: Plantation Society and Anglo-Barbadian Politics 1627—1700*. New York: New York University Press, 1984.

Stuart, Andrea. *Sugar in the Blood: A Family's Story of Slavery and Empire*. New York: Vintage, 2013.

Totally Barbados. https://www.totallybarbados.com.

INDEX

INDEX

SECRETS *of* ART

Uncovering the mysteries and messages of great works of art

Debra N. Mancoff

FRANCES
LINCOLN

CONTENTS

INTRODUCTION

The Night Watch
Rembrandt van Rijn (1606–1669)
1642
Oil on canvas
379.5 x 443.5 cm (149.4 x 177.6 in)
Rijksmuseum, Amsterdam

Every work of art has a story. It may reflect the time of its creation or the originator's innovation and imagination, and the more we know about a work, the more we can deepen our appreciative engagement. But sometimes we notice something in a work that seems at variance with what we know about the artist, the subject or the era in which it was created. There may be something odd in the physical or pictorial features: a thickening of paint, a blurred reflection in a mirror, an inconsistent or incomprehensible detail. We may even catch glimpses of ghostly traces of another image beneath the surface. We begin to suspect that there is more to the work than meets the eye, and we wonder if the conventional story is the whole story. The familiar work acquires an aura of mystery, and our engagement turns from appreciation to enquiry. We wonder: Does this work harbour a secret?

To uncover the mysteries hidden in a work of art, we must ask questions about its history: Who commissioned the work? Where was it displayed? Who saw it? And has who owned it over the years? Questions about the physical state of the work also raise issues that demand further investigation. Did the artist use an unusual material or an unorthodox method? Does the work appear as the artist intended or has it been altered or damaged? Was it completely finished? Has it deteriorated due to unstable pigments, overexposure to light, an unsafe location, or well-intentioned but misguided methods of restorative care? These are questions that we, as viewers, cannot answer, so we turn to the expertise of art scholars, conservators and scientists whose findings uncover the life of a work beyond its appearance, bringing to light its hidden history, its cultural context and its evolving condition.

The integrated discoveries of archival research, physical evaluation and scientific analysis have revealed fascinating twists in the private lives of popular works of art. Take, for example, Rembrandt van Rijn's acclaimed painting *The Night Watch*. Installed in the most prominent gallery in Amsterdam's Rijksmuseum, it is seen by more than two million visitors a year. It was commissioned in 1640, as part of an ensemble of seven group portraits by Amsterdam's leading artists, featuring the prominent citizens that comprised the voluntary companies of civic guardsmen. Rembrandt's painting accompanied the others in 1642, in the great hall of the Kloveniersdoelen (headquarters of Kloveniers division of civic guards). Aside from an evacuation for safekeeping during the Second World War, as well as removal for periodic cleaning and repair, *The Night Watch* has been on continuous public display. Blazing with colour and brimming with energy, the life-size figures seem ready to burst out of the canvas and into the gallery; modern viewers feel an instant connection with the cinematic sweep of this

centuries-old painting. Looking at it today we feel as if we are granted a glimpse into Rembrandt's world. It is hard to conceive that such an open, exuberant and popular work could hide any secrets from its admiring public.

Since its initial installation in 1642, the public has enjoyed remarkable access to *The Night Watch*. The great hall of the Kloveniersdoelen hosted meetings, banquets and other civic celebrations, and outside of such official events visitors were allowed to come in and view the paintings. After the consolidation of the civic guard units, *The Night Watch* moved, in 1715, to another public space, the Small War Council Chamber on the upper floor of the Town Hall (currently the Royal Palace). In 1808, two years after Napoleon I's brother, Louis Napoleon, was declared the king of Holland, the painting moved again, exhibited with other outstanding Dutch works to herald the foundation of a royal museum. With the collapse of the French occupation in 1815, *The Night Watch* became part of the new national collection, the Rijksmuseum, housed in the Trippenhuis (Trip family mansion) and open to the public. The current home of the Rijksmuseum was built in 1885; architect P.J.H. Cuypers's design features a purpose-built gallery to showcase its most significant painting.

The documented history of the painting is also remarkable. *The Night Watch* is signed and dated; an ambitious painter on the rise, Rembrandt was keen to build his reputation and get his name before the public. The work is first cited in an official record in 1653, when a town council member, Gerrit Shaep Pietersz, compiled a list of paintings in the three *doelens* (guards headquarters). He describes *The Night Watch* as: 'Frans Banning Cocq, captain, and Willem van Ruytenburg, lieutenant, painted by Rembrandt in the year 1642'. At roughly the same time, the Cocq family acquired a small drawing of the painting and preserved it in an album with the inscription 'Sketch of the painting in the great hall of the Kloveniersdoelen, in which the young lord of Purmerland, as captain, orders his lieutenant, the lord of Vlaardingen, to march out his company of civic guardsmen'. The sketch features two figures who are not in the painting. Furthermore, there is a large shield in the painting that does not appear in the sketch. These small differences spark interest. Do we see *The Night Watch* exactly as Rembrandt intended?

The mystery of the missing figures is explained in the historical record. When the painting was moved to the Town Hall in 1715, it proved too large for the intended location and it was trimmed, removing a strip of canvas on every side. The loss on the left side spared the gold-helmeted guard holding a pike, but sacrificed two minor figures behind him. The problem of the shield (centre right background) is not so easily solved. There is no known record of when it was added or by whom or why. Could Rembrandt have added it himself? There have been long-standing rumours that some of the guardsmen felt slighted at the size and position of their portraits; each individual had paid to be included. Given that the shield lists the names of all the guardsmen, its addition could have been to satisfy those who felt they were not fairly represented. Complaints of disgruntled sitters have not been verified, so we cannot be sure exactly when or why the shield was added to the painting. As for the sketch, we can only guess that the artist made it before the adding of the shield, but it is equally possible that the artist simply left it out.

Seventeenth-century descriptions of the painting present yet another discrepancy. None of them refers to the work as *The Night Watch*. In fact, the Rijksmuseum officially lists the painting as *Civic*

Guardsmen of District II under the Command of Captain Frans Banning Cocq, known as the 'Night Watch'. The current title is not documented until 1797, when the National Council of the Batavian Republic registered a receipt for an etched copy of *De Nagtwagt* (*Nachwacht* in Dutch; *Night Watch*). An earlier document may suggest the source of this evocative name. In 1758, city art restorer Jan van Dijk reported on the condition of the painting, calling it 'admirable' as 'a strong sunlight scene'. But he laments that multiple coats of 'boiled oil' and 'varnishes' made it impossible for him to discern 'what kind of company' was depicted. The civic guard held both day watches and night watches; was the varnish on the painting so discoloured that it had turned day into night?

Over the decades a painting changes. Protective coatings can degrade; so can pigments. Smoke, dust and other pollutants can accumulate on the surface. *The Night Watch* is known to have been cleaned at least twenty-five times. And it has suffered several deliberate assaults. In 1911, a man wielding a knife scratched the top layer of varnish. In 1975, another man sliced into the canvas, making twelve cuts that required extensive repair. Acid was sprayed on the surface in 1990, but it did not penetrate the varnish. Each time the painting was cleaned, studied and, where needed, repaired. Each cleaning and repair has presented an opportunity to assess the condition of the painting. The latest initiative was launched on 8th July 2018. In advance of a major preservation project, the Rijksmuseum has assembled a team of more than twenty art scholars, conservators and scientists for Operation *Night Watch*. Using such cutting-edge technologies as high-resolution photography, macro X-ray fluorescence scanning and hyperspectral imaging they will gather and interpret an unprecedented catalogue of data. And,

in contrast to past studies, they will carry out the work right in the gallery, within a protective glass chamber, in full public view. Those who cannot visit the museum can watch the research team in action online via live feed. Operation *Night Watch* will not bring the painting back to its original appearance, but the new information, shared by the experts with an enthusiastic public, may get the painting to relinquish a few more of its secrets. The project demonstrates that, no matter how closely we study a work of art, or how well we think we know it, there is always more to learn.

While Operation *Night Watch* benefits from the use of twenty-first century technology, the key to unlocking a work's secrets is as likely to be found in a letter or a poem, in an obsolete tradition, a play on words or a cryptic emblem, or in a subtle gesture or fashion statement. It might even be embedded in the imagery itself, hiding right there, in plain sight. To augment our own observations and appreciation, we need the collaborative insights of the scholars and scientists who have worked together to coax out what has been covered, concealed – even obliterated – over the ages. And those insights guide us in the chapters that follow, as we look into some of the art world's most intriguing secrets to discover what is hidden from view. We shall peer through layers of paint to chart an artist's change of mind or to bring to light another hand's alterations. We shall untangle the bewildering effects of optical illusion and search for hidden identities. We shall consider the results of censorship, read secret symbols and decode the decorum of dress. And we shall look at works that were never finished, or were broken or lost, to see if the part can tell us the story of the whole. Each case presents a fresh encounter with a familiar work in a tale of secrets that are revealed through facts, but prove to be as fascinating as fiction.

1

1

Seeing Through Paint

AN ENCOUNTER WITH A WORK OF ART BEGINS WITH A SIMPLE QUESTION: WHAT DO WE SEE? The elements that draw our initial attention are contained within the object; its shapes, lines, colours and textures invite us to look and linger. As we do, we augment what we see with our own associations; we forge a relationship with the work based on the knowledge and information we bring to our viewing, our individual preferences and our emotional response. Through sight and thought we can experience a meaningful and enjoyable connection, but there is more to a work of art than just what meets the eye.

Every work of art has a history. Someone made it at a particular moment in time, in a certain place and out of distinctive materials. We may be able to glean that information from the work itself if it is signed and dated, if the maker's biography is well known and if the materials can be identified by their appearance. But sometimes the work is anonymous or undated. The materials might be rare or unrecognizable. To fill in these gaps, art scholars search beyond the visual content of an object for documentary evidence that links the work to a wider world of understanding. Letters, literature and even lore can situate a work in a time or place. They can verify an artist's name or workshop and even trace the work through centuries of ownership, exhibition and critical reception. Even if a precise date or an exact attribution cannot be recovered, the careful analysis of written evidence can construct a context through which the scholar can comprehend and interpret the work.

Documentary research can create a frame of reference for an object; scientific analysis can draw meaning from its physical properties. The presence of a rare material can link a work to a time or a place or to a costly commission. Detection of an unexpected element – particles of dust or a substance invented after the work was created – can expose an alteration, change an attribution or overturn an authentication. During the last century, the use of X-ray and ultraviolet analyses has revealed that telling information hides beneath the surface. Ghostly images may indicate a design change, an addition or a cover up that the unassisted eye cannot see. In this century new technologies, such as multispectral scanning and imaging devices, use a full range of light waves to delve even deeper, providing precise information in greater detail. These scientific tools – many originally devised for medical research – have given scientists and scholars an unprecedented ability to see through the paint.

Seen through the lens of the integrated findings of technology, archival research, scientific analysis and old-fashioned curiosity, familiar works acquire new and richer meanings. The examples that follow reveal how the pigments in a wall painting not only hint at the overall splendour of a lost interior design, but suggest the original function of a puzzling chamber. Images generated using a multispectral camera unveil a series of changes in a portrait of a duke's mistress that chart various stages of their affair. X-ray and ultraviolet analyses uncover surprises hidden in one well-known work and confirm a scandalous tale about another. And the use of digital imaging and projection allow twenty-first century viewers to get a brief glimpse of a suite of works ruined beyond rescue in the twentieth century. The alliance of art history, science and technology does not alter the appearance of the works, but the secrets that are disclosed change how we see them.

MATERIAL MATTERS AND MEANING

Detail of St Michael, Byward Tower
c. 1390s
Tower of London
Historic Royal Palaces, London

In 1953, art restorers removing the lime wash from a wall in Byward Tower in the Tower of London made a stunning discovery. Hidden beneath the centuries-old covering was a medieval painting of the Crucifixion. A massive chimney breast, installed during the Tudor era, had obliterated most of the central figure of Christ on the cross, but the flanking figures – John the Baptist and Mary on the left; John the Evangelist and the Archangel St Michael on the right – were in surprisingly good condition. The depiction of Richard II's patron saint, John the Baptist, raised the possibility that the work dated from late in his reign (r. 1377–1399); the elegant style supported that speculation. Most significantly, the newly revealed painting was the sole surviving example of the original interior embellishment that graced the finer quarters of the vast stronghold.

Few medieval wall paintings have survived the centuries in Britain's damp climate, so preservation was an immediate concern. Given that the surface was fragile, it was deemed best to limit the size and number of fragments extracted for analysis, even though this hindered historic research. More than a half century later, Dr Hadira Liang was invited by Historic Royal Palaces to carry out a new investigation using noninvasive technology. Assisted by a team from Nottingham Trent University, she scanned the paint layers using an optical coherence tomographer (OCT), a portable medical imaging device developed for three-dimensional mapping of the eye. Using portable remote imaging systems for multispectral scanning (PRISMS), she produced high-resolution images via wavelengths across the spectrum, revealing pigments that were rare and expensive. These splendid materials suggested that something important happened in this room.

Byward Tower, which was built during the reign of Henry III (1238–1272), marks the southwest corner of the outer ward. Its two rounded towers flank a portcullis; once a gatehouse with a drawbridge over the moat, it currently serves as the main tourist entrance to the whole venue. The name 'Byward' is a contraction referring to its proximity to the Warders' Hall (by the warders). From 1279 to 1810 Byward Tower housed the Royal Mint; with the guards close by it was a highly secure location. It has long been assumed that the gallery over the portcullis played some role in the mint's operations, and the discovery of the brilliant and costly decor suggests it was the room in which bouillon was sold to the mint to make the coin of the realm. If this was the original function, then St Michael, holding his scale at the site of the Crucifixion, warns the merchants to be honest. Just as their gold is weighed in the present, at the end of days Michael will weigh their souls.

Delicate features and artful postures typify the elegance of the International Style. Seen throughout the courts of Europe from the later fourteenth through to the fifteen centuries, the typical International Style figure was graceful and aristocratic, whether it represented a knight, a peasant or an archangel.

The medieval painter used brilliant and costly mineral pigments: azurite derived from copper ore and vermillion ground from cinnabar. The later analysis also revealed red lac, made from the secretions of the lac insect, which is native to India.

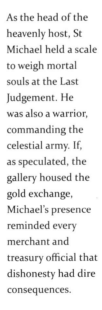

As the head of the heavenly host, St Michael held a scale to weigh mortal souls at the Last Judgement. He was also a warrior, commanding the celestial army. If, as speculated, the gallery housed the gold exchange, Michael's presence reminded every merchant and treasury official that dishonesty had dire consequences.

The lustrous green background, painted in verdigris made of copper, simulates a silk drape. It is embellished with royal symbols – fleur-de-lis and Plantagenet lions – in gold leaf. There are also collared parakeets, traditional symbols of trust and loyalty. The combination enriched the appearance of the chamber while asserting royal authority.

Byward Tower was built in the thirteenth century, when Henry III surrounded the whole of the twelfth-century fortress with an extra layer of defence. It served as a secure gatehouse, with a drawbridge and a double portcullis. During the 1281 poll tax protest known as Wat Tyler's Rebellion, Richard II ordered further fortifications of the tower and remained there for the duration of the uprising.

The exact date of installation of the stone chimney breast is not known, but the construction suggests the Tudor era. As can be seen behind the later brick facing, it was decorated with a painted Tudor rose. Built over the centre of the medieval wall painting, the addition destroyed the heart of the Crucifixion scene, although a bit of the arm of the cross remains visible on the right.

MEANINGFUL LAYERS

The Lady with an Ermine
Leonardo da Vinci (1452–1519)
c. 1489–1490
Oil on panel
54.8 x 40.3 cm (21 x 16 in)
Czartoryski Museum, Krakow

When the stoat (*Mustela erminea*) moults its sparse brown coat and grows dense white winter fur it is called an ermine. Agile and aggressive, this sharp-toothed predator makes an unlikely pet, but the sitter in Leonardo da Vinci's *Lady with an Ermine* is fully at ease with the sinewy animal resting in her arms. Their bodies twist in unison expressing a physical, and even emotional, bond.

A letter discovered in 1900 confirms the sitter's identity as Cecilia Gallerani (1473–1536). Her father served as a financial agent to the duke of Milan, and the ermine may have been a play on her family name: contemporary art scholars cite the word *galée* as a reference in Greek to the ermine. She, too, had court connections: beautiful and well educated, Cecilia was the mistress of Ludovico Sforza (1452–1508), uncle and regent to the reigning duke of Milan. Ludovico had two nicknames: Il Moro, for his dark complexion, and l'Ermelino, or the White Ermine. In 1488, shortly before his liaison with Cecilia began, Ludovico joined the chivalric Order of the Ermine. Founded by King Ferdinand of Naples in 1464, the order's motto, *Malo mori quam foedari* (Death over dishonour), drew on the ermine's legendary purity; it would die rather than soil its snowy coat.

Within a year of his investiture, Ludovico engaged Leonardo to paint Cecilia, the artist's first commissioned portrait since joining the ducal household as resident painter in 1482. Whether a tribute to Cecilia's character, a pun on her name, or an allusion to her bond with her lover, the ermine is an integral feature of the portrait. However, recent scientific analysis revealed that it was not part of Leonardo's initial conception.

In 2014, the French engineer Pascal Cotte, working with Lumière Technology, employed the layer amplification method (LAM), in which a multispectral camera, used to record the effects of thirteen different wavelengths of light directed at the surface, generated more than 1,600 images. When analysed, these images track the material variants within the painting's layers – Cotte compares this to peeling an onion – documenting the artist's process in unprecedented detail.

Cotte discovered two earlier stages beneath the finished portrait. In the first, Cecilia is alone. She is joined by an ermine in the second stage, one much smaller, milder, and greyer than the lithe and muscular animal in the final version. Do the changes chart the rising intensity of the relationship, or perhaps something more? In 1490 Giacomo Trotti, Ferrara's ambassador to Milan, wrote to Ercole d'Este, duke of Ferrara, that Ludovico – betrothed to the young daughter of the duke since 1480 – did not look forward to his upcoming political marriage due to the fact that his mistress, described as being as beautiful as a flower (*bella come un fiore*), now carried his child. The powerful presence of the ermine in the final stage may refer to another enduring association: steadfast and pure, the ermine protected pregnant women.

The ermine is an integral feature of the portrait. However, recent scientific analysis revealed that it was not part of Leonardo's initial conception.

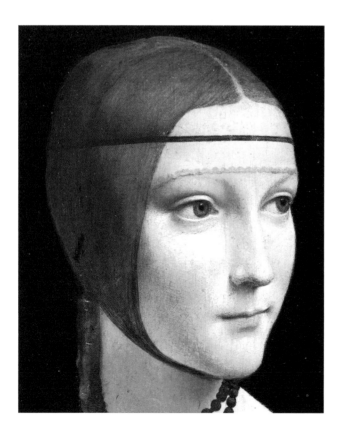

A sonnet written in 1492 by the Ludovico's court poet, Bernardo Bellincioni, asked Nature if she envied Leonardo's exquisite portrayal of Cecilia, 'one of your stars'. In his praise for Ludovico's generosity and Leonardo's skill, Bellincioni authenticated the patron and the painter. Cecilia also mentioned the painting six years later, in a letter to Isabella d'Este, lamenting that it was 'painted when I was much younger. Since then I have greatly changed'.

A distinct optical effect is produced when a wavelength bounces off a type of matter. The LAM uses thirteen different wavelengths to penetrate the layers of a painting, exposing the slightest distinction in the density and composition of pigments. The data retrieved and assembled here reveals an unprecedented account of Leonardo's supple capacity to change his ideas as he worked, but it does not explain his motives behind these changes.

The Ermine as a Symbol of Purity
Leonardo da Vinci
c. 1494
Drawing (brown ink, black chalk, paper)
91 mm (3.6 in) diameter
The Fitzwilliam Museum, Cambridge

Poised on the edge of a bog, the ermine in Leonardo's drawing turns back towards the hunter, ready to surrender rather than muddy its pristine coat. Leonardo recorded this lore in a notebook (Ms. H 1494) along with the belief that, as a model of moderation, the ermine ate only once a day.

SCIENCE AND SPECULATION

The Blue Boy
Thomas Gainsborough (1727–1788)
c. 1770
Oil on canvas
179.4 × 123.8 cm (70.6 × 48.7 in)
The Huntington Library, Art Collections,
and Botanical Gardens, San Marino, CA

From the time it was painted, questions have swirled around Thomas Gainsborough's most recognized work. With no date inscribed, its debut possibly occurred at the 1770 exhibition of the Royal Academy of Arts in London, as suggested by Mary Moser's comments to a fellow academician: 'Gainsborough is beyond himself in a portrait of a gentleman in a Van Dyke habit'. But that year, Gainsborough exhibited four portraits of men – two full-length and two half-length – and he had already painted his nephew, Edward Richard Gardiner, in a 'Van Dyke habit' in the previous decade. The Blue Boy's identity remained in question until 1808, when Edward Edwards asserted that it was 'a Master Brutall [sic] whose father was then a very considerable ironmonger, in Greek-street [sic] Soho.' The painting had been owned by Jonathan Buttall (1752–1805), the son of a successful Soho hardware merchant; it was sold as part of a bankruptcy auction of his possessions in 1796. Buttall would have been in his late teens when the work was painted, and Gainsborough knew the family from his days in Ipswich (1752–*c.* 1759). Closer confirmation has not been found.

In 1921, once a substantial layer of discoloured varnish was removed, pentimenti appeared near the top of the canvas. An X-ray analysis, in 1939, revealed the head of an older man wearing a white stock beneath that of the sitter. This provided a sound explanation for two uncharacteristic features of the painting. The canvas was 60 cm (2 ft) shorter than the conventional height for a full-length portrait, and the paint application on the face and the surrounding area was much heavier than Gainsborough's typical feathery touch. Clearly he had reused a canvas, cutting it down and painting over a discarded portrait. While this did not shed light on the sitter's identity, the repurposed canvas made a strong case that Gainsborough was painting the work for his own pleasure, perhaps featuring the son of a friend.

There were more surprises to come. Extensive examination in 1994 – employing microscopic, infrared and ultraviolet analyses – revealed a ghost of a large white dog, resembling an English water spaniel, on the young man's left. Its position and prominence indicated that Gainsborough originally gave his sitter a canine companion and then replaced it with a pile of rocks. Scientific analysis cannot explain this decision; that is a puzzle for art history to solve. More information may be found when a new round of conservation – launched at the time of this writing – reaches its conclusions. Whatever the findings, the work of science, coupled with that of art history will certainly shed even more light on a familiar and beloved painting.

Edward Edwards's 1808 claim that the sitter was Jonathan Buttall was readily accepted and remains the consensus attribution. But some scholars, wary of the nearly four-decade gap between the creation of the painting and Edwards's publication, speculate that Buttall was merely one of the owners and that the sitter has yet to be identified.

The pentimenti noticed prior to the 1939 examination raised speculation that the elegant young man initially wore the hat rather than holding it in his hand. This was disproved by the X-ray analysis. As with the variety of silks portrayed in the whole ensemble – the soft breeches, the tight-knit hose, the stiffened bows on the shoes – the soft plume on the hat demonstrates Gainsborough's subtle ability to simulate sumptuous surfaces.

The brilliant-blue silk doublet is a perfect line-by-line replica of what a privileged youth would wear in Van Dyke's day. It appears at least four times in Gainsborough's portraits of young men, suggesting that he owned the ensemble.

On the left, X-radiography reveals the ghost figure beneath the Blue Boy, rising above the stretcher – a sure indication that the canvas was cut down. The reflectographic image on the right presents the dog seated rather than standing and reveals that Gainsborough changed his mind about the dog more than once.

Gainsborough Dupont
Thomas Gainsborough
1773
Oil on canvas
51.6 x 38.8 cm (20.3 x 15.3 in)
Waddesdon Manor, Aylesbury

Gainsborough painted other young men in the blue Van Dyke ensemble. Here, the collar, shoulder treatment and sleeve slash match that of the doublet worn by the Blue Boy. Some scholars speculate that Dupont – Gainsborough's nephew and studio assistant – also sat for the earlier portrait, but his sharp features seem distinctly different.

TRACKING THE TRACES OF A SCANDAL

Madame X (Madame Pierre Gautreau)
John Singer Sargent (1856–1925)
1883–1884
Oil on canvas
208.6 x 109.9 cm (82.1 x 43.3 in)
Metropolitan Museum of Art, New York, NY

As an ambitious young portrait painter in Paris, John Singer Sargent was on the lookout for a glamorous sitter whose image would establish his reputation. He found her in the American-born socialite Virginie Gautreau (1859–1915). She was known throughout Paris for her dramatic sense of style and her extraordinary looks, and many young artists vied to paint her; Sargent was the first to persuade her to sit. But in the summer of 1883, after months of work, Sargent was struggling with the portrait. As was his practice, he had chosen a gown from her own wardrobe, a tightly fitted black velvet and satin sheath from the Maison Félix, with a deep decolletage, supported by delicate diamond straps. The daring and severe silhouette showcased her statuesque proportions and her pale yet luminous complexion, which she always enhanced with a lavender-toned powder. Sargent lamented to friends that her beauty was 'unpaintable' as he repeatedly modified the grey-brown hue of the background with translucent rose glazes to temper the unearthly glow of her skin.

Sargent's tonal adjustments to the area around his sitter's right shoulder are clearly visible on the finished canvas, but X-radiographic examination has exposed his uncharacteristic uncertainty about the pose of his sitter. Sargent made many preliminary sketches, focusing on the sinuous line of Madame Gautreau's arms, neck and shoulders, as well as her pointed profile. Yet, as the X-radiograph reveals, he continued to revise as he painted, modifying the contour of her head and her right arm, raising the neckline of her dress, and moving the placement of her hand on her hip. The profile proved troublesome as well, seen in at least eight different attempts. A murky shadow over her shoulder indicates that he twice shifted the position of her diamond strap, and his final decision to let it ride low on her arm sealed the fate of his work when it debuted at the 1884 Paris Salon. Rather than a striking likeness of an unorthodox beauty, Sargent's portrait of Madame Gautreau was derided as an audacious and vulgar bid for attention on the part of a pair of ambitious Americans.

Today, that strap sits firmly on Madame Gautreau's shoulder; hurt by the *succès de scandale*, Sargent took the painting back to his studio immediately after the exhibition and repositioned it. Until recently, only a grainy black-and-white photograph and a wood engraving portrayed the painting as it appeared at its debut. In 2015, Don Undeen, senior manager of MediaLab at the Metropolitan Museum of Art examined a full-scale digital version of the painting, using an infrared flashlight and an infrared camera. The light, tracked by the camera, 'burned through' the surface layer, revealing the seductive slip as seen by Sargent's original audience. Through cutting-edge science, twenty-first-century viewers can now get a truer glimpse of a time when an artist's – and a woman's reputation – could dangle on a thin band of diamonds.

FAR LEFT Using a full-scale digital replica and an infrared flashlight that creates a circular mask on the surface, an infrared camera burns through the over paint without damaging the surface.

LEFT For more than a century, this 1884 photograph was the prime document of Sargent's original concept. It is not known whether Sargent commissioned the photograph, and it was not widely circulated.

This 1885 photograph of Sargent's studio presents the painting as it appears today. It is not known exactly when Sargent repainted the slipped strap, but clearly he did it in the immediate aftermath of the scandal. Sargent remained reluctant to exhibit the portrait, but kept it, regarding it as one of his best works.

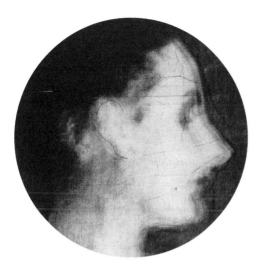

These X-radiographic images expose Sargent's subtle adjustments to the precise lines of his sitter's head, arms and shoulders. At least eight profiles can be discerned, and he considered placing her right hand on her hip. He raised the gown's low decolletage and, most intriguing, in his initial rendering, the strap was firm and high on her shoulder.

Fascinated by his sitter's languorous contours, Sargent sketched her in poses that emphasized her long neck, broad shoulders and corseted waist. Here, as she leans back into the settee, one of the diamond straps on her dress slides down the crest of her shoulder. Perhaps this sketch gave him the idea to allow the strap to slip into its suggestive position.

NEW LIGHT ON FADED GLORY

Harvard Art Mural Triptych
Mark Rothko (1903–1970)
1962
Egg tempera and distemper on canvas
Panel #1: 267.3 × 297. 8 cm (105.2 × 117.2 in)
Panel #2: 267.3 × 458.8 cm (105.2 × 180.6 in)
Panel #3: 267 × 243.8 cm (105.1 × 96 in)
Harvard Art Museums, Cambridge, MA

The commission to paint five murals for the new Holyoke Center at Harvard University, in 1962, presented Mark Rothko with an ideal opportunity. Believing that nothing should stand 'between the idea and the observer', he preferred an immersive environment for the installation of his large, colour-saturated canvases. He hung the suite of unframed paintings low on the east/west walls of the dining and special events room on the top floor of the modernist building designed by Josep Lluís Sert. Two panels were mounted on one side to flank the open door; the three panels known as 'The Triptych' were installed on the opposite wall. Rothko requested that the floor-to-ceiling windows of the north/south walls be covered with light-blocking fibreglass curtains. But the curtains were rarely closed, and the paintings suffered from exposure to light, as well as the lack of Rothko's intended 'close quarters' with the viewer.

Within fifteen years, the paintings were light damaged, dented and torn, and marred with food stains and graffiti. In 1979, the university removed the murals and placed them in storage.

Rothko's use of an unstable or fugitive pigment – Lithol red – mixed with an unstable animal-skin glue binder had hastened the deterioration of the paintings. He worked on untreated canvas, resulting in a porous and fragile surface. Ektachrome colour transparencies of his radiant colour scheme had been taken in 1964, but they, too, had faded. While twentieth-century attempts to verify Rothko's original hues fell short of intended objectives, more satisfying results were achieved through twenty-first-century technological research prompted by the desire to give the public a better idea of the original appearance of the murals. A digital restoration of the degraded transparences established a baseline example for Rothko's crimson-based palette. A software program, developed for the project by a joint team from Harvard University and the Massachusetts Institute of Technology, isolated colours and allowed pixel-by-pixel analysis of each painting. This data charted discrepancies between the dulled murals and the brilliant tones still observable in a stored canvas that Rothko chose not to include. Never exposed to light, it provided another example of colours now irrecoverably lost.

A set of 'compensational' digital images was created to simulate the original tones. The public experienced this virtual recreation in a 2014-2015 exhibition featuring the five canvases in a space that approximated the horizontal dimensions of the dining hall. Five cameras 'corrected' the paintings through digital projection. According to critic Louis Menand, the effect brought the ruined canvases 'back from the dead'. Near the end of the day, the projectors were switched off one by one to reveal the actual state of the faded murals. Although technology could not reverse the damage, it offered a way to experience the intended glory of the murals without causing them further harm.

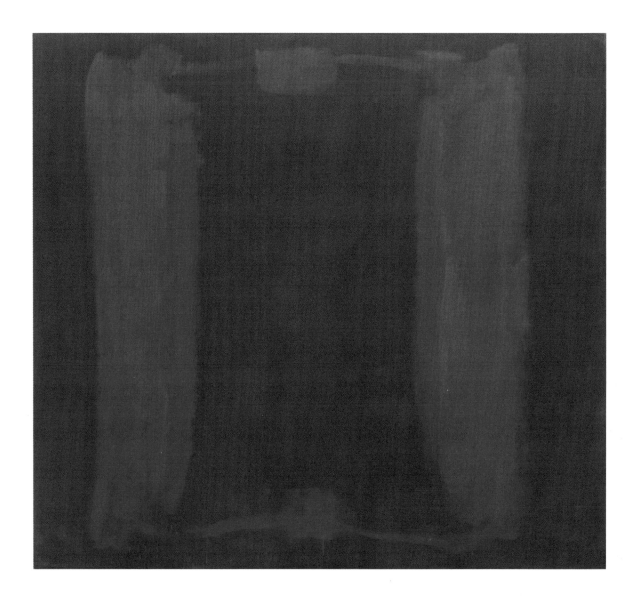

Rothko achieved his vivid saturated tones by brushing transparent veils of colour on an untreated, highly absorbent canvas. Mixing Lithol red pigment with animal-skin glue and whole eggs, he created a radiant crimson that he not only used in pure form, but mixed with other colours to unite the ensemble. The light sensitivity of the pigment and the instability of the binder accelerated surface deterioration.

With similar dimensions to the original site in the Holyoke Center (now the Smith Campus Center), the exhibition gallery at the Harvard Art Museums met Rothko's desire that viewers share 'close quarters' with his paintings. The three panels known as 'The Triptych', filled one wall of the original site; the two remaining panels flanked the open doors on the opposite wall. The absence of windows allowed complete control of the lighting for the murals' safety and the viewer's aesthetic experience.

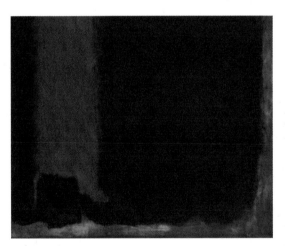

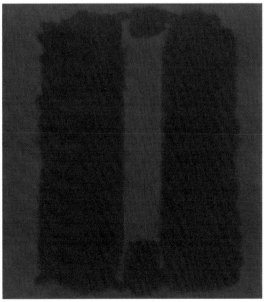

Rothko applied his paint in layers that ranged from diaphanous staining to impenetrable opacity. His brushwork is an essential element of his work. Current conservation practice demands that inpainting be observable and removable; for these works it is not a viable solution. Inpainting with light only simulates the colours; it does not restore the full effect of the original surface. But kept to a low level, it does no further damage.

Rothko's formal architecture was based on the rectangle, which he floated on a distinctively brushed, edge-to-edge surface. The forms in the triptych panels suggest portals that evoke dimension through colour variation rather than perspective.

2

Under the the Surface

THE SURFACE OF A WORK OF ART STAGES
THE VIEWER'S VISUAL EXPERIENCE. Whether
colourful or monochromatic, rough or smooth,
crafted from a single substance or a combination
of materials, what lies on the surface ignites our
interest. We build a relationship with the work in
our imagination as colours and shapes, forms and
textures all coalesce into meaning. The work may
trigger an emotional response, reminding us of an
event or a story, or it might prompt us to ponder what
inspired its creation. The surface can be perceived as
a window, drawing us in for a closer look. But what
if the surface is a curtain that conceals the artist's
own intentions, or acts as a door that locks away an
earlier stage of endeavour? In order to uncover these
secrets we must find a way to penetrate the surface
and see what is hidden within its layers.

Many works of art bear visible traces of what
lies beneath the surface. The term 'pentimento'
(from the Italian *pentirsi*, to repent), describes the
presence of a lost line or image that can be glimpsed
beneath a thin veil of pigment or through faded
paint. A loss of material can expose a lower layer or
a repair can leave a visible scar. These traces hint at
the life of the work beyond what is readily visible,
but to understand them we must delve deeper and
turn to the collaborative expertise of those who
examine every aspect of the work, from its physical
fabric to the history of its creation. Art historians
and curators can research an artist's practice. Did
they use elaborate underpainting or glazing to give
the surface its distinctive appearance? Did they
paint on an unorthodox support that mutates the
medium? The conservator may uncover a surprise

when cleaning a work; an old layer of varnish or a
later veneer of paint may mask the artist's original
image. Was the work altered in some way or created
on a repurposed panel or canvas found in a market
or in a dusty corner of the studio? Scientific analysis
now gives the conservator and the curator the ability
to see beneath the surface, revealing things that
have been hiding for centuries.

In recent decades, advances in light-scanning
technology have made it possible to separate and
examine even the sheerest layers of paint and the
most complex components in pigments, as well as to
detect the minutest material inconsistencies. These
methods are noninvasive, gathering information
without damaging the integrity of surface. But
material evidence does not hold all the answers,
and new information sparks further enquiry and
even raises curatorial and interpretative dilemmas.
As the following examples reveal, removing a patch
of paint may transform the power of a picture, but
the reason for the cover-up remains unexplained. An
alteration once attributed to the artist proves to be a
later addition; perhaps a seller or an owner wanted
to transform the work so that it better conformed
to the artist's signature style. Did an artist reuse
a canvas as a measure of economy or to edit the
arc of their development? Can a simple cleaning so
transform the appearance of a work that it changes
our understanding of an artist's developmental
chronology? And what if an artist paints in such a
way that the layering of their medium is part of the
visual experience? In every case, there are secrets
to be found beneath the surface.

DISCOVERY ON THE SHORE

View of Scheveningen Sands
Hendrick van Anthonissen (1605–1656)
c. 1641
Oil on wood panel
56.8 × 102.8 cm (22.4 × 40.5 in)
The Fitzwilliam Museum, Cambridge

This modestly scaled marine painting came to The Fitzwilliam Museum as part of a bequest from Richard Edward Kerrich in 1873. The Cambridge-born clergyman and amateur artist inherited a fine collection from his father Thomas that included oil sketches by Peter Paul Rubens and drawings by Albrecht Dürer. In value and significance those works overshadowed Hendrick van Athonissen's coastal scene, but *View of Scheveningen Sands* presented an appealing, albeit unassuming example of Dutch Golden Age painting. Van Anthonissen was a minor master who specialized in seascapes featuring volatile skies, rolling waters and ships in full sail. *View of Scheveningen Sands* marked a nuanced departure from this formula; the skies are relatively calm, sands rather than sea dominate the composition and small groups of people cluster across the foreground. No clear narrative could be discerned, and the subject appeared to be the coast itself with staffage figures placed to add life to an otherwise unremarkable vista.

Time had taken its toll on the painting. Over the years the natural resin varnish, brushed on to enrich and protect the surface, darkened and yellowed. In 2014 the work arrived at the Hamilton Kerr Institute, the conservation laboratory affiliated with the museum, for cleaning. As conservator Shan Kuang began the meticulous task of removing the varnish, she noticed a variance in the painted surface around the horizon in the lower-right quadrant. She recognized it as overpainting – a later addition – and removed a bit of it to see what was underneath. A puzzling figure appeared. A man seemed to be standing on the horizon looking at an undersized sail. The conservation team agreed to remove the overpainting, and with the aid of a microscope, Kuang took it off with solvents and a scalpel. She discovered what had drawn the crowds to the shoreline: a stranded whale, lying upright so that its fin looked like a little sail against the sky.

Although hardly unprecedented, a giant sea mammal beached on the shore would certainly have drawn a crowd in seventeenth-century Netherlands. The figures now have a purpose: they have come to get a first-hand look at a real-life leviathan, known to most only through mythology and the Bible. Given the sight line, van Anthonissen seems to have been there too, making accurate sketches for his portrayal of a natural phenomenon. The man revealed in the cleaning had climbed up on the whale, perhaps to measure its magnificent proportions. Two mysteries remain: Why was the whale painted out of the picture? And when did it happen? There is no mention of the whale in the painting's provenance, so we may never know the answers.

When the painting came into the museum's collection, it appeared to be a highly conventional shore scene. The rough seas and volatile sky suggested harsh weather, as did the small boats pulled up on the sands. The presence of what seemed to be a sail on the near horizon seemed consistent with the boats in the distance.

The hazy form on the horizon had been taken for a sail, but something just did not look right.

As the conservator removed the yellowed resin, the figure of a man appeared. The shadowy mass on which he stood was clearly not a boat, and further work revealed a dorsal fin, leading the conservator to uncover the hulking body of the whale.

Removing the over paint revealed the focus of the painting: a beached whale that drew a curious crowd to the shoreline on a blustery day. The careful observation and clear depiction suggests that the painter was there, too.

During the Dutch Golden Age the appearance of a beached whale was regarded as a portent of disaster. But it was also regarded as a rare opportunity to observe an extraordinary creature at close range. The man perched on top of the massive mammal may have climbed up there for sport, but was just as likely to have been measuring the whale.

PICTURE WITHIN A PICTURE

Girl Reading a Letter at an Open Window
Johannes Vermeer (1632–1675)
1657–1659
Oil on canvas
83 × 64.5 cm (33 × 25.4 in)
Gemäldegalerie, Dresden

In 1979, an X-ray analysis hinted that a painting once hung on the back wall of Johannes Vermeer's exquisite depiction of a woman alone in a chamber, reading a letter. The concept of a picture within a picture was consistent with Vermeer's other work. More than twenty of his thirty-six authenticated canvases feature either a map or paintings in the background to add context or commentary to his subtle narratives. Here, the covered image appeared to be of Cupid; the tonal quality of the overpainting, as well as the way in which the neutral background of the blank wall set off the intimate isolation of the figure, suggested that Vermeer himself had made the change.

Nearly three decades later new analyses undermined this conclusion. In 2017, prior to formulating a conservation programme to remove the top layer of yellowed varnish (possibly applied in the nineteenth century), the Gemäldegalerie gathered fresh data through a microscopic surface study and infrared reflectography. X-ray fluorescence spectroscopy – employing wavelength dispersal technology similar to that used in an electron microprobe – investigated even further beneath the surface, revealing a fine layer of dust trapped between the overpainted patch and the original coat of varnish. Although the results could not pinpoint the date of the overpainting, they indicated that the layer of dust had accumulated after Vermeer varnished his canvas.

Following a thorough consultation with a panel of scholars, the museum formulated a conservation plan that began in 2018. They would remove the overpainted patch along with the yellowed varnish.

In order to detach the over paint, conservator Christoph Schözel plied a scalpel under high magnification; even the gentlest solvent might dissolve Vermeer's delicate varnish. This painstaking work takes years, but the removal of the yellowed varnish and the exposure of Cupid's body, completely transform the painting. The tones, once golden ochre as seen through the discolored coating, are now cooler, greyer, and far subtler. Even a partial exposure of the figure of Cupid – just the head and upper torso – links it with at least two other paintings that feature the same, plain-framed image on the back wall. An inventory of Vermeer's possessions compiled after his death indicates that he owned a 'picture of Cupid', but the figure is not described. As painted here, with a bow in his right arm and a card marked with the Roman numeral 'I' in his upraised left, Cupid's pose recalls that of the emblem advocating monogamy in Otto van Veem's popular emblem book, *Amorum Emblamata* (1608). As with a motto that accompanies an emblem, this picture within a picture adds a commentary to Vermeer's once austere composition. Rather than providing an intimate glimpse of a very private moment, the painting now offers a lesson about love.

As the overpainted patch is removed, the figure of Cupid is revealed. The sheer size and bright tonality of the depiction completely changes the mood of the painting from contemplative to either anecdotal or didactic.

While the layer of dust discovered beneath the overpainted patch reveals that the painting was altered after Vermeer applied his final coat of varnish, it is not possible to explain the addition. Theories include changing taste, a prudish reaction to the naked Cupid or a preference for Vermeer's more restrained compositions.

The altered composition enhances the intimacy of the moment. The ample green curtain on the right and the carpet-covered table in the foreground isolate the figure; the neutrality of the wall emphasizes her solitude. The viewer can only guess at the contents of the letter, but the woman's rapt attention and parted lips suggest a personal message.

Amorum Emblamata
Otto van Veem (1556–1629)
1608

Emblem books, pairing images and
mottos, were popular in Vermeer's
day. In Otto van Veem's *Amorum
Emblemata*, the subject was love.
Here the motto instructs the reader
to be faithful, declaring 'A lover
ought to have only one'.

A Young Woman Standing at a Virginal
Johannes Vermeer
c. 1670–1672
Oil on canvas
51.7 × 45.2 cm (20.4 × 17.8 in)
National Gallery, London

Vermeer featured the
painting of Cupid raising
a card in several works. It
is believed to have been in
the painter's collection and
is attributed to Cesar van
Everdingen. The distinctive
pose and the thick brown
frame match the painting
now revealed in *Girl Reading
a Letter at an Open Window*.

UNDERLYING INFLUENCE

Man with a Leather Belt
Gustave Courbet (1819–1877)
1845–1846
110 × 82 cm (39.3 × 32.2 in)
Musée d'Orsay, Paris

As an aspiring artist in Paris, Gustave Courbet replaced the rigorous curriculum of formal training with intense self-guided study of masterworks in the Musée du Louvre. He was particularly drawn to the art of the seventeenth century, and the influence of Spanish, Dutch and Italian painting of the era is evident in more than twenty self-portraits painted between 1842 and 1855. It had long been common practice for artists to paint their own likeness to save the expense of hiring models. But for Courbet, testing the lessons he learned in the Louvre by portraying himself in a range of emotions and characters linked his work to tradition and helped him forge what he called an 'independent sense of my own identity'. His assimilation of seventeenth-century portraiture can be seen in the realist vision, contemplative pose and golden-brown palette of this painting, originally titled *Portrait of M. X****.

Nine years later, Courbet exhibited the work under a new title: *Portrait of the Artist/A Study of the Venetians*. He did not comment on the change, but in 1973, when the work was subjected to X-ray analysis, an explanation was revealed. Beneath the surface of the work now known as *Man with a Leather Belt* was a copy of Titian's *Man with a Glove* in Courbet's own hand. Like many struggling artists, Courbet often reused his canvases, and the copies he

made in the Louvre were intended for study rather than exhibition. Titian's portrait of an elegant but anonymous Venetian courtier had been in the Louvre's collection since 1792, and while Courbet did not acknowledge its influence, the similarities – and the differences – between the paintings are striking and significant.

In both, the half-length figure of the sitter looms close to the surface of the picture plane, emerging from a dramatically shadowed background and bathed in warm light. Neither looks out at the viewer; both have an enigmatic, side-long gaze. Even their garments are similar: dark jackets, open collars, white cuffs. Courbet also copied the way Titian painted his sitter's hands, although he inverted the position on the left so that the extended forefinger draws back his flowing hair. On the right, he rotated the hand slightly, and, instead of holding a soft glove, Courbet's figure grasps his thick, roughly crafted belt. With the addition of a sketchbook and chalk on the left, Courbet asserts his 'independent' identity. The painter's tools, his rustic garments and his large capable hands mark Courbet as a modern man of purpose – a working man – who supplants the Venetian man of privilege painted just under the surface.

Combining grace and strength, Courbet's arched right hand recreates the position portrayed by Titian. But in contrast, he uses the relaxed gesture to call attention to his flowing hair. And while Titian's sitter wears a ring and has a frilled cuff, Courbet's hand is unadorned and his shirt is plain.

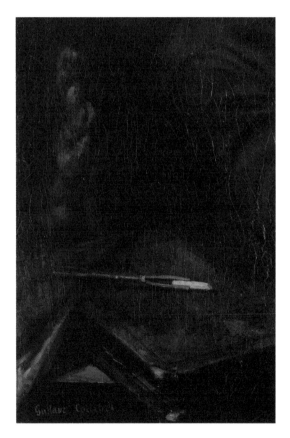

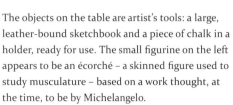

The objects on the table are artist's tools: a large, leather-bound sketchbook and a piece of chalk in a holder, ready for use. The small figurine on the left appears to be an écorché – a skinned figure used to study musculature – based on a work thought, at the time, to be by Michelangelo.

The thick leather belt is old and worn but serviceable, and the hand gripping it is large and strong. Although Courbet's composition refers to Titian's sitter through gesture, his choice to replace the soft expensive glove with a crude belt makes an important social distinction.

Man with a Glove
Tiziano Vecellio (1488/90–1576)
c. 1520
Oil on canvas
100 x 89 cm (39 x 35 in)
Musée du Louvre, Paris

Artists practised technique and honed their skills by copying esteemed works of art. For Courbet, Titian's moody and mysterious portrayal of a man roughly his own age provided not only a lesson in the drama of shadow, lighting and contrast, but a challenge to create a modern counterpart featuring his own likeness. The fact that he painted his portrait directly over his copy of Titian's suggests that he had gleaned all he could from the older work and no longer needed it in the studio.

Desperate Man
Gustave Courbet
1843–1845
Oil on canvas
45 x 54 cm (17.7 x 21.3 in)
Private collection

With a startled stare, tensed brow and flared nostrils, Courbet's Desperate Man seems to lunge forward, as if to break out of the picture plane. His skin flushes and he parts his lips, but he seems frozen on the spot. There is no explanation for his desperation; in fact the cause does not matter. Courbet – recognized by his soulful eyes, flowing hair and powerful hands – did not seek to tell a story in this self-portrait. Following Rembrandt's example, he used his own likeness to master facial expression.

NEW IDEAS, NEW INSIGHTS

Woman Ironing
Pablo Picasso (1881–1973)
1904
Oil on canvas
116.2 × 73 cm (45.7 × 28.7 in)
Solomon R. Guggenheim Museum, New York, NY

Pablo Picasso first visited Paris in 1900, to see his painting *Last Moments* (1899) in the Spanish display at the Exposition Universelle. Restless and striving for recognition, he spent the next several years moving back and forth between Paris and Spain. His new surroundings initially inspired him to paint nightlife subjects in vibrant colours, but personal loss and financial hardship turned his vision in a striking new direction. Limiting his palette to a single hue, modulated with white, ochre and grey, Picasso turned to themes of poverty, introspection and loneliness in what is now called his Blue Period (1901–1904).

Painted in the spring of 1904, *Woman Ironing* features the nuanced range of tone from deep midnight blue to icy blue-tinged silver that he mastered through his monochromatic experiments. The emaciated figure embodies the melancholic spirit of the Blue Period, quietly resigned to her numbingly hard work. Hidden beneath the surface, *Woman Ironing* features another hallmark of the Blue Period; with little money for supplies, Picasso painted it on a used canvas. An X-ray analysis in 1989 confirmed the existence of an underlying image: a standing male figure in three-quarter length.

More than twenty years later, infrared imaging spectroscopy amplified the limited findings of the X-ray analysis. Using hyperspectral cameras that break infrared light into hundreds of distinctive bands, Dr John Delany, senior imaging scientist at the National Gallery of Art, Washington, D.C. was able to suppress the surface image and gather the information beneath it. The three-quarter-length portrait now had a distinctive face, with clear, strongly drawn features. Subtle tonality, variants in hue and details of dress could be read. The extent and clarity of this data also facilitated the study of paint application and brushstroke, leading curators to authenticate that the hidden painting was also by Picasso.

Infrared imaging spectroscopy provided a wealth of visual information, but it raised an intriguing question: Who was this man? Without an inscription on the painting, or a document that refers to the hidden work, scholars compared the man's facial features to those in Picasso's circle. The strongest resemblance is seen in an undated self-portrait by Ricard Canals – Picasso's friend and sometime rival – most notably in the round contours of his face, his curling forelock and his intense brown eyes. There is even a suggestion that it might be Picasso himself. The new analysis has also changed the way we see *Woman Ironing*. Prior to the spectroscopic analysis, the painting was meticulously cleaned and conserved, revealing previously unseen touches of pink pigment in the background and on the woman's dress. Here, once hidden in an iconic work, are the first glimmers of transformation from the cold despair of the Blue Period to the warmth and luminosity of the Rose Period (1904–1906).

Julia Barten, the senior conservator at the Guggenheim Museum, completed an extensive cleaning and conservation of the painting in 2012. As she removed patches of discoloured glue that had been applied to the surface as part of a repair in 1952, she was amazed to see the surface brighten with lively brushstrokes and touches of pink. Once regarded as an iconic example of the Blue Period, the cleaned painting now forecasts Picasso's next development: the Rose Period.

The 1989 X-ray analysis revealed a ghost image of man with a moustache standing beside an unidentifiable object. Infrared imaging spectroscopy augmented that image, revealing a distinctive face, details of dress and traces of colour. The form on the right, though still blurred, appears to be an easel, suggesting that the man might be a painter or that he posed in Picasso's studio.

No more than skin and bones, the woman leans the full force of her weight into her task. Her hair tumbles with the effort, but her face, with its strong profile and deeply shadowed eyes, lends her weary form a monumental dignity.

The skilful shading of the woman's arms and hands evokes the effort of pressing on the iron, warming her skin tone with a muted but rose-toned flush of exertion. The paintings of the Blue Period are never solely blue.

La Vie
Pablo Picasso
1903
Oil on canvas
196.5 × 129.2 cm (77.4 × 50.9 in)
Cleveland Museum of Art, Cleveland, OH

Picasso repeatedly painted over his early work. Although the deathbed scene *Last Moments* marked an important milestone in his career, Picasso used the canvas to paint one of his most ambitious Blue Period compositions: the enigmatic *La Vie*. Did Picasso reuse canvases to save money or did he intend to edit the arc of his artistic development?

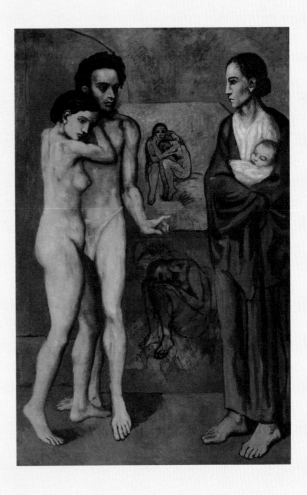

ICON INTO ART

White Flag
Jasper Johns (b. 1930)
1955
Encaustic, oil, newsprint, charcoal on canvas
198.9 x 306.7 cm (78.3 x 120.7 in)
Metropolitan Museum of Art, New York, NY

Jasper Johns tells a surprisingly mundane creation story about his most iconic subject: 'I dreamt one night that I painted the flag of America. The next day I did it.'

He began the first of his flags in 1954. To handle the large scale (107 x 152 cm/3.5 x 5 ft) Johns crafted three separate sections, which he assembled after rendering the stars and stripes in an authentic palette of red, white and blue. The resulting image was straightforward and familiar, yet at the same time, ambiguous and strange. The next year, Johns pushed his new theme into truly unfamiliar territory. *White Flag* marked the first of his monochromatic iterations in his ongoing series of flags, and it remains the largest and most provocative of them all. The disturbing effect, however, owes more to what can be seen beneath the surface than his wry and equivocal engagement with a revered symbol of his nation.

To paint his flags, Johns revived an ancient technique using molten wax infused with pigment. Encaustic – derived from the Greek *enkaustic*, meaning to burn in – provides a fast-setting medium in which each touch of the brush is preserved as a distinct and pristine mark. Johns adopted this demanding medium out of frustration; oil paint dries slowly and becomes blurred and muddy when overworked. Seeking a richly layered yet articulated surface, Johns combined collage with coats of encaustic to fabricate a range of effects from transparent to opaque. While glimpses of the collaged materials can be seen at close inspection in his coloured flags, the white palette gives them far more visibility and makes them an essential element in the visual experience.

As he did for his initial *Flag*, Johns worked on three separately stretched sections: the stars, the upper stripes on the right and

the stripes in the lower half. He used unbleached beeswax as a ground layer, and then built his forms with torn newsprint, miscellaneous pieces of paper and shreds of fabric, all dipped in beeswax. Once the waxed layers adhered, Johns joined the panels and overpainted them with more beeswax, now augmented with white pigment and oil, brushing on his mixture with varied pressure to leave veils of different thicknesses. The result can be seen in the luminous and dimensional finish, as well as through areas of the topcoat to the collaged materials below. Drained of colour, the ghostly image of stars and stripes are in no way diminished in impact. Johns has repeatedly stated his preference to paint ordinary objects, 'things that the mind already knows'. But the way he paints them transforms them, and in *White Flag*, he forces the viewer to literally look through an icon to see the means by which he turned it into art.

The print on the newspaper emerges through the top layer of pigment and wax. In some sections, the words are almost legible. But it would be a mistake to try to link the meaning of the words to the content of the work. For Johns, the newsprint served as medium not message.

The stars seem to rise up from the surrounding negative space. Johns achieved this effect with collage, heightened with touches of charcoal. All the details are seen through veils of wax, white pigment and oil. In this version, Johns portrayed forty-eight stars; the fifty-star flag was adopted in 1960, after the statehood of Alaska and Hawaii.

Working with three separate sections enhanced Johns's control over his surface. He used a topcoat of encaustic, oil and white pigment to unify the sections after he joined them. But the seams are clearly visible; Johns had no desire to hide them.

Flag
Jasper Johns
1954–1955
Encaustic, oil and collage on fabric
107.3 x 153.8 cm (42.2 x 60.6 in)
Museum of Modern Art, New York, NY

The inaugural work in his series of flags also introduced Johns's unique method of encaustic collage. His layered mix of beeswax, paper strips and pigment deliberately created an uneven surface, and the difference in opacity between the primary colours and white modulated the visible presence of the newspaper beneath the paint. His choice of subject confounded critics, who questioned whether this was a painting of a flag or a flag made of paint.

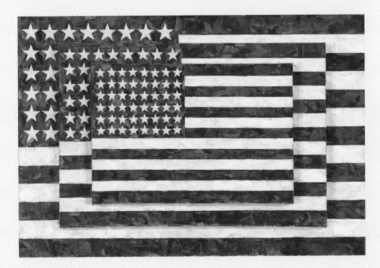

Three Flags
Jasper Johns
1958
Encaustic on canvas
77.8 x 115.6 cm (30.6 x 45.5 in)
Whitney Museum of American Art, New York, NY

Johns created more than forty flag paintings; drawings and prints bring the tally of renditions to more than one hundred. He has remained adamant that his choice was rooted in visual expression rather than an intended political comment, noting that the flag is 'seen and not looked at, not examined'. His treatment of such a revered and recognizable image reminds viewers that, in essence, a flag, like a painting, is no more than a surface to which we have assigned a particular significance.

3

3

Optical Illusion

IMAGINE DRAWING A CUBE. With a simple arrangement of two squares and four connecting lines, you can depict a three-dimensional form on a two-dimensional surface. Much of art involves this type of artful deception, creating a credible image out of the manipulation of line, shape and colour. The subtle gradation of tone on the outline of a curved form transforms a circle into a sphere. The skilful application of brushstrokes turns pigments into other substances: textiles, precious metals, wood and even flesh. One small dash of colour in the corner of an eye adds vitality to the depiction of a face. And the mastery of perspective allows an artist to conjure depth and distance on a flat plane. Optical illusion is part of the visual experience and, over the centuries, artists have developed techniques that engage the mind by fooling the eye. Some of these are simple and intuitive; others rely upon mathematical formulae, complex theories or trickery. The secret to a convincing optical illusion lies in the practitioner's expertise; they must know the rules well enough to bend and even break them.

In the past, whenever artists sought to mirror the natural world in their work, a test of their ability was the extent to which their art simulated the experience of sight and the perception of actual objects. Tales abound of birds trying to peck at the depiction of glistening grapes, of water so deftly painted that it appeared to flow, of a marble mouth that seemed mobile, breathing and ready to speak. The quest to create a sense of physical space where none existed fuelled the development of systematic perspective, notably in European painting. During the Middle Ages, the Latin term *perspectiva* comprised the whole of optical science, including the working of the human eye and the activity of light in reflection and refraction. By the fifteenth century, with the rising interest in spatial representation, writers and theorists began to narrow the definition to refer to linear perspective, a structured system of arranging forms along parallel lines on a flat surface so that they appear to have weight, depth and volume, just as they do in real space. Within a century, many artists became masters of spatial illusion, able to evoke the appearance of great depth, to position forms and figures in recessive distance, and to suggest to viewers that they could actually see through a painted window, walk through a painted door or look up at the sky through an opening painted on a ceiling. By the seventeenth century, art writers formulated the term trompe l'oeil (fool the eye) to describe the most sophisticated – and successful – visual fictions.

An optical illusion can thrill, amuse or disorient a viewer. It can serve to expand a claustrophobic environment or to embellish a plain interior with what appears to be silk, velvet, marble and gold. Fooling the eye can be used to heighten spirituality, to shock the viewer or to play a prank. In the examples that follow, a painter transforms a plain little room into a grand and glorious chamber. Another uses deliberate distortion to disguise a secret meaning in plain sight. The mastery of architecture, engineering and stage design gives one artist the ability to make an impossible structure seem viable. Another uses his consummate skill to portray mundane objects with an ironic twist. Visual effects that we know cannot exist are portrayed as if they are real in a painting intended to stimulate altered states of mind. And even the humble square can move and morph when the rules of drawing a square are pushed to their limit to make a static form give up its secrets.

CREDIBLE SPACE, INCREDIBLE ILLUSION

The Oculus, Camera degli Sposi
Andrea Mantegna (1431–1506)
1465–1474
Fresco and dry tempera
270 cm (106 in) diameter
Ducal Palace, Mantua

In a virtuoso display of perspective, Andrea Mantegna transformed a nondescript room in the northeast tower of the Castello di San Giorgio, Mantua, into an opulent chamber fit for the personal pleasure of his noble patron. The *Camera degli Sposi* (Marriage Chamber, also known as the *Camera picta*) was intended to provide a reception room for honoured guests, a place for family gatherings and, on occasion, to serve as the bed chamber for Ludovico Gonzaga, the second Marchese of Mantua. But the cubic proportions (8-m [26-ft] wide walls; 7-m [23-ft] high ceiling) and shallow-vaulted ceiling of the room created a closed-in, uninviting space. Using only paint and optical illusion, Mantegna turned that unpromising chamber into an open-air pavilion, decorated with gilding, foliage, carved architectural mouldings and a view of a brilliant cerulean sky through an oculus in the centre of an elaborate dome.

Although not used in Mantegna's day, the term trompe l'oeil (fool the eye) describes the sophisticated level of illusion achieved in his design for the *Camera degli Sposi*. To simulate the appearance of three dimensions on a two dimensional surface, Mantegna drew upon the work of architects and painters of the previous century – notably Filippo Brunelleschi, Leon Battista Alberti, Donato Bramante and Piero della Francesca – in their quests to formulate a rational and repeatable system of perspective. Each experimented with a converging pattern of orthogonal lines into a single vanishing point that provided a template for rendering architectural forms with credible depth. Mantegna furthered the effect using foreshortening, a modulation of the size and shape of objects and figures so that they seemed to be occupying actual space. His masterful replication of surface textures – carved stone, gilded plaster, worked leather – turned the painted walls and ceiling into a luxuriously appointed environment. And most remarkably, he broke through the ceiling to extend his illusion into an imagined space beyond the confines of the chamber.

Classical architects situated a round opening called an oculus (eye) in the crown of a dome to let in light and air. Mantegna designed his to reveal a carved balustrade ringed with active figures to suggest the existence of a rooftop terrace. Five women peer down at the spectators below, a peacock perches on the ledge and ten putti dart in, out and around the openings in the balustrade. The heavy planter balanced on a rod over open space, as well as the rude behaviour of the putti, were clearly meant to disconcert and delight the visitors standing beneath them. This effect, known as *de sotto in sù* (seen as if from below) brings the viewer to the exact spot for the optimal experience of Mantegna's soaring perspective and conjured space.

The 8-m (26-ft) ceiling height allowed Mantegna to cover the interior with life-size figures in naturalist settings. On the north wall, above an actual fireplace, he devised an open-air terrace, where Ludovico and his whole family have assembled. The lower walls are veneered with faux marble and the vault spandrels are ornamented with feigned stucco portrait roundels. A heavy leather curtain, painted as if blown back by the wind, hangs from hooks that mimic the form of real hooks in the opposite corner, made to hold bed curtains.

Here, on the north wall, Ludovico and his sons welcome important visitors to Mantua. The fortified walls of the city and the surrounding hills can be seen in the distance behind them. Mantegna positions his figures so close to the edge of the picture plane that some, for example the man on the far right, protrude out into the viewer's space.

Looking up, spectators might be jolted by the sight of a heavy planter balanced on a relatively slender rod directly above them. The women on either side smile as they look back down, as if amused by the effect of Mantegna's masterful illusion.

Playful putti enhance the illusion, standing on the inner edge of the oculus and even peeping out of the openings in the balustrade. The putto on the left crowns himself with a champion's wreath, while the one on the right hoists an apple, as if he is ready to drop it.

Mantegna's skill at foreshortening adds ribald wit to the ensemble. One putto leans over the rim, exchanging a glance with two others who push their heads up from openings in the balustrade. A tiny arm pokes out at the left, waving a wand, while the little winged fellow next to him presents a very rude view to the viewers below.

DISTORTION BY DESIGN

Jean de Dinteville and Georges de Selve ('The Ambassadors')
Hans Holbein the Younger (1497/98–1543)
1533
Oil on panel
207 x 209.5 cm (81.5 x 82.5 in)
National Gallery, London

This double portrait by Hans Holbein the Younger presents a convincing scene. The two men – the French ambassador Jean de Dinteville and the French envoy to the Diet of the Holy Roman Empire Bishop Georges de Selve – are depicted near life size and inhabit a shallow but plausible space. Their highly individualized portraits convey distinct personalities, just as their superbly painted garments represent their status. The precisely rendered objects on the table between them demonstrate Holbein's expertise in foreshortening, light and shadow; the detailed recreation of every surface texture heightens the impression of material reality. But something strange and supernatural intrudes into this naturalistic setting. The odd, oblong shape floating across the floor in the lower foreground is an optical illusion known as an anamorphic image. It cannot be read from the conventional position in front of the painting; it must be seen from a different point of view.

To create an anamorphic image, the artist must distort the natural shape of an object so that its intended form can only be seen at an oblique angle, through a viewing device or reflected in a specialized mirror. It is a visual ruse born out of the mastery of perspective. Leonardo da Vinci experimented with anamorphic images in his notebooks, and they occasionally appear in fifteenth-century prints. But

to Holbein it was no mere trick; he included it in an important double portrait in the context of an iconographic ensemble. When the viewer stands to the immediate right of the picture plane and looks at the painting from the side, the contorted shape takes the form of a skull. The enduring importance of objects that represent worldly knowledge and pleasure – globes of the heavens and the Earth, measuring devices, a mathematical text, musical instruments – is diminished by the ultimate symbol of human morality.

The meaning of Holbein's skull can be deciphered, but the means by which he painted it and intended it to be seen are a matter of speculation. The high level of anatomical accuracy suggests that he painted from a real skull. To calculate the lateral stretching needed for anamorphosis, he likely mapped his image on a trapezoidal grid. The original frame of the painting has not survived, so it is not known if there was an indication of where to stand or if a viewing device was attached. But it is clear that the symbolic message of the painting does not end with the visual illusion of the skull. Walking back to the front and looking high in the upper-left corner, the viewer sees the silver crucifix nearly hidden behind the folds of the damask drapes. It adds an element of redemption to this meditation on life, earthly vanity and death.

These objects – including a celestial globe, a
pair of quadrants, and a polyhedral sundial –
represent the desire to map and measure the
heavens. The humanist interest in the sciences
mark de Dinteville and de Selve as modern men,
open to new ideas about the world.

Here the objects represent the arts and letters. Along with the terrestrial globe, there is an open hymnbook, an arithmetic book, a case of flutes and a lute with a broken string. Each object – expertly lit and foreshortened – occupies real space, revealing that Holbein excelled at all types of visual illusion.

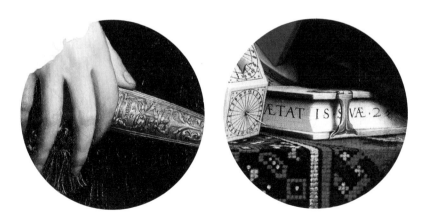

An inscription on the embossed sheath of de Dinteville's dagger states that he is twenty-nine years old; another on the book beneath de Selve's elbow reveals that he is four years younger. Holbein has inserted information about the men throughout the painting, drawing the viewer deeper into their world.

It is easy to miss the silver crucifix in the upper-left corner. Holbein has half covered it with the heavy damask drapes. As with the skull, it demands that the viewer engage with the imagery to better understand the painting.

To see the skull in its recognizable form, the viewer must stand to the right of the painting and look slantwise across the picture plane. There are many theories about the intended viewpoint: the painting might have been hung so that someone entering from the right would immediately see the skull or that the skull could be seen from the front with the aid of a glass cylinder tilted at a slight diagonal. No written accounts exist, so all explanations remain speculative.

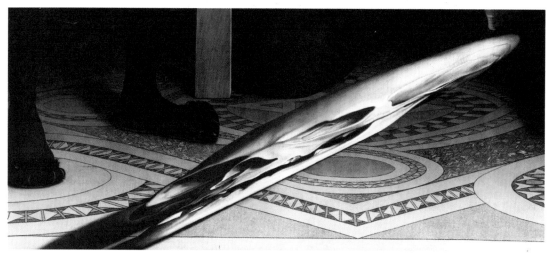

Distinctively handsome, with an alert gaze and a mildly amused expression, de Dinteville appears as a young man of privilege and importance, just as he was in life. The flush of his complexion gives the vital impression of the blood beneath his skin. This is a real man wearing real garments of satin, fur, linen and velvet. Holbein's ability to capture a breathing likeness won him the position of court painter to Henry VIII in 1535.

Allegorical Escutcheon of Death, from 'The Dance of Death'
Hans Holbein the Younger
c. 1525
Woodcut
6.5 × 5 cm (2.5 × 2 in)
British Museum, London

Holbein designed more than forty images for his woodcut series, 'The Dance of Death'. The Grim Reaper, in the form of a skeleton gathering men and women of all stations, emerged as a powerful and enduring motif in late medieval iconography. In *The Ambassadors*, De Dinteville wears a skull-shaped pin on the lower-right face of his hat; it was a *memento mori* (remember death), a pragmatic reminder that all must die.

SINISTER SPACES

'The Drawbridge' from *Carceri di invenzione* (Plate VII)
Giovanni Battista Piranesi (1720–1778)
1761
Etching
Sheet: 64 × 49.2 cm (25.2 × 19.4 in); Plate: 54.5 × 40.7 cm (21.5 × 16 in)

In 1740, Giovanni Battista Piranesi travelled to Rome in the entourage of the Venetian ambassador. Trained in structural and hydraulic engineering, he sought to launch a career as an architect, but at twenty, his youth and lack of connections limited his opportunities. Piranesi was already an accomplished draughtsman with experience in engraving and stage design, so he easily found work in the lucrative market for *vedute* (views) that depicted the architectural monuments of Rome and its environs. Visitors avidly collected these as souvenirs of the Grand Tour. To distinguish himself from older, better-established *vedutisti* (view makers), Piranesi drew upon his deep understanding of elaborate perspective systems and produced meticulously detailed imagery that presented renowned buildings in convincing space and settings, as seen in his most acclaimed series *Vedute di Roma* (1748–1778). But, he particularly excelled at *capriccio* (architectural fantasy), and in 1750, he published *Invenzione capric di carceri*, a suite of fourteen, unsigned views of prison interiors based solely on his imagination.

A decade later, at the height of his fame, Piranesi released a new, signed edition with two additional prints. More importantly, he revised the original images, darkening the atmosphere and inserting architectural elements that heightened the viewer's sense of claustrophobia and disorientation. As seen in 'The Drawbridge', the ramps and bridges create a labyrinth in the towering and cavernous space. Spiral staircases appear to writhe as minute figures make their perilous ascent. Through the manipulation of light and the confounding complexity of the architectural elements, Piranesi crafts the illusion of a forbidding and mysterious space, where stairs, spans and passageways appear more threatening than the instruments of torture. As the title, *Carceri di invenzione*, states, these prisons were the artist's own devising, but their disturbing reality derives from his real world architectural expertise.

For visitors from abroad, Piranesi's *vedute* defined Rome. Many tourists planned their itineraries based on the monuments he depicted; on his first visit, German author Johann Wolfgang Goethe expressed disappointment that what he saw did not measure up to Piranesi's views. In a similar vein, the artist's *Carceri* became the model for sinister settings.

As early as 1760, the first edition inspired the stage design for Jean-Philippe Rameau's opera *Dardanus* (1760). Romantic writers, including William Beckford and Thomas de Quincy, matched their words to his visions, and such artists as John Martin and Gustave Doré emulated his elaborate spatial effects. The influence of the *Carceri*'s ominous atmosphere can be seen in cinema classics ranging from Fritz Lang's *Metropolis* (1926) to Ridley Scott's *Blade Runner* (1982). But more than modelling menace, Piranesi's *Carceri* demonstrated how the most disorienting fantasy can be built upon a thoroughly rational system of representation.

'THE DRAWBRIDGE' FROM CARCERI DI INVENZIONE (PLATE VII)

The layering of elements – from the giant rope and pulley at the front of the picture plane, to the rising drawbridge in the mid-ground and the spiral staircase snaking around the column in the distance – reflects Piranesi's command of effective stage design.

Piranesi's deep understanding of structural engineering gave him the tools to build his imaginary prison. The broad-spanned arches and the sturdy columns have architectural integrity; they could work in an actual building. But the dizzying mass of elements creates a bewildering atmosphere, projecting the illusion of chaotic space.

A gigantic spiked rack and the heavy chains remind the viewer that this prison is a place for punishment as well as incarceration. But the shadowed corners and disorienting pathways are even more disturbing. Piranesi pioneered the Gothic idea that what we imagine is more terrifying that what we actually see.

'View of the Temple of the Sybil in Tivoli',
Vedute di Roma
Giovanni Battista Piranesi
c. 1761
Etching
42.2 × 63.5 cm (16.6 × 25 in)
V&A Museum, London

Piranesi secured his reputation with *Vedute di
Roma*. He began the series around 1748 and worked
on it until his death. Piranesi regularly released
portfolios of new images throughout the project,
ultimately completing 101 views. His depiction
of ruins – with broken columns and shattered
pediments, overgrown with moss and trees – blur
the line between real views and architectural
caprice. The figures that climb the temple's
walls and shelter in its crumbling niches add a
picturesque element, as well as a sense of scale.

'Over London—By Rail',
London, A Pilgrimage
Gustave Doré (1832–1883)
1872
Engraving

The French illustrator, Doré, teamed up
with British journalist William Blanchard
Jerrold to document mid-Victorian
London. They sought out every aspect of
life, including the squalor of the modern
metropolis. Upon seeing the published
suite of 180 plates, British critics accused
Doré of sensationalism and claimed that
he exaggerated the appalling conditions
of the poor. The dark shadows, crowded
spaces and twisting pathways of Doré's
compositions owe their spirit to Piranesi's
Carceri, but rather than a flight of fantasy,
Doré presented his work as an exposé of
harsh and neglected reality.

SLEIGHT OF HAND AND BRUSH

Rack Picture for William Malcolm Bunn
John F. Peto (1854–1907)
1882
Oil on canvas
61 × 50.8 cm (24 × 20 in)
Smithsonian American Art Museum, Washington, DC

From ancient times, the history of art brims with tales of an artist's uncanny ability to create a visual illusion. Grapes depicted by fifth-century Athenian painter Zeuxis were so realistic that birds tried to steal them. As a child prodigy in thirteenth-century Florence, Giotto pranked his master by painting flies on the noses of his figures, laughing as Cimabue tried to whisk them off. Dutch and Flemish still-life painters of the seventeenth century simulated surface textures and the play of light to create compositions in which the objects appeared as real as anything else in the room. Among their subjects, most typically food and floral arrangements, was a humble yet useful object: the letter rack. Found in homes and businesses, an actual rack was simply a grid of fabric tape, tacked to a board to hold letters and other ephemera. In the late nineteenth century, John F. Peto gave the subject a modern American twist, painting trompe l'oeil 'office boards' on commission for Philadelphia businessmen.

William Malcolm Bunn was a self-made man with political ambitions. In 1878, he bought the *Sunday Transcript*, and over the next decade used the newspaper as a forum to advocate for Republican policies, to support party candidates and advance his own career. Peto's ensemble presents a portrait of a busy man. The board is well used and a bit worn; one of the bottom tapes has torn and dangles off the four-box grid. There are the remains of business cards – upper right and lower right – that appear to have been glued on and then ripped off the board. Chalk numbers near the bottom remain from a hasty, but unexplained calculation. There is a photo of Bunn, as well as a folded copy of the paper. Any of these objects could have existed, but further investigation reveals that Peto was as inventive with his ideas as he was with the art of illusion.

X-ray and infrared analysis uncovered a number of changes. Originally, Peto had inscribed 'V[ery] Truly yours/Wm Bunn' below the photograph. In the lower-left corner there was a playing card and an envelope marked 'The contents might be of interest to you'. But Peto painted that over with a rough profile sketch marked 'McFod to the Fore' and a letter addressed to 'Garabaldi McFod' at the *Sunday Transcript*. No one with that name has been connected with the paper or with local politics. Was he a character in a now-lost private joke? Just as Peto blurred illusion and reality, he merged fact and fiction, a double sleight of hand meant to amuse the patron as well as fool his eye.

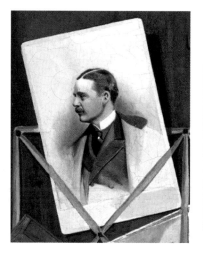

Bunn was known for his good looks and polished personal style. He enjoyed a high social profile in Philadelphia as a club man, an influential editor and a popular after-dinner speaker. Peto often included a simulated photograph in his trompe l'oeil ensembles, personalizing the content.

As in an actual, well-used letter rack, the wood backing is notched and worn. Remnants of a torn, yellowed card – scraped off in haste – can be seen in the corner. The newspaper's banner ties the ensemble to Bunn; the 1881 date on the green-covered report notes when Peto began the painting.

The unskilled profile portrait and the legend 'McFod to the Fore' contrast with Peto's fine rendering of the photograph and the newspaper. In scale and quality, the little sheet seems to be a homemade promotional flyer. It may mock Bunn's more calculated political activities, but since McFod cannot be identified, its meaning cannot be discerned.

The careful rendering of stamps, postmarks, letterhead printing and various handwritings serve to enhance the illusion of Peto's ensemble. One envelope has been roughly torn open; the coarse brown lining can be seen beneath the outer yellow layer. The fabric tapes of the grid are stretched and frayed, as they would be from regular use.

*A Trompe l'Oeil of Newspapers, Letters and Writing Implements
on a Wooden Board*
Edward Collier (*c.* 1640–1710)
Oil on canvas
c. 1699
58.8 × 46.2 cm (23.1 × 18.2 in)
Tate Britain, London

The Dutch-born artist Edwaert Colyer possibly anglicized his name to Edward Collier
when he moved to London. His trompe l'oeil technique reflected continental practice,
but the objects on his letter rack are English. From the curled corners of the newspapers
to the translucent tortoiseshell comb and the sturdy leather straps, Collier displays his
mastery of visual illusion. The canvas is not dated, but curators discovered that in 1699,
15th May fell on a Monday, matching the date on one of the newspapers.

ALTERED PERCEPTIONS

Swans Reflecting Elephants
Salvador Dalí (1904–1989)
1937
Oil on canvas
51 × 77 cm (20.08 × 30.31 in)
Private Collection

Salvador Dalí's mastery of illusionistic representation fuelled his objectives as a Surrealistic painter. His ability to manipulate form and perspective allowed him to present what he described as 'the world of delirium unknown to rational experience'. Dalí's unsettling visions challenged the concept of a concrete physical reality. For example, in *Swans Reflecting Elephants*, a trio of graceful swans appear to be seen twice: perched on the shore and reflected in the mirror-like surface of the water. But with a slight shift in focus those shimmering reflections transform into images of elephants; the swans' lithe necks become trunks, their feathered breasts faces and their spread wings ears. Dalí painted this evocative work after nearly a decade of developing a theory he called the paranoiac-critical-method, through which the repetitive, obsessional thinking associated with the mental disorder paranoia disrupts conventional perception. Everything that one sees has the potential to be something else.

Collaboration with Luis Buñuel on the film *Un Chien Andalou* (1929) brought Dalí into the Parisian Surrealist circle. In 1930 he wrote an essay on his new theory; *'L'ani pourri'* appeared in *Le Surréalisme au service de la révolution*, the journal founded by the movement's principle theorist André Breton. Dalí intended his theory as a counterpoint to Breton's own emphasis on automatic expression as the best means to unleash the unconscious; he also exchanged ideas about paranoiac perceptions with French psychoanalyst Jacques Lacan. Dalí promoted his method through lectures and articles, most notably *'La Conquête de l'irrationel'* (1935). He even planned to publish a journal, but that did not materialize. The fullest and most enticing demonstration of his theories can be found in his paintings of the 1930s, which

employ the motifs of doubling, metamorphosis and reflection as a visual equivalent of the obsessional misreading of the external world associated with paranoiac disorders.

In contrast to many of his paranoiac-critical paintings, Dalí gave *Swans Reflecting Elephants* a straightforward, descriptive title. The vista is serene, yet disquieting, reminiscent of the deeply recessional landscapes of Northern Renaissance paintings. In the same year that he painted *Swans Reflecting Elephants*, Dalí explored the myth of Narcissus, most notably in his painting *Metamorphosis of Narcissus* for which he wrote an accompanying poem. But here Dalí invokes neither a myth nor a narrative; the destabilizing possibility of irrational perception is the content of the painting. The swans maintain their physical presence on shore while their reflections transform. In *Swans and Elephants* Dalí asserts a lyrical yet disturbing concept: forms are ever in flux and a multitude of deviations reside even in the most recognizable imagery.

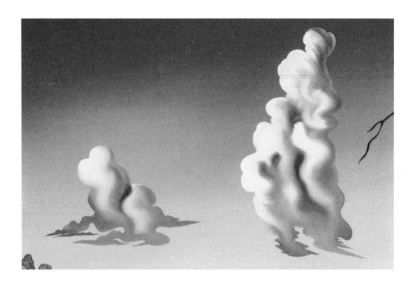

To fool the eye and trick the mind, Dalí often included evocative forms in his paintings. Here the clouds take on zoomorphic (left) and anthropomorphic (right) forms, but there is no rational explanation for the suggestion of a crouching dragon or struggling human figures in the sky.

Dalí did not identify the man on the left who turns away from the swans. One possibility is that it is a portrait of the British poet Edward W.F. James. A Surrealist patron, he was particularly generous to Dalí, collecting and promoting his work, paying his expenses and commissioning the original design for the Mae West sofa.

The right side of the tree appears to have the contours of a woman's figure, with arms raised and torso arched, leaning against the bare trunk. With deliberate ambiguity, Dalí provokes viewers to question their own perceptions.

Mae West's Face which May be Used as a
Surrealist Apartment
Salvador Dalí
1934–1935
Gouache with graphite on a commercially printed
magazine page
28.3 x 17.8 cm (11.1 x 7 in)
Art Institute of Chicago, Chicago, IL

Fascinated with her flamboyant beauty, Dalí
transformed Mae West's face into a luxurious
sitting room. He turned the lower half into
the floor with tiles that delineate one-point
perspective. He framed her sultry eyes and
hung them on a red wall. Her platinum waves
became curtain swags, and her plump red lips a
cushioned sofa. In 1974, he recreated the image
as a three-dimensional installation. In each
iteration – film star, painting, sculpture – West
existed as an optical illusion.

In transforming the swan's image into that of an
elephant, Dalí drew upon a highly conventional
form of optical illusion: one form literally reading as
another. Seen upside down, the extended neck and
opening wings of the swan appear to be the head of
the elephant. The mirrored image of rough-barked
trees provides the pachyderm with legs.

THE SECRETS OF A SQUARE

Movement in Squares
Bridget Riley (b. 1931)
1961
Tempera on hardwood
123.2 × 121.2 cm (48.5 × 47.7 in)
Arts Council Collection, Southbank Centre, London

In 1961 Bridget Riley set out to answer a simple question: 'Was there anything to be found in drawing a square?' Drawing square after square, she lined them up maintaining a consistent height, but as she progressed from left to right she narrowed their width until they took on a 'new pictorial identity'. The individual blocks turned into pulsating bands, creating the optical illusion of three-dimensional movement on a static two-dimensional surface. *Movement in Squares* represents Riley's breakthrough moment, launching her on a career-long investigation of the kinetic potential of geometric forms. She discovered that, through repetition and reconfiguration, she could make the motionless elements in painting undulate and rotate as well as advance and recede.

Despite the rigorous appearance of Riley's abstract imagery, she is guided by her own aesthetic instincts rather than scientific or mathematical principles. She has never studied optics and cites Impressionist and Post-Impressionist painters as her 'closest historical relatives'. Her formal enquiry rose directly out of her close studies of nature.

Well grounded in landscape painting, Riley stripped back her visual vocabulary to the most fundamental forms of representation. The square appealed to her for its simplicity and symmetrical integrity. Everyone recognizes a square, defined as having four equal sides and four equal angles.

But her slight adjustments unleashed the square's dynamic potential, and what Riley found in the process of painting *Movement in Squares* led her to consider the inherent possibilities of other conventional shapes. She worked with circles, triangles and curves, and she expanded her austere black and white palette with grey, followed by the incorporation of colour. Over the decades, Riley's art has revealed what form can do, and she has worked by trial, error and discovery rather than theory and presumption.

Riley refutes the claim that she started a movement, but critics positioned her complex optical imagery as the iconic catalyst of Op Art. The term itself, a word play on optical, became widespread after a landmark exhibition. *The Responsive Eye*, at the Museum of Modern Art in New York (1965), which featured Riley's work. The often disorienting effect of her visual expression resonated with the free-wheeling visual culture of the Swinging 60s, and, to her dismay, her illusionistic imagery was allied to the growing appetite for hallucinatory experiences and experimentation with psychedelic drugs. Riley bristled when the patterns produced through her diligent research were adopted for such commercial products as posters, fashions and decor. In her quest, the optical illusion was never the desired intention, but a result of her endlessly inquisitive process.

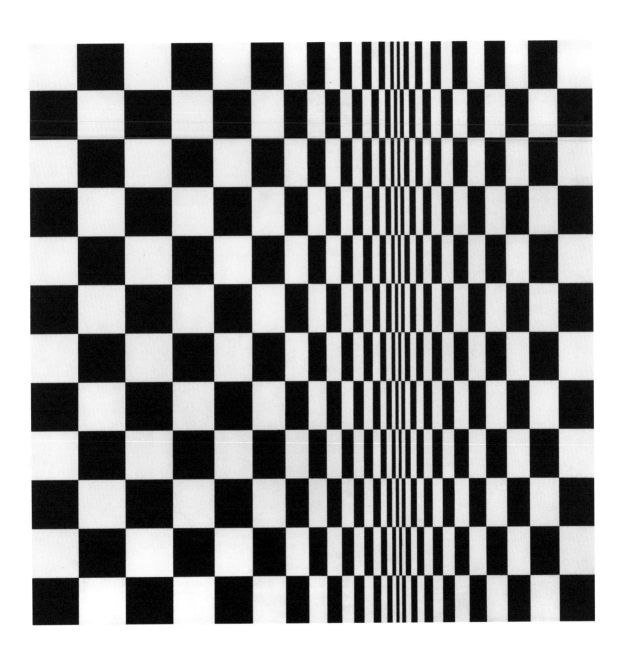

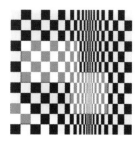

As Riley moved right, she narrowed the width of each square without adjusting the height, and then widened out again. While she was transforming her squares into standing rectangles, the visual effect suggests compression, creating the illusion of tension along each horizontal band.

BELOW Riley confined her early investigations to black and white. This heightens the contrast between the shapes. It is hard for the eye to take in that stark difference, and that is what makes the static squares seem to vibrate. The optical illusion is one of movement, even though the mind is fully aware that the painted surface is still.

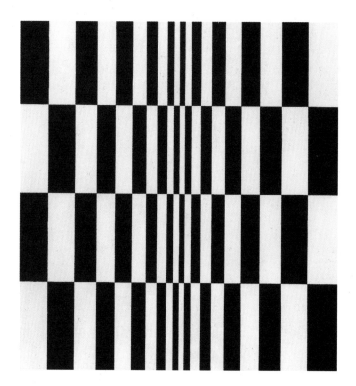

ABOVE The narrowing of the squares makes it appear that the bands sink into a groove, like the gutter in a book. This is simply the illusion created by the diminution of the manipulated shapes. At the same time, the bands seem throb, swelling up on each side of the gutter. Riley regarded the effects she achieved as more a matter of sensation than perception, giving the viewer a physical as well as a perceptual experience.

'The Car for the OP Art Girl' *Daily Mirror*
1966
Photograph

The craze for Op Art fashions made Riley furious. When she saw a selection in department store windows on Madison Avenue in New York, she wanted to sue the designers, convinced that 'it will take twenty years before anyone looks at my painting seriously again'. Her fears were unfounded, but the commercialization of optical patterning became a signature of the Swinging 60s look, enhancing everything from album covers and attire to interior decoration and automobiles.

4

Hidden
Identities

THE PRESENCE OF A HUMAN FIGURE IN A WORK OF ART SETS OFF A SERIES OF ASSOCIATIONS IN A VIEWER'S MIND. Does the size, posture or silhouette tell us something about the figure's age or gender? Do their clothes reveal something about their social situation or profession? Do we sense a type of temperament or a fleeting emotion in their gestures or facial expression? Even if we do not know their name or are unfamiliar with their features, we assign them an identity, and that, in turn, is a catalyst for understanding the image and its ideas. But an artist can adjust the visual elements of identity to better suit the story or circumstance. They can make a plain face beautiful, a modest physique magnificent or indicate a heightened social status by creating an imagined ensemble of splendid fabrics and glittering jewels. They can merge the likeness of an individual with another character – a legendary hero, a goddess or saint, a tortured soul – to create a hybrid identity that lends meaning to both the factual and fictional narrative. Or an artist can create an identity that harbours a secret to add layers of meaning to the message.

There are numerous covert ways in which an artist can inscribe an identity into a work of art. A recognizable figure may mingle in a crowd, hiding in plain sight. Their place in the composition – off to the side or deep in the distance – may make it hard to find them or suggest that they, like the viewer, play the role of observer rather than participant. A portrait of a recognizable person can be presented as a picture within a picture: a painting on the wall, an image in a mirror, the subtle shimmer of a face reflected on such shining surfaces as metal, glass or still water. One individual can appear in the guise of another. Or the figure can be given a disguise: a costume, a mask, a veil. Sighting a clandestine figure in a work of art draws the observer into a more intimate relationship with the artist and their intentions. Once we see through the imposed identity, we want to know what is the figure hiding.

Of all the identities an artist might conceal in their work, the most intriguing is their own. The elements they use to cover or transform their intent acts as a barrier of protection as well as portal to deeper meaning. And by decoding the disguise, we understand that the likeness is more than a portrait; it is an assertion of identity from the artist's point of view. In the examples that follow, a young painter declares that she has surpassed her master in a work that appears to honour him. Another painter modifies a biblical reference to ask for compassion from a powerful ally while appearing to confess contrition. And the assumption that the person with the highest rank is the most important figure in a composition is challenged in a work that is filled with recognizable portraits but riddled with interpretative ambiguity. The modern medium of photography was first promoted as an objective means to capture an image. How then, could a sitter defy this level of exposure and maintain anonymity? Could the agency of the artificial authority be subverted by wearing a mask or staging a masquerade? Finally, we are made aware of the power of selfhood and communal identity when an artist defies social erasure and refuses to hide.

SUBVERSIVE SELF-PORTRAIT

Bernardino Campi painting Sofonisba Anguissola
Sofonisba Anguissola (c. 1532–1625)
c. 1559
Oil on canvas
111 × 110 cm (43.7 × 43.3 in)
Pinacoteca Nazionale, Siena

When Sofonisba Anguissola painted this unconventional double portrait, she was about to leave her home in Cremona, northern Italy, and take a position in the court of King Philip II of Spain as portrait painter and lady-in-waiting to Queen Isabel of Valois. Campi had been her painting master, but he had left Cremona a decade earlier to advance his career in Milan. It is uncertain whether Campi made an undocumented visit to Cremona at this time, but Anguissola could easily have used a portrait as her model or even painted him from memory. The dominance of her image over his in the double portrait raises the question whether Anguissola intended it to be a tribute to her former teacher at a crucial turn in her career or a subversively witty self-portrait.

Few sixteenth-century artists – and certainly no female artists of the era – painted as many self-portraits as Anguissola. More than a dozen have been identified, spanning her long career from youth to old age. Anguissola had the good fortune of being born into a wealthy family headed by an enlightened father who determined that his six daughters deserved the same quality of education as men. When his eldest daughters demonstrated talent in the visual arts, he arranged to have esteemed local artists – Campi (1546–1549) and

Bernardino Gatti (1549–1552) – give them the same training as articled apprentices. Anguissola painted most of her self-portraits between the conclusion of her studies with Gatti and her departure for Spain. More than a record of appearance, these portraits chart her accomplishments: she portrays herself with an open book, seated at a clavichord and painting a devotional image of the Virgin and the Christ Child. In every portrait, she appears self-possessed and serious, modestly dressed in a dark *corpetto* (fitted jacket) trimmed at the neckline and cuffs with simple lace.

In the double self-portrait, Anguissola presents herself as an elegant, serenely confident woman, without a single attribute that identifies her as an artist. Campi's face and hand are brightly illuminated but, dressed in black garments, he fades into the foreground shadows. It is her portrait that is the subject of the composition. Campi turns away from the easel, and in doing so, he looks directly at the woman who is painting the double portrait. Through this exchange of glances, Anguissola asserts her prowess through her unseen presence as the prevailing artist, and Campi's deferential glance suggests that he agrees. She has overturned the traditional hierarchy of master over pupil – even he must acknowledge that she has surpassed him.

Most women who became painters followed their fathers into the profession. Even in her day, Anguissola's recognition was attributed to her rare talent rather than family connections. Giorgio Vasari, author of *The Lives of the Artists* (1568), hailed her as a *miracolo* whose talent and determination outshone 'any other woman of our time'.

Campi (1522–1591) was born into a family of artists based in Cremona. He left home in his youth for training in Mantua, and when he returned in 1541, he won local acclaim for his painting *The Assumption of the Virgin* (1542) in S. Agata and for frescoes in the nave of S. Sigismondo (1546). Wider fame came later, after he moved to Milan.

In most of her self-portraits, Anguissola wears attire that befits a serious young woman: a simple *corpetto* solely relieved by black lace trim. Here she appears stylish, but modest, in a gown of padded and embroidered brocade. Her attire is appropriate for her new position in the Spanish court, reflecting Baldassare Castiglione's advice to women in *The Book of the Courtier* (1528) to avoid 'vain' or 'frivolous' apparel.

Painters used a mahlstick for fine detail. Hooked to the edge of the canvas, the tool provided a firm support to steady the brush hand. Anguissola also used a mahlstick, as seen in her self-portraits at the easel.

Self-Portrait
Sofonisba Anguissola
1556
Oil on canvas
66 x 57 cm (26 x 22.4 in)
Muzeum Zamek, Łańcut

Anguissola portrayed herself as a working artist twice; in both she paints a Virgin and Child. The paintings within the portraits seem to be pure invention. They do not match any of her known work. But she felt fully capable of the ambitious subject, inscribing the later example (1561) with the boast: 'I, the maiden Sofonisba, equalled the muses and Apelles in performing my songs and handling my colours'.

A PLEA FOR MERCY

David with the Head of Goliath
Michelangelo Merisi da Caravaggio (1571–1610)
1609–1610
Oil on canvas
125 × 101 cm (49.2 × 39.8 in)
Borghese Gallery, Rome

On the night of 29th May 1606, when a dispute over a tennis match turned violent, Caravaggio killed Ranuccio Tomassoni. Hot tempered and quick to use his dagger, the painter had previously run afoul of the law for assault and vandalism, but this was murder, and at the height of his success, Caravaggio fled Rome. The Papal Authority charged Caravaggio in absentia, declaring a *bando capitale* (capital sentence) that allowed anyone to take his life and collect a reward upon the presentation of his severed head. Caravaggio's sensational exploits have often coloured the interpretation of his work, but in the case of *David with the Head of Goliath*, his art truly mirrored his life.

Giovanni Pietro Bellori, writing in *The Lives of the Artists* (1572), identified the image of the slain giant in the 'half-length David holding by its hair the head of Goliath', as 'Caravaggio's own portrait'. According to Giovanni Baglione's *Lives* (1642), Caravaggio had used a mirror to capture his own likeness since his youth, presenting himself in such alarming guises as an ailing Bacchus (*c.* 1593) and the monster Medusa (*c.* 1598). Caravaggio first interpreted David's triumph over Goliath in 1600, and although a passing resemblance can

be discerned in the giant's coarse features to the painter's own rugged appearance late in life, when Caravaggio painted this version he still had his youthful good looks. In another version, painted in 1607, the giant's features are distinctly different. But in all three versions, David embodies the message. He is the unlikely hero in the first, beheading his fallen adversary. In the second he is impassive but triumphant, displaying his grisly trophy. Here, in this last version, David's face expresses compassion for the opponent he has justly defeated.

The *bando capitale* forced Caravaggio to remain in exile from Rome, but he arranged to send *David with the Head of Goliath* to a Roman patron. Cardinal Scipione Borghese, the nephew of Pope Paul V, had already acquired several of the painter's works for his private collection, including a depiction of the Madonna and Child with Saint Anne (1605; Borghese Gallery, Rome) after it was rejected by the College of Cardinals as too vulgar, and the ailing Bacchus. Caravaggio sent the work to the influential cardinal as a personal petition to lift the *bando capitale*. Sadly, the artist died before his painting reached Borghese.

In a mid-seventeenth-century inventory of the Borghese collection, Jacopo Manilli identified Caravaggio's model for David as *suo Caravaggino* (his little Caravaggio). There is speculation that Cecco del Caravaggio, a studio assistant, posed for the artist several times, but this case cannot be verified. It was also rumoured that they were lovers.

The inscription on the sword – H-ASOS – long thought to be the swordsmith's mark, is now believed to derive from an Augustinian commentary on the Psalms equating David's victory over Goliath with Christ's triumph over Satan. The letters abbreviate the dictum *humilitas occidit superbia* (humility kills pride).

Throughout his years in exile, Caravaggio managed to secure important commissions. But he also continued his violent behaviour. Jailed after wounding a man in Malta in 1608, he escaped and fled to Sicily. Restless and failing in health, he moved on to Naples in 1609, where a near fatal attack by armed men left him disfigured. Goliath's ravaged features reflect the toll of the painter's misfortune, as well as his misdeeds.

Portrait of Caravaggio
Ottavio Leoni (1578–1630)
c. 1621
Chalk on blue paper
23.4 × 16.3 cm (9.2 × 6.4 in)
Biblioteca Marucelliana, Florence

At a trial for libel in Rome in 1603, Caravaggio testified that he knew the fashionable Roman portraitist, Ottavio Leoni, but had never spoken with him. Leoni's portrait, the only known likeness of Caravaggio by a contemporary, was rendered from memory.

Saint Bartholomew, det. from
The Last Judgement
Michelangelo Buonarroti (1475–1564)
1536–1541
Fresco
Sistine Chapel, Vatican

Michelangelo depicted his own suffering by hiding a portrait of himself within the flayed skin of Saint Bartholomew in his fresco on the altar wall of the Sistine Chapel. Given Michelangelo's fame, Caravaggio certainly knew the work. Cristofano Allori, a follower of Caravaggio, painted his own portrait as a severed head in *Judith with the Head of Holoferenes* (1613; The Queen's Gallery, London). He cast his former mistress as the triumphant heroine.

THE UNSEEN PAINTING

Las Meninas
Diego Velázquez (1599–1660)
1656
Oil on canvas
320.5 cm x 281.5 cm (126.2 x 110.8 in)
Prado, Madrid

On a life-size canvas, Diego Velázquez creates an illusion of absolutely credible space. The dimly lit room, hung with paintings, is a hive of activity as a group of attendants hover around the Spanish infanta, Margarita Teresa. But her facial expression and the line of her gaze – as well as that of the painter (a self-portrait of Velázquez) and the second figure on the right – suggests that she has suddenly become aware of another presence just beyond the picture plane. The heavily framed mirror on the back wall reveals the object of her attention; it reflects the image of the king, Philip IV, and his wife, Mariana. As early as 1724, author Antonio Palomino, in his three-volume study of Spanish art (*El Museo pictório y escala óptica*), named every figure and identified the room as the Cuarto del Príncipe, in the Alcázar in Madrid. Yet over the centuries, ambiguities in the composition have ignited ongoing debates about the position of the king and queen, the perspective of the viewer and who is posing for the painter. The answers reside on the one element that the painter has deliberately withheld from viewers: we can only see the back of his imposing canvas.

The assumption that Velázquez is painting a portrait of the king and queen can be traced back to Palomino's laudatory discussion of the work. Given the formality of their reflected presence in the mirror, he assumed that the royal couple was posing for the painter. But a significant factor undercuts this supposition. The canvas in the painting is far too large for a standing double portrait. No such painting exists, and if it ever did, it was never mentioned in a royal inventory. The first known title of the work, cited in a 1660 inventory, calls attention to the Infanta: *Retrato de la señora emperatriz con sus damas y una enana* (portrait of the Empress with her ladies and a dwarf). But she is too close to the painter to pose; she might be taking a break from a sitting or she and her entourage may have interrupted her parents' session.

These speculations raise another question: Must the hidden canvas be a royal portrait? Standing in front of *Las Meninas* the viewer occupies the same space as the king and queen. Rather than seeing who is being painted, the viewer is granted an intimate glimpse from the monarchs' point of view. As the painter leans back from his enormous canvas – roughly the size of the actual painting – and looks knowingly out at the viewer, we understand the scope of his privilege and another explanation arises. Velázquez might have painted himself painting *Las Meninas*.

The reflection of Philip IV and his second wife, Mariana of Austria, in the mirror is hazy yet unmistakable. Their formal position suggests that they are posing, but the alert response to them by the other figures in the room hints that their presence was not expected.

Menina, a word of Portuguese derivation, designated a young lady in waiting in service to the queen's household. María Agustina Sarmiento kneels to the right of the infanta, offering her a *bucaro*, a terracotta vessel holding perfume or a liquid refreshment. Isabel de Velasco stands to her left. The figures on the far right are Maribárbola and Nicolasito Pertusato; as adult dwarfs retained by the court they were regarded as fit companions to the royal children.

Portrait of the Infanta Margarita Teresa of Spain
Diego Velázquez
1660
Oil on canvas
212 × 147 cm (83 × 58 in)
Kunsthistorisches Museum, Vienna

Velázquez painted the infanta repeatedly through her childhood. Here she is portrayed at the age of eight, three years older than when she posed for *Las Meninas*. In every portrait, her garments are miniature versions of a female courtier's dress. This is more than a sign of status; in the sixteenth century, children of every social level were dressed as adults as soon as they could walk.

Over the course of his remarkable career, Velázquez earned many court appointments. From chamberlain to the king and superintendent of Royal Works (1643) to grand marshal of the palace (1652) he held positions rarely granted to a painter. The red cross, seen here on his black doublet, was added to the painting after his death, to mark his posthumous investiture as a knight of the Order of Santiago.

José Nieto Velázquez (no relation to the painter) served as *aponsentador*, marshall to the queen's household. One of his duties was to hold the door for the queen. Does his presence indicate that the Queen has just entered the room or that she is about to exit? Perhaps Velázquez included him to add illumination, visual complexity and depth to his composition.

AUTHENTIC ANONYMITY

Untitled (*Woman in Mask*)
Rufus Anson (active 1851–1867)
1858
Daguerreotype
10.8 × 8.2 cm (4.3 × 3.2 in)
Art Institute of Chicago, Chicago, IL

Sitting for his first daguerreotype portrait in October 1841, poet Ralph Waldo Emerson felt compelled to fix his gaze and compose his features into an expression that would represent his character to posterity. He lamented that his efforts to control his likeness failed; the results looked more like a 'mask than a man'. The new photographic process, introduced in the United States just two years earlier, was credited with capturing a sitter's authentic appearance, unmediated by an artist's interpretation, through the agency of light and the objectivity of technology. Within a decade, the process was widely available – from professional studios in cities to peripatetic practitioners making the rounds of towns and farms – and Americans sought to take a picture to pass down the generations. With such emphasis on visual authenticity, it is curious that this sitter chose to hide behind a mask when seated in front of the camera.

In 1837, French artist Louis Daguerre improved upon the early experiments of his late associate Joseph Nicéphore Niépce to produce a fixed, positive image with a camera. In the process that bears his name, a copper plate coated with light-sensitive silver iodide is exposed in order to record an image, which is then developed using mercury vapour and stabilized with a salt solution. This produces a unique, richly detailed reproduction of the desired scene on a mirror-like surface.

Daguerre believed his technique was best suited for landscape and still-life subjects, but when his 1839 pamphlet explained the process to the public, aspiring American photographers exploited its potential for portraiture. Over the next two decades, daguerreotype portraits reached their zenith of popularity in the United States, and a small, glossy image of a friend or relative, protected in a metal and velvet-lined case, became a favourite keepsake. Due to its scientific origins, the process was believed to capture an absolutely authentic likeness: 'a transcript of the beloved features, ever at hand, wearing the very expression that revealed the soul'.

Going on the premise that accurate expression 'is everything in a daguerreotype', such articles as 'Suggestions for Ladies Who Sit for Daguerreotypes' (1852) instructed readers how to enhance their natural appearance through flattering attire. But the sitter in this untitled portrait is dowdily dressed with an overwhelmingly fussy bonnet, and a stiff, out-of-date coiffure. By covering all but the sitter's mouth, the mask raises a range of possibilities, including that of cross-dressing, a practice banned throughout New York State where the portrait was taken. Whatever the reason, the sitter's attempt to disguise identity in an image heralded for its accuracy ironically testifies to the power of the daguerreotype. The only way to evade the camera's truth was to hide behind a mask.

While the stiff, moulded mask hides more that half of the sitter's face, the ruffled bonnet obscures the head shape and covers most of the hair. Beneath the bonnet, the rolled coiffure appears rigid and unnatural. Perhaps the sitter is wearing a wig.

A poorly tied fichu covers the bodice of the sitter's ill-fitting gown. The sleeves are enormous and pulled down to partially cover the hands. This clumsy ensemble completely engulfs the sitter's body, going against popular advice to accentuate a feminine silhouette.

Rufus Anson ran a busy and successful studio in New York City from around 1851 to 1867. The stamp on the frame suggests that it was supplied with the daguerreotype. These plush lined cases were more than decorative. The slightest abrasion could mar the delicate surface, and many daguerreotype frames were designed with a thin sheet of protective glass and a cover.

Comtesse de Castiglione
Pierre-Louis Pierson
(1822–1913)
c. 1864
Daguerreotype
Pierson-Mayer

A daguerreotype is a unique image; to be reproduced it must be
re-photographed. In the early 1850s, new techniques allowed
photographers to create negative images from which multiple
positive images could be printed. Photographs of family, friends and
celebrities could now be shared and collected. Renowned for her
flamboyant beauty, the Comtesse de Castiglione was photographed by
Pierson more than 400 times. She poses here with a passe-partout in a
flirtatious pose that calls attention to her face.

PERFORMING FOR THE CAMERA

Untitled Film Still #14
Cindy Sherman (b. 1954)
1978
Gelatin silver print
24 x 19.1 cm (9.4 x 7.5 in)
Museum of Modern Art, New York, NY

The scene looks so familiar. A sultry woman in a black dress gazes to her left at something or someone outside the frame. The reflection in the mirror reveals a martini coupe on a table and a jacket hanging on the back of a chair. The woman looks distraught and holds an unidentified, sheathed object in her right hand. The stylistic details – the woman's bouffant hair, her cinch-waist dress, the floral-patterned table covering, the double photograph frame behind her – evoke an aesthetic and an era. The image appears to be a film still from the early 1960s, but just as the focus of the woman's attention remains elusive, the film cannot be named. The photograph is part of a series of seventy images, staged, shot and modelled by Cindy Sherman that stir a viewer's cinematic memory without any narrative link to an actual film.

As a child, Sherman loved to dress up, and as a teenager she began to haunt second-hand shops to collect clothing, wigs and accessories. Rather than simply wearing the items, she used them to construct characters, and her fascination with the way wardrobe transforms the wearer inspired her career-launching series Untitled Film Stills (1977–1980). Each features an ambiguous cinematic scenario focusing on a female film stereotype: the ingénue, the bombshell, the farm girl, the woman scorned. Sherman triggered a story without telling one by tapping into the common memory of film noir and B movies from the later 1950s and early 1960s. By manipulating the recollection of what viewers have seen, Sherman forces them to create the script, and she saw it as a mark of her success when her viewers claimed to remember the movie. 'In fact', she states, 'I had no film in mind at all'.

In making the film stills, Sherman played the role of director, designer and actor. But ultimately her leading role is photographer, using a shutter-release cable to take the shot. The 8 x 10 format, the grainy surface and high-contrast tonality of her photographs deliberately simulate the mass-produced film stills created to promote movies and to be collected by film stars' fans. Presenting herself in character, Sherman links her work to the subversive self-photographs of Marcel Duchamp (as Rrose Sélavy) and Claude Cahun. But rather than traversing gender boundaries, Sherman's dramatis personae interrogate the mass media's depiction of women. Although Sherman almost exclusively photographs herself, explaining 'I am the one who is always available and I know what I want', her images are never portraits. Her face and body provide the screen on which she projects a provocative convergence of photography and performance.

Sherman exploits the visual elements of the film still. She stuck to the 8 x 10 format associated with these popular prints and didn't strive for sharp detail or balanced tonality. 'I wanted them to seem cheap and trashy', she explained, 'something you'd find in a novelty store and buy for a quarter'.

Using wigs and cosmetics Sherman takes on a new character. More than a putting on a disguise, she seems to dissolve into a cinematic leading lady. Often, as here, her facial expression is hard to read; her refusal to title the individual stills heightens the ambiguity. In her later work, Sherman has employed face and body prostheses, constructing shocking characters, but the Untitled Film Stills portray recognizably normal types, tapping into a viewer's memories from mass media.

The mirror reveals that there is a cocktail glass on the far side of the corner of the table. The nearby chair is pushed a bit back, as if someone has got up and abandoned the drink. A man's jacket is casually hung on the back of the chair. Sherman tells us just enough to make us want to know more.

Untitled Film Still #21
Cindy Sherman
1978
Gelatin silver print
19.1 x 24 cm (7.4 x 9.5 in)
Museum of Modern Art,
New York, NY

Dressed in a prim suit and a modest hat, a young woman is seen against the background of New York's skyscrapers. Her wide-eyed youth and her cautious expression define her as an ingénue. Perhaps she is new to the city, seeking a job in an office. Her character appears again in the series (#22), but her story is waiting to be told.

What is this woman holding? She seems to grip the handle of a knife that is sheathed in a velvet cover. Her cuff bracelet draws the viewer's eye to that mysterious object, as well as the bruise on her forearm. These clues may be tantalizing, but they fall short of telling her story.

One half of this double frame holds a photograph of the woman. Her hair is shorter – a gamine cut – and she looks seductively at the camera. But it is impossible to see whose image is in the other frame.

INVISIBLE IN PLAIN SIGHT

Portrait of the Artist as a Shadow of His Former Self
Kerry James Marshall (b. 1955)
1980
Egg tempera on paper
20.3 × 16.5 cm (8 × 6.5 in)
Private Collection, Steven and Deborah Lebowitz

Kerry James Marshall found a new direction in his art shortly after reading Ralph Ellison's *The Invisible Man* (1952), a groundbreaking novel about the alienation of African American life in a white dominated society. In previous work, Marshall had focused on abstract painting and collage, but after years of 'pushing around paint' he felt he had come to a 'dead end'. His first foray into figurative work was small – confined to the dimensions of a sheet of typing paper – but its impact was enormous. Although the bust portrait of a gap-toothed, grinning man bore little resemble to the artist, it gave Marshall a platform for the ideas he wanted to explore in his art – technique, identity and the emotional and aesthetic conditions of blackness – with his medium carrying his message.

The opening lines of Ellison's novel – 'I am invisible, understand, simply because people refuse to see me' – struck a chord in Marshall's imagination. Not only did it expose a harsh reality of the African American experience, it inspired Marshall to seek a visual counterpart for this state of 'simultaneous presence and absence'. Drawing upon his deep engagement with the history of European art, Marshall approached his subject as a tonal challenge: a black figure upon a black ground. He further linked his work with the past by adopting the compositional format of early Italian portraiture and painting in egg tempera. The medium demanded painstaking control, but it also provided an absolutely matte surface, heightening the subtle variation of black tones and emphasizing the contrast between black and white. Marshall exploited the power of his restricted palette: 'I was aware of using the black as a rhetorical device'.

Over the next few years the grinning man came to haunt Marshall's paintings, as the artist acknowledged that *Portrait of the Artist as a Shadow of His Former Self* served as a 'manifesto'. He paired it with a blank, white panel in *Two Invisible Men (The Lost Portraits)* and inserted the work as a framed painting on a wall in *Portrait of the Artist and a Vacuum* (both 1985). The antic face topped a barely visible body – black on black with a black contour – in *Invisible Man* (1986). Like a trickster figure – familiar, and yet provocative and strange – the grinning man led Marshall to his mature mode of expression, portraying African American life with grace, dignity and the proud assertion of visibility. The common element is the matte-black skin tone, for, as Marshall realized in painting his first portrait, the 'idea of those paintings is that blackness is non-negotiable'.

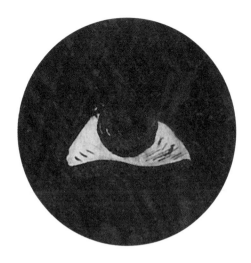

Marshall intentionally referenced early Renaissance portraiture in the three-quarter, bust portrait position of the figure. He built his composition and his technique on his study of the history of European art as a means to both challenge and expand the canon.

The brilliant white serves to heighten the power of black. With deep black irises against the clear white, the eyes are captivating, but the intent of that gaze – soulful or joyful, passive or dismissive – is impossible to read.

The wide, gap-toothed grin may be read as comic or sardonic. The prominent white teeth seen in contrast to the pitch-black skin summons up offensive racial images but, for Marshall, the reference is confrontational and redemptive. And the ambiguity is deliberate, making the viewer feel as off balance as the man being viewed.

The Invisible Man
Gordon Parks (1912–2006)
1952
Gelatin silver print
33 × 41.9 cm (13 × 6.5 in)
Art Institute of Chicago, Chicago, IL

After the landmark publication of *The Invisible Man*, novelist Ralph Ellison and photographer Gordon Parks collaborated on a feature article for *Life* magazine (25th August 1952) titled 'A Man Becomes Invisible: Photographer recreates the emotional crises of a powerful novel'. Marshall acknowledges the profound effect of Ellison's novel on his early figurative work, and while he does not mention this staged photograph of the protagonist emerging from his subterranean hiding place it instantly gained iconic status and may have also been an influence.

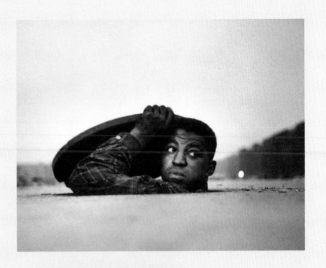

Untitled
Kerry James Marshall
2009
Acrylic on PVC panel
155.3 × 185.1 × 9.8 cm
(61.1 × 72.9 × 3.9 in)
Jack Shainman Gallery,
New York, NY

In contrast to the shadow effect – being seen and not being seen – in Marshall's early portrait, the sitters in his mature work have a compelling presence. Magnificently dressed, this unnamed artist proudly holds her palette as an emblem of her identity and levels an unflinching gaze out to the viewer. But the matte-black skin tone marks the legacy of what Marshall discovered in the early portrait: black is not-negotiable.

5

Censorship

A WORK OF ART IS REMOVED FROM A GALLERY. Another is covered with a curtain. A painting or sculpture is modified with the addition of a drape, a barrier or an explanatory text. Police intervention is summoned to close an exhibition or to call a halt to a performance. Whatever the reason – and whatever the result – the history of censorship is entangled with the history of art. Typically the power to curtail artistic expression is in the hands of a sanctioned authority: a government official, an institution or a representative of a society or sect. Rationales range from trigger warnings about sensitive issues to the professed desire to protect the public from images and ideas that are deemed transgressive. The controversial content may be political, religious, critical or sexual; the intent of the artist to stir controversy may be deliberate or accidental. Every case of sanitizing, silencing or shutting down a work of art contends with the artist's freedom of expression and the individual's right to see and judge for themselves. But censorship can backfire; public condemnation can give a work wider exposure to rally support, change minds and challenge authority. The secret of censorship is that it reveals more about the motives and morals of the censor than what the artist wished to express.

Censorship is hardly a contemporary phenomenon. Over the centuries, many works have been banned, altered or destroyed in the name of the public good. What appears to be chaste and beautiful in one era can be perceived as distasteful and corrupt in another, as seen in the defacement of ancient classical sculptures during the Middle Ages. The association of the body with sin diminished with the rise of humanist thought in the fifteenth and sixteenth centuries, and artists emulated the classical ideal. Michelangelo's magnificent frescos in the Sistine Chapel, for example, celebrated the nude as the purest expression of the human condition. But just as he was finishing *The Last Judgement* (1536–1541), the final work in the ensemble, the Catholic church adopted retrograde restrictions on religious imagery and, in 1565, a year after Michelangelo's death, the Vatican hired the painter Daniele da Volterra to drape the offending figures; he became known as *Il Braghettone* or the breeches maker.

Expurgation can be used to cloud a community's memory or revise its history. An individual who has fallen out of favour with a ruling authority can be effaced from a painting or a photograph. The altered image stands as proof that they held no power; that they were never there. In the 1920s the Nazi party in Germany attempted to obliterate a whole movement in the arts. Condemned as degenerate, modernist works were removed from national collections; artists who advocated modern aesthetics were banned from exhibiting and fired from their teaching posts. This purge culminated with the display in Munich of 650 objects in the 1937 exhibition '*Entartete Kunst*' ('Degenerate Art'). The installation, including works by Max Beckmann, Henri Matisse, Marc Chagall and Pablo Picasso, purported to expose the inherent depravity in works of art that the Nazi regime described as an insult to the German people. The exhibition attracted more than three million visitors, triple the number that attended the '*Grosse Deutsches Kunstausstellung*' ('Great German Art Exhibition') held at the same time.

There is nothing intrinsically immoral in a work of art. But if the physical object endures, the interpretation can change. In the examples that follow we see how careful restoration can bring back an artist's original vision. Another artist stands up to censure, only to censor himself in a later version of the same subject. A governmental official 'kills' images to promote a social agenda. A painter strikes back when his work is destroyed, replicating and revising his work in retaliation. A once-shocking performance is muted when the circumstances of presentation – as well as social attitudes – change. And a modest work in a minor exhibition sets off a national reaction, empowering the artist's message far beyond any expectations.

NAKED EMOTIONS

Expulsion from the Garden of Eden
Masaccio (Tommaso di Ser Giovanni di Mone Cassai; 1401–1428)
c. 1426–1428
Fresco
213.36 × 88.9 cm (84 × 35 in)
Brancacci Chapel, Santa Maria del Carmine, Florence

When Adam and Eve tasted the forbidden fruit, they sensed that there was something wrong with their bodies. According to the book of Genesis in the Old Testament, for the first time they experienced shame in being naked, and they sewed fig leaves into 'aprons' to cover their loins (Genesis 3:7). From the Early Christian era onwards, the large, flat leaf of the fig tree appeared in depictions of their expulsion, and the multi-lobed leaf soon became both a symbol and a solution for hiding something distasteful. Yet, when Masaccio painted the first man and woman being driven out of Eden, he painted them fully nude. The fresco was part of a series of works in the private chapel founded by the Brancacci family in the church of Santa Maria del Carmine in Florence. Masaccio's *Expulsion* is located on a pier just within the threshold of the chapel. Masolino da Panicale's painting of the Temptation is on the opposite pier.

In both depictions, the painters reflect the new ideals of humanism emerging in the intellectual and artistic circles of Quattrocento Florence. The bodies they portray appear to have weight and the potential for movement; the positions and proportions are modelled on the example set by classical sculpture. Masolino's figures seem to pose as if to be admired. In contrast, Masaccio propels his figures into expressive, muscular action. Adam sobs into his hands, contracting his diaphragm with each laboured breath. With a clutching gesture,

Eve attempts to cover her breasts and genitals, indicating her sense of shame. And although they are clearly being expelled from the garden, Masaccio did not depict their fig leaf 'aprons', as if their transgressive behaviour – rather than their nudity – caused their shame. From the humanist perspective, the nude body was the ultimate symbol of the human experience in all its beauty, power, emotion and nobility.

Within little more than a century, this attitude changed. To counter the rising influence of the Protestant Reformation, the Roman Catholic Church convened the Council of Trent (1545–1563). Along with clarification and affirmation of Catholic doctrines, the council produced a set of guidelines for imagery, warning that the emphasis of beauty in the depiction of the human body stimulated lust. No matter the subject or context, lasciviousness had no place in religious art. In 1658, under the reign of Duke Cosimo III d' Medici, an anonymous artist added garlands of leaves around the hips of both depictions of Adam and Eve in the Brancacci Chapel. These 'fig leaves' remained in place until the 1980s, when they were removed as part of an extensive programme of restoration (1984–1990). When the doors reopened to the public, Masaccio's figures once again appeared as he intended, reasserting their nudity as an essential and profoundly moving expression of their humanity.

The Temptation of Adam and Eve
Masolino da Panicale (1383–c. 1440)
c. 1425
Fresco
208 × 88 cm (81.8 × 34.6 in)
Brancacci Chapel, Santa Maria del Carmine, Florence
Post-restoration

Like his younger colleague Masaccio, Masolino's
conception of the human body is based on classical
sculpture. But in contrast to Masaccio, who used
the classical example as a departure point, Masolino
imitated the poses as well as the proportions.
His figures, while beautiful and serene, seem
inexpressive and static by comparison. Note that the
serpent has a little human head, recalling a vestigial
form from the Middle Ages.

Over the centuries the grime and pollution
produced by oil lamps and votive candles
completely obscured Masaccio's clear colours.
The purpose of the restoration programme was
to clean the frescoes and make any necessary
repairs; it also provided the opportunity to
remove the seventeenth-century addition of the
leafy branches wrapped around the figure's hips.
Although Masaccio intended his figures to be
nude, his representation of the narrative shows
Adam and Eve leaving the garden, when they
would have been wearing their 'aprons'.

BELOW With a sword in hand, a powerful angel drives Adam and Eve out of the garden and points them towards the unknown. Over the centuries, the face of the angel had so deteriorated that it could not be fully restored. Similarly, the sky has lost its top layer of fresco, exposing the preparatory layer of blue-grey plaster.

ABOVE Eve's position – arms across her body to cover her breast and pubis with her hands – augments the shame and sorrow she expresses on her face. Masaccio adapted the gesture from the classical *Venus pudica*, a pose in which the Goddess of Love gracefully arranges her arms to feign modesty while drawing attention to the parts of her body that Eve so poignantly covers.

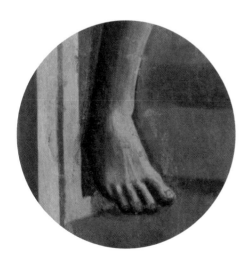

Masaccio's figures convey real movement as well as human emotions. As Adam takes his final step out of the Garden of Eden's gate, his right heel lifts off the ground, transferring his weight to the ball of his foot. It is known that Michelangelo admired Masaccio's frescoes; this influence is clear in the physical expression of his monumental figures.

Although Adam hides his face, his heaving abdominal muscles reveal that he is sobbing. It is well known that Masaccio studied classical sculpture, but his grasp of anatomical action suggests he looked at actual bodies in motion.

WHAT HAVE I DONE TO OFFEND YOU?

Phyllis and Demophoön
Edward Burne-Jones (1833–1898)
1870
Watercolour and body colour
91.5 x 45.8 cm (36 x 18 in)
Birmingham Museums and Art Gallery, Birmingham

Shortly after the opening of the 1870 spring exhibition, Frederick Taylor, president of London's Old Water-Colour Society, approached Edward Burne-Jones with a delicate matter. The society had received a letter of complaint concerning one of his five paintings on display. The letter has been lost, but Taylor's request that Burne-Jones modify one of the figures with removable chalk suggests that the writer, 'Mr. Leaf', was offended by its nudity. The artist flatly refused and found Taylor's alternative suggestion – that he choose a work by another artist to replace the now controversial painting – humiliating. With the discussion at an impasse, the society went ahead and removed *Phyllis and Demophoön* from the gallery, hanging two other works in its place. Late in July, when the exhibition closed, the artist ended his six-year association with the group.

Burne-Jones based his depiction of the star-crossed lovers on a tale from Ovid's *Heroides* (*The Heroines*; late 1st century BCE). On his journey home from the Trojan War, Theseus's son, Demophoön, briefly stopped in Thrace, where he courted the king's daughter, Phyllis. Promising to return, Demophoön departed for Greece, but during his long absence, Phyllis fell into despair and took her own life. An almond tree grew on her burial site. When Demophoön finally returned and learned of her demise, he embraced the tree, and Phyllis emerged to forgive him. The classical origins of the subject validated the portrayal of nude figures, and Burne-Jones's pairing echoed that of Zephyrus and Chloris in Botticelli's much admired *Primavera* (c. 1482). But he broke an unspoken rule of Victorian art decorum. Male figures were never portrayed fully frontal in the nude.

There is a Latin inscription on the back of the work in Burne-Jones's hand: 'Tell me what I have done, except to love unwisely?' (*Dic mihi quid feci? Nisi non sapienter amari*). It might well be Phyllis's own lament, but it has also been read as a personal confession. For several years, Burne-Jones was embroiled in a passionate, extra-marital affair with the sculptress, Mary Zambaco. She often modelled for him; Phyllis bears her likeness. But it is unlikely that this connection played into the controversy. While his friends were well aware of his liaison, the general public was not, and the inscription on the verso could not be read in the gallery. The line Burne-Jones crossed was public, not private. In his letter of resignation to the Old Water-Colour Society, he cited a 'want of sympathy between us in matters of Art', emphasizing that to flourish his art required 'absolute freedom'. Yet, a decade later, when he painted *The Tree of Forgiveness*, reprising his vision of Ovid's doomed lovers, he covered Demophoön with a well-placed fluttering drape.

The physicality of Phyllis grasping her long-lost lover also made the critics uneasy. In *The Times*, Tom Taylor described it as 'a love chase' with 'a woman follower', declaring that as a subject it 'is not pleasant'.

LEFT Burne-Jones added the detail of the tree bursting into flower as Phyllis emerges to claim her lover. Neither Ovid nor Chaucer, who included the tale in his *Legend of Good Women*, describe the blossoming; it was probably the artist's invention.

RIGHT Burne-Jones's watercolour technique was as unorthodox as it was masterful. He worked on an unusually large scale, often across multiple sheets of paper, and applied thick layers of pigment with a dry brush. Without the characteristic visible washes and pooling effects, he created a flat, matte surface more like that of tempera than conventional watercolour.

The Tree of Forgiveness
Edward Burne-Jones
1881–1882
Oil on canvas
186 × 111 cm (73.2 × 43.7 in)
Lady Lever Art Gallery, Liverpool

In this later version, the figures are far more monumental, facial expression more dramatic and gesture more vigorous. Phyllis's body now fully bursts out of the tree, as Demophoön writhes in her grasp. But the composition is basically the same with one small difference: Demophoön now wears a modest little drape.

Drawing of Mary Zambaco
Edward Burne-Jones
c. 1869–1870
25.9 × 32.2 cm (10.2 × 12.7 in)
Private collection

Burne-Jones first met Mary Zambaco through her mother, who commissioned the artist to paint Mary. Her strong features and wide dark eyes, intrigued the painter, and for a time she was a constant presence in his studio and in his art. Long after the affair ended, Burne-Jones remarked that the head of Phyllis in the 1970 painting 'would have done for a portrait' and described it as 'a glorious head'.

CONTROVERSY AND CONSEQUENCES

Man at the Crossroads and Looking with Uncertainty but with Hope and High Vision to the Choosing of a Course Leading to a New and Better Future
Diego Rivera (1886–1957)
1933–1934
Fresco
5.2 x 19.2 m (17 x 63 ft)
RCA Building, New York, NY
Destroyed

In the early 1930s Mexican muralist Diego Rivera crisscrossed the United States courting collectors and seeking public commissions. The most prestigious came in 1932: a vast fresco for the lobby of the RCA Building (now 30 Rockefeller Center), the skyscraper that anchored New York City's Rockefeller Center. It was to be funded by the Rockefeller family, whose fortunes came from the Standard Oil Company. Rivera, as famous for his progressive politics as for his public art, responded to the general theme of 'New Frontiers' with an ensemble that celebrated the social role of labour, industry and scientific discovery. By the end of the year his sketches were approved and, with six assistants, he set to work in March 1933 intent on meeting a May 1st deadline.

A provocative article, written by Joseph Lilly for the 24th April edition of the *New York World Telegram*, brought the project to a halt. Under the headline 'Rivera paints scenes of communist activities and John D., Jr. pays the bill', Lilly branded the design socialist propaganda, citing a portrait of Vladimir Lenin and noting that the colour scheme was predominantly red. Nelson Rockefeller, John D. Rockefeller, Jr.'s son, wrote to Rivera on 4th May asking him to remove the Soviet leader's portrait. Rivera replied two days later, offering to counterbalance the offending likeness with such American advocates of freedom as Abraham Lincoln, Nat Turner, John

Brown, and Harriet Beecher Stowe. But he insisted that Lenin's image would remain. Without further discussion the project was terminated on 9th May. Rivera received full payment ($21,000, meant to cover assistant's salaries and materials as well as the artist's compensation), and the unfinished fresco was covered with heavy white canvas.

There were protests, as well as debate about transferring the unfinished work to the Museum of Modern Art, but by the end of the year the controversy died down and Rivera had returned to Mexico City. On the morning of 13th February 1934, the building opened to the public as usual, but the fresco was gone. Overnight, a work crew had chiselled the fresco from the wall, destroyed the fragments and covered the damage with a fresh coat of plaster. Asked for his response by *The New York Times*, Rivera called the act 'cultural vandalism'. But he had already prepared a strategic counterattack. In the furore that followed Lilly's article, he had his assistant, Lucienne Bloch, smuggle a camera into the site to document the work. He used the photographs to replicate the design at a reduced scale in Mexico City's Palacio de Bellas Artes with a new title: *Man, Controller of the Universe*. Along with the portrait of Lenin, he added those of Karl Marx, Friedrich Engels, Leon Trotsky and Charles Darwin, as well as an image of a scornful John D. Rockefeller, Jr., sipping a cocktail with syphilis bacteria hovering over his head.

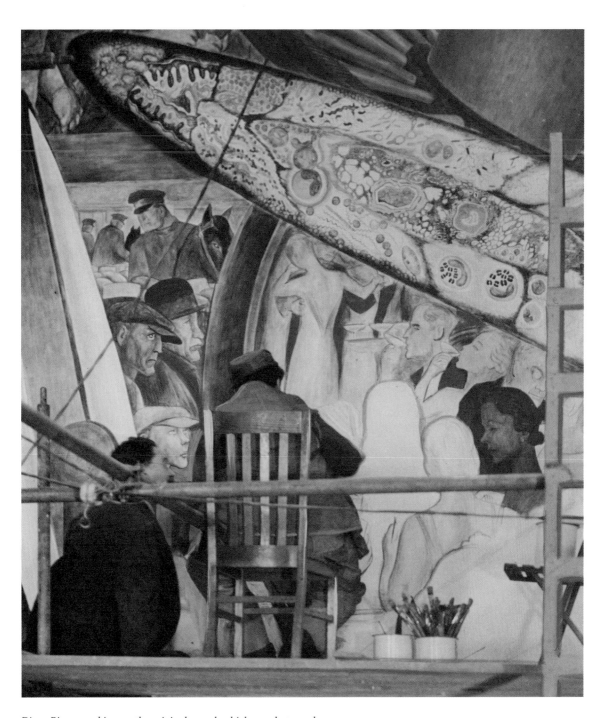

Diego Rivera working on the original mural, which was destroyed.

Man, Controller of the Universe
Diego Rivera
Fresco
4.85 x 11.12 m (15.91 x 36.48 ft)
Palacio de Bellas Artes,
Mexico City

Rivera spent more than a decade (1907–1921) in Europe, where he studied traditional art and learned to paint in fresco. The centuries-old technique uses a prime layer of plaster enhanced with marble dust. Working section by section, the artist paints on the prime layer when it is damp; as the prime layer dries it bonds with the pigment layer. This is why Rivera's painting had to be chiselled off the wall. The technique is designed to endure.

The reduced replica of the destroyed mural features a few changes, but it provides the best surviving evidence of Rivera's intentions. The heroic central figure represents the modern worker who has at his command the power of science, technology and industry. The crossroads he must navigate oppose the political systems of capitalism, represented on the left, and socialism, represented on the right.

When he replicated the destroyed mural, Rivera inserted John D. Rockefeller, Jr. nursing a cocktail in the nightclub scene; in reality, Rockefeller was a teetotaller. The propeller wing above his head houses all types of microbes to represent the benefits of scientific analysis. Syphilis bacteria is right above Rockefeller's head.

The red headscarves and banners indicate a May Day celebration, revealing that the *New York World Telegram*'s criticism of the dominance of red in Rivera's palette was about more than colour. Rivera never hid his political beliefs; he had joined the Communist Party in 1922, but his work in the United States for capitalist magnates led to his expulsion.

Although Rivera claimed that Lenin was depicted in the original sketches, the figure's face was generalized. When painting the fresco, Rivera worked from a photograph; there is no doubt that he wanted a recognizable likeness.

EDITING THE ARCHIVE

Untitled photograph, possibly related to *Wife and Child of a Sharecropper*
Arthur Rothstein (1915–1985)
August, 1935
Nitrate negative
35 mm
Library of Congress, Washington

The extraordinary photographic archive compiled by the Farm Security Administration (FSA) from 1935 through to 1944 presents an enduring record of rural poverty in the United States. Over the course of a decade, renowned photographers, including Walker Evans, Ben Shahn, Carl Mydans, Paul Carter, Russell Lee and Dorothea Lange, travelled throughout the country, from Florida to California, documenting family farming communities in the aftermath of the 1929 stock market crash and devastating droughts of the early 1930s. As chief of the historic section in the Division of Information of the FSA, economist Roy E. Stryker had full control to select photographers and hand out assignments. He also designated those images that would be printed and shared with the public in newspapers, magazines and government publications. Stryker advocated a straightforward use of the camera to capture objective reality, and when a negative fell short, he 'killed' it.

The term 'killed negative' indicates some form of intentional mutilation that renders a negative unusable. Photographers regularly shoot more frames than they intend to print, editing from contact sheets or negatives. A killed negative cannot be printed, but it might be kept for reference. Stryker, who claimed his mission was 'to collect documents' assumed the role of editor in what would become the largest federally funded photographic project in the nation's history. But he never explained his standards for selection. And the sheer number of negatives that he killed was staggering: of more than 170,000 35 mm negatives collected, he punched a hole in 100,000 so that they would not be printed. Photographer Edwin Rosskam called the method 'barbaric', while Ben Shahn characterized Stryker as 'a little bit dictatorial . . . he ruined quite a number of my pictures'.

Arthur Rothstein, who worked for Stryker from the launch of the project, had no insight into how his supervisor decided what to print and what to kill. He speculated that killed images were 'duplicates' or 'weren't the best'. His own image of a mother tending to her distraught toddler, as two older children huddle close by, seems to comply with the mandate of capturing an unmediated view, but reasons for its elimination went unrecorded. And Stryker's constant monitoring of his staff undermined his own claims of objectivity. When they took to the road, he bombarded photographers with instructions of what to shoot, specifying such subjects as 'needy families – people evacuating, migrants on the road'. Stryker's project did more than document circumstances; it rallied support for New Deal policies. To that end, Stryker deployed photographs as propaganda, in a persuasive American narrative of struggle and resilience, highlighting a stereotype of rural life that persists to this day.

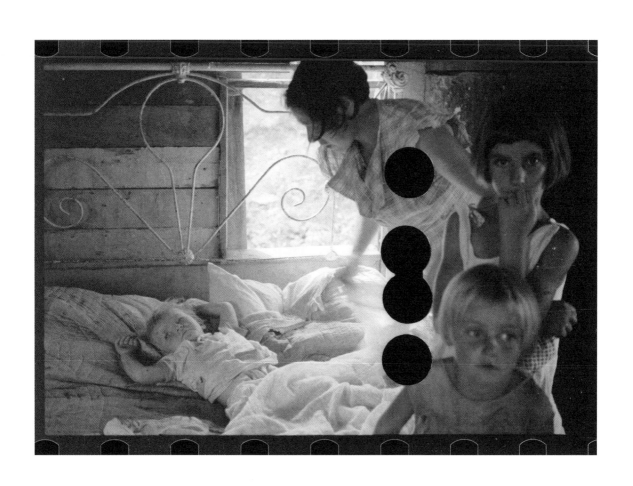

The holes were made using a hole punch of the type used on tickets in theaters and trams. The placement was generally random, and usually no more than one hole was punched. Killed negatives can, in fact, be printed; the hole appears as a black circle that disrupts the composition.

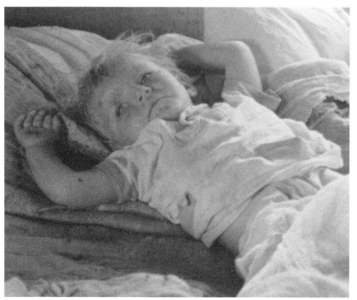

ABOVE The older girl stares unflinchingly at the camera. With her arms crossed over her body, and her left fist covering her mouth, she may be defiant or she may be defensive. Rothstein seems to have followed the instructions to capture rather than compose his image, but as a document, it is hard to interpret.

LEFT Dirty-faced and crying, the toddler lies on a rumpled bed. The mother's passive presence muddies the message. Is the child ill? Hungry? Or perhaps the child is just exhausted from throwing a tantrum.

Untitled photo, possibly related to: *Daughter of sharecropper, Mississippi Country, Arkansas*
Arthur Rothstein
August, 1935
Library of Congress

Stryker killed negatives for any number of reasons. Although the central figure of the young man is compelling, this portrait of a family group is marred by cut off figures and blurred details. The lack of calculated composition demonstrates that Rothstein is following the mandate to just shoot, but the photograph is more a family snapshot than pictorial evidence. Perhaps that's why it didn't make the cut.

Destitute Pea Pickers in California. Mother of Seven Children. Age Thirty-two. Nipomo California
Dorothea Lange
March 1936
Library of Congress

This now iconic work, commonly known as *Migrant Mother*, offers a different perspective on the theme of maternal concern. Lange took five different shots of Florence Owens Thompson and her children. In this one, Thompson gazes sadly but resolutely into the distance, holding her infant while the older children hide behind her shoulders. This powerful portrait conveys the sitter's essential dignity as well as her circumstantial pathos. Can such an emotionally charged image truly be regarded as objective?

OPPOSITE PAGE
Killed negatives, untitled photographs from the FSA archive by Ben Shahn, 1935 (above); Paul Carter, 1936 (below)

THIS PAGE
Killed negatives, untitled photographs from the FSA archive by (clockwise from top left) Carl Mydans, 1935; Russell Lee, 1938; Carl Mydans, 1935; Russell Lee, 1937

PROVOCATIVE PASSAGE

Imponderabilia
Marina Abramović (b. 1946) and Ulay (1943–2020)
June 1977
Performance
Galleria d'Arte Moderna, Bologna

Imponderabilia, staged by Marina Abramović and her creative partner Ulay (Frank Uwe Laysiepen), provided an unsettling welcome to the 1977 performance festival held at the Galleria d'Arte Moderna in Bologna. Stripped of their clothing, Abramović and Ulay stood statue-still and facing one another within the museum entrance, which had been narrowed for the exhibition. Visitors quickly realized that there was no other way to get in; they had to squeeze between the bare bodies of two strangers. The photographs documenting the performance record visitors' embarrassment as they turned sideways and tried to make their own bodies smaller to minimize the forced physical contact. Some tried to appear to be unperturbed, while others could not hide their expressions of distaste, fear, shock and even shame. Abramović and her partner remained impassive – gazing into each other's eyes – until the police arrived and stopped the performance less than halfway through its planned six-hour duration.

Abramović's art makes demands on the body. Her work has tested her capacity for pain, endurance, immobility and trusting strangers. *Imponderabilia* turned the tables on visitors, drawing them – unwillingly – into the centre of her performance. To attend the festival they had to violate a significant social taboo: physical contact with an unfamiliar nude body. The doorway provided the only access into the gallery, forcing each visitor to make several choices. How to protect their own body? Whether to use their hands as they made their way through the narrow passage? And, since they had to turn sideways, who to face? The unrehearsed actions of the visitors revealed that they felt far more vulnerable than Abramović and Ulay, who, after all were willing participants.

In 2010, Abramović trained a group of thirty-nine young artists, actors and dancers to re-enact her best-known performances as part of a career retrospective at the Museum of Modern Art in New York. From their number she selected pairs to to recreate *Imponderabilia*. They worked in rotation – now same-sex pairs as well as male and female – standing as she and Ulay had decades earlier: nude, immobile and gazing into each other's eyes. But this time there were a number of significant differences. The doorway was wider, leaving enough room for visitors to avoid contact if they so desired. There was an alternate entrance; visitors could circumvent *Imponderabilia* without missing the rest of the exhibition. And just outside the doorframe, two fully clothed security guards stood still and silent. Their positions mirrored that of the nude figures standing within the passageway, but their uniformed presence tempered what was once a shocking and risky performance.

Visitors' faces betrayed their discomfort as they squeezed between the bodies that blocked their way. Some attempted to maintain composure, but appeared tense with effort. Others looked directly at one of the artists, trying to break through their disengagement. Still others seemed to hold their breaths as they concentrated on the uncomfortable choreography that they were forced to perform just to enter the exhibition.

Passing in or out of *Imponderabilia* compelled the visitor into a social transgression. No matter what they did, they had to press up against the bare body of a stranger. And even though visitors were dressed, they felt exposed and violated.

Abramović and Ulay remained motionless throughout their performance. They fixed their gaze upon one another, keeping their faces as devoid of expression as humanly possible. *Imponderabilia* was only one of many collaborative works they staged together during their twelve-year romantic and creative partnership (1976–1988).

The Artist is Present
Marina Abramović
14 March – 31 May 2010
Performance
MoMA, New York, NY

For *The Artist is Present* – the work that gave the 2010 Museum of Modern Art retrospective its name – Abramović sat in a bare gallery at one end of a table. Anyone was welcome to sit in the empty chair at the opposite end and stare at the artist for as long as they desired. Abramović sat silent and returned the gaze. Many participants found the wordless exchange challenging; many left in tears. Abramović performed the work daily for the duration of the almost three-month exhibition.

Imponderabilia (re-enactment)
Marina Abramović
19 April 2018
Performance
Bundeskunsthalle, Bonn

With extra room to manoeuvre – and the option of entering through another door – visitors to the retrospective experienced *Imponderabilia* in a way that made them feel more secure. While the modifications to the work reduced the original impact of the performance, the new version was free from police intervention.

TAKING A STANCE ON FREE SPEECH

What is the Proper Way to Display a US Flag?
Dread Scott (Scott Tyler; b. 1965)
1988
Silver gelatin print, US flag, book, pen, shelf
203.2 × 71.1 × 152.4 cm (80 × 28 × 60 in)

Dread Scott's installation in the 1989 minority students' juried exhibition at the School of the Art Institute of Chicago posed a quandary. The title, written on a photomontage hung above a wall-mounted shelf, asked 'What is the Proper Way to Display a US Flag?' Scott placed a ledger on the shelf for visitors to record their answers, but an American flag, spread on the floor, blocked the way. To participate, the visitor would have to defy Illinois state legislation, which decreed it illegal to 'walk on, trample, mutilate, deface or defile the flag'. An activist as well as an artist, Scott's adopted name honoured Dred Scott, the first enslaved American to sue for citizenship. He believed that art had the power to 'propel history forward', and his provocative work did just that by igniting friction between a revered object and the rights it was meant to symbolize.

Prior to the opening of the exhibition on 17th February, the school administration consulted its legal council who advised that the state ordinance did not prohibit placing the flag on a clean floor. Scott was asked to consider replacing his installation with another work, but he declined, stating: 'I'm not going to censor myself'. The installation had been exhibited without controversy in November 1988, and it was the culminating work in a series of twelve installations titled American Newspeak

... Please Feel Free (begun 1987) that invited public opinion on contentious topics. Within a week of the opening, a local radio host rallied veterans' groups to take a stance against Scott's installation. Demonstrations, held on the front steps of the Art Institute of Chicago, eventually swelled to thousands of protestors. A rotation of veterans in full uniform visited the gallery daily. They repeatedly picked up the flag, folded it according to military protocol, and placed it on the shelf. Each time, a gallery staff member unfolded the flag and repositioned it on the floor. The school received bomb threats, and Scott received death threats. To review safety issues, the exhibition closed to the general public for a week (17th February to 3rd March); when it reopened uniformed police stood at the door and six security guards were stationed in the gallery.

The exhibition became a national issue when Republican Senator Bob Dole – declaring 'I don't know much about art, but I know desecration when I see it' – introduced legislation in the Senate to make any mistreatment of the American flag a federal crime. His initiative failed to get his colleagues' support. By the close of the exhibition on 16th March there was a different endorsement. The two ledgers – two hundred pages each – were filled with positive and negative comments, all bearing witness to the power of freedom of expression.

The photomontage featured American flag-draped coffins and images of student protesters in South Korea holding signs stating 'Yankee Go Home'. These anti-war and anti-intervention sentiments provided the context for the title of the installation, hand-lettered by Scott at the top of the montage.

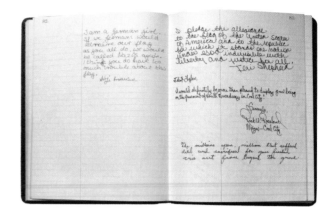

The comments in the ledger ranged from hostile – 'In Russia you would be shot' – to reflective, amused and supportive. More than one person noted that the installation inspired them to reconsider their own patriotism and their notions of freedom of expression. One viewer described the experience as a 'moment of self-awareness' prompting him to wonder when the nation would value 'human life and liberty' above property and symbolic representation.

The student protests of the late 1960s ignited debates about respect for the flag, resulting in the 1968 Flag Desecration Act. The Supreme Court revisited the issue in 1989 and 1990 to define the flag's status as 'symbolic speech', which posited that since many forms of desecration were, in fact, free speech they were protected under the First Amendment. Scott's installation was cited as one example.

Waving flags and chanting such slogans as 'One, two, three, four/Get the flag off the floor', demonstrators gathered in front of the Art Institute of Chicago. Near the end of the exhibition the crowd swelled to 7,000, forcing the Chicago Police Department to close off a portion of Michigan Avenue near the main entrance. Although affiliated with the museum, the school had full jurisdiction over student exhibitions; the gallery was part of school facilities with a separate entrance at the back of the building.

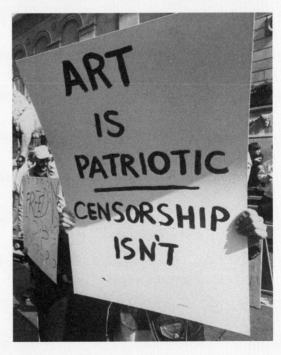

6

Secret Symbols

WHEN WE LOOK AT A WORK OF REPRESENTATIONAL ART WE ENGAGE IN A RAPID AND SEAMLESS ACT OF PERCEPTION. The lines, shapes and colours coalesce into objects we recognize, name and then associate with things that are familiar through prior knowledge or experience. This approach identifies the object as a sign – this stands for that – allowing us to decipher what is depicted in the same way that we read a set of characters or a code. But the meaning of those signs in the context of the work may require more than straightforward decoding. Throughout the history of pictorial representation, images have carried meanings that are larger and more complex than what is pictured. More than a sign, an individual image must be understood as a symbol, encapsulating a concept beyond the form and function within its familiar identity and connecting to issues and ideas outside of the object itself. To uncover and amplify the meaning contained within a work, we are required to situate it in a context of issues and ideas that may not be familiar or that differ greatly from those of our own. And sometimes we can never fully comprehend what the work was intended to convey; we discover that its meaning was a secret to all but a privileged few.

Within a cultural context, some symbols retain a consistent meaning over time. For example, take the rose. Over the centuries it has appeared in European art as an unparalleled icon of beauty. This meaning is overt, presumably linked to the appearance of the flower and the enduring opinion that the rose is beautiful. But the rose may also stand for an abstract idea connected with beauty such as love or desire. In this way, the visible meaning – the rose is beautiful – serves to comment on the abstract reference: love is beautiful; beauty arouses desire. The distinctive way that the symbol is depicted adds another layer of meaning. A white rose may signify chastity. Pink can indicate tenderness, while red evokes passion.

The stage of development can be significant: Is the rose budding, in full bloom or overblown? These factors shade overt meaning without displacing it. But the familiar form may have a disguised meaning, an assigned association with an external idea that is revealed only through the knowledge of cultural concepts, historic circumstances or community beliefs. The rose may be an attribute of an individual: the Virgin Mary presented in a bower as the rose without thorns or Aphrodite welcomed with a shower of petals as the goddess of love. It can stand as an insignia of a country, a device for an order of chivalry or spirituality, or it can be the badge of a clan. Each of these meanings can coexist or remain separate. Only the context reveals how to read the rose.

Meanings are neither forged nor exist in isolation, and over time that message can be muted. To recover the original concepts, scholars consult historical records and literature as well as compilations of symbols – iconographic indices; emblem books; dictionaries of flowers, colours and other visual motifs that correspond with the relevant culture and time. But some meanings remain elusive or esoteric and require deeper investigation into obsolete ideas, clandestine beliefs, covert societies or the eccentric views of an individual artist, patron or audience. The following examples uncover some intriguing secrets in the art of symbolic expression. New information can overturn a meticulously researched and widely accepted interpretation without providing an alternative solution. An enduring message is modified to suit a new audience. A portrait devoid of a human presence offers an intimate view of one man's regard for another. Familiar symbols are used in an unconventional context to deliberately generate ambiguity. And a rendering of an earlier era's masculine ideal allows a contemporary artist to simultaneously critique and appropriate the power of the past.

SYMBOLS AND SPECULATION

The Arnolfini Portrait
Jan van Eyck (*c.* 1390–1441)
1434
Oil on oak panel
82.2 × 60 cm (32.4 × 23.6 in)
The National Gallery, London

The prosperous couple in Jan van Eyck's double portrait welcomes viewers into their beautifully appointed reception room. Rendered with a sharp eye and a deft brushstroke, each object is purposefully placed. The convincing tactility of every surface – lustrous velvet, polished brass, planed wood, reflective glass – evokes the material wealth of a fifteenth-century merchant household. Justly proud, Van Eyck signed his work above the mirror at the heart of the composition, with a declaration of his on-the-spot observation: *Johannes de eyck fuit hic*, 1434 (Jan van Eyck has been here).

Despite Van Eyck's masterful command of surface illusion, the painting itself reveals little about this couple beyond their financial status. Their identity was first asserted in the earliest known record of the work, an inventory of the collection of Margaret of Austria, compiled in 1516, that cites 'a large picture which is called Hernoul le Fin and his wife', painted by 'Johannes'. The sparse documentary trail repeats the surname in some form of Flemish vernacular until 1857, when art scholars Joseph Crowe and Giovanni Battista Cavalcaselle linked it with the Arnolfini family, successful merchants based in Lucca with five members living in Bruges.

Writing in 1604, Karel van Mander suggested that this might be more than a portrait of a married couple, noting that their gestures appear 'as if they are contracting a marriage'. Three centuries later, art historian Erwin Panofsky crafted an erudite analysis of the visual evidence, making a persuasive case that the painting was a 'pictorial marriage certificate'. Noting that, in Van Eyck's world, marriage was a sacrament – and that Van Eyck was fluent in medieval iconographic traditions – Panofsky read the material objects as symbols: the single burning candle marks a divine presence in a 'nuptial chamber'; the discarded shoes reveal that the couple stands on holy ground; the little dog embodies the concept of fidelity; and the image of St Margaret, carved on the bedpost, protects any pregnancy that will result from this union. Sealing his argument, Panofsky proposed that the two additional figures reflected in the mirror are witnesses, and the declaration in the signature – Jan van Eyck was here – equalled a legal 'affidavit'.

New evidence, uncovered in the 1990s, undermines this analysis. Two Arnolfini cousins, both named Giovanni, lived in Bruges. The younger, Giovanni di Arrigo, traditionally identified as the husband, did not marry until 1447, six years after Van Eyck's death. The more likely sitter, Giovanni di Nicolao, married in 1426, but according to a letter written by his mother-in-law, his wife Constanza Testa died a year before this work was painted. There is no evidence that Giovanni di Nicoloa remarried. No longer regarded as a marriage portrait, the meaning of the work is again a matter of scholarly speculation.

Van Eyck signed ten paintings with the motto *als Ich kann* (as I can). Only this one time did he declare his actual presence, but did he do so as a witness to an event or to boast of first-hand observation?

The mirror reflects the backs of Arnolfini and his partner. Beyond them, two figures enter the room, a man in red and another in blue, who raises his hand, perhaps to return Arnolfini's greeting.

Gathering the ample folds of her *houppelande* (overdress) the woman displays her expensive ensemble. Often interpreted as a maternity garment, the full-fronted gown was, in fact, fashionable for all affluent women. The gesture reveals the luxurious miniver lining as well as a fitted kirtle (underdress) edged with the same fine fur.

Portrait of Giovanni Arnolfini
Jan van Eyck
1438
Oil on panel
29 × 20 cm (11.4 × 7.9 in)
Gemäldegalerie, Berlin

The striking similarity of facial features –
hooded eyes, sharp cheekbones, cleft chin –
links this sitter with the *Arnolfini Portrait*. He
appears older, but no less prosperous, wearing
a scarlet chaperon (the wound head piece) and
a fur-lined cloak. These likenesses prompted
speculation that the painter and patron were
friends, but that has yet to be authenticated.

Once thought to symbolize sacred ground,
the discarded clogs were more likely a real life
detail. Arnolfini would have worn these pattens
(wooden overshoes) to protect his expensive
dyed leather boots from Bruges's muddy streets.

Legends of canine fidelity made a dog an apt
icon of loyalty in friendship and marriage.
While the Brussels griffon may attest to the
bond between this man and woman, it could
just as likely a pampered pet.

SIGNS OF TRANSIENCE; SIGNS OF THE TIMES

Vanitas Still Life
Hendrick Andriessen (1607–1655)
c. 1650
Oil on canvas
63.8 × 84.1 cm (25.1 × 33.1 in)
Mount Holyoke College Art Museum, South Hadley, MA

With hollowed-eyes and a gap-toothed grimace, the skull at the centre of Hendrick Andriessen's still life grimly evokes human mortality. But the collection of objects surrounding the skull add layers of meaning to its long-standing warning: *memento mori* (remember death). As is typical in *memento mori* imagery, the ensemble includes representations of worldly desires: position, knowledge, wealth and power. These are joined by references to the passing of time, through which those pursuits are proved to be futile. This pictorial statement of *vanitas* – the recognition that earthly gratification is elusive and ultimately fleeting – marks a distinctive development in seventeenth-century still-life painting that found its greatest popularity with the Netherlands' newly affluent middle class.

This category of still life takes its name from the preacher's repeated warning in the Old Testament book of Ecclesiastes: 'Vanity of vanities. All is vanity' (1:2; 12:8). While the Latin noun *vanus* (empty) is usually cited as the word's origin, in this context the Hebrew noun *hevel* (vapour) adds the correct nuance. Rather than devoid of importance, the rewards of earthly pleasures are decreed to be no more enduring than mist dissolving into the air. 'Vanitas' first appears as an art term in Dutch household inventories in the early 1600s. Small in scale, yet masterfully painted, these still-life ensembles were generally purchased for upper-middle-class homes, where the potent message of mortality and material transience cautioned against overindulgence and self-satisfaction. This vivid reminder that all things must pass transcended religious differences, as seen in Andriessen's skilful combination of Catholic and Calvinist iconography.

The jewel-encrusted crown and golden sceptre represent political power. The lustrous silk and gold-banded mitre behind them proclaim religious authority. The skull sits upon an unfolded document and a massive book: the conventional emblems of human knowledge. But the other exquisitely painted objects emphasize that all power, authority and knowledge wanes over the passage of time. An open watch sits on the left corner of the table; the hands approach twelve o'clock. The darkened room reveals that it is almost midnight. The flowers – possessing beauty that is doomed to wither – include morning glories and four o'clocks. The delicate bubbles that float in the air are doomed to pop. Even the stalk of wheat – a symbol of abundance that crowns the skull – has dried. Like the burned-down candle, whoever owned this painting had a limited life. But there is more than a touch of irony in the realization that the painting would go on to warn future generations. And, with his reflection seen on the shining surface of the candlestick, Andriessen makes a bid for his own immortality despite his eloquent discourse on vanitas.

ABOVE The morning glory and the four o'clocks are temporal symbols. Named after the messenger to the Olympic gods, the iris often appeared in early Northern Renaissance scenes of the Nativity as as a harbinger of Christ's sacrificial death. In Andriessen's day the tulip was an acronym for Calvinist principles: 'T' for Total Depravation; 'U' for Unconditional Election; 'L' for Limited Atonement; 'I' for Irresistible Grace; 'P' for the Preservation of the Saints. The tulip may also refer to the collapse of the tulip market in 1637.

RIGHT Still-life painting demanded the ability to reproduce the rich visual experience of the material world. Here Andriessen demonstrates his consummate skill in every surface, from the sheen of a silk ribbon to the delicate incising on the gold watch. Most astonishing is his depiction of the bubbles: air-borne, transparent and ready to burst.

BELOW The wheat circlet on the skull links it to Christ's crown of thorns; the holly's spiny edges reinforce that association. But the dry, brittle stalk is also a reference to transience, recalling the lines in Psalm 103, that compare the days of a lifetime to the grasses of the field, 'for the wind passes over it, and it is gone' (16).

BELOW The extinguished candle is an enduring symbol for life's end. But Andriessen secures a kind of immortality by painting a tiny self-portrait reflected on its bulb. As long as the work he painted exists, he will be remembered.

In contrast to the origin of the term in the Latin word *vanus* (empty), every object in a vanitas still life carries meaning. The medal of St George (patron saint of England), hanging on its blue ribbon below the crown and sceptre, may refer to the recent Civil War in England, which ended with the execution of King Charles I and abolition of the monarchy.

Still Life with a Skull and a Writing Quill
Pieter Claesz
(1596/97–1660)
1628
Oil on wood
24.1 x 35.9 cm
(9.5 x 14.1 in)
Metropolitan Museum of Art, New York, NY

The skull, the book and the candlestick were almost constant elements in vanitas imagery. Small in size but masterful in execution, a work like this by Claesz would have hung in an affluent household as an object to admire, but with a message to be heeded. The glass of the goblet – overturned and empty – reflects the windows of a typical domestic interior.

A PORTRAIT IN STILL LIFE

Gauguin's Chair
Vincent van Gogh (1853–1890)
1888
Oil on canvas
90.5 x 72.7 cm (35.6 x 28.6 in)
Van Gogh Museum, Amsterdam

Vincent van Gogh furnished a house on the Place Lamartine in Arles with a specific goal in mind. He had journeyed from Paris to Provence in February 1888 to escape the pressures of city life, the dreariness of the northern winter and to 'paint nature under a brighter sky'. Within a few months, lonely for companionship, he rented four rooms in a building with a bright yellow exterior and whitewashed interior walls. He hoped to welcome like-minded visitors, and in September he informed his brother, Theo, that he had purchased two beds and two mattresses, as well as twelve rush-bottomed chairs. He set up his own room in the 'Yellow House' to be simple and serviceable but purchased 'dainty' things for the guest room – including an upholstered armchair – and he painted bright bouquets of sunflowers to decorate the white walls.

On 23rd October, Paul Gauguin joined van Gogh in the Yellow House. Roughly a month later, van Gogh painted a pair of unusual portraits, arranging household objects to represent absent sitters. For *Gauguin's Chair*, he covered the red tiles of the studio floor with a floral rug. He brought the armchair down from the guest room and placed two books and a lighted candle on the cushion. Each object was freighted with meaning. Traditionally a chair with arms belonged to the head of the household; van Gogh felt Gauguin to be superior both as a painter and

as a man. Although untitled, the books have the yellow paper covers associated with contemporary novels, a reflection of Gauguin's cultural sophistication. The burning candle signified the enduring power of creativity, a symbol that van Gogh adapted from the lithograph, *The Empty Chair*, designed by Luke Fildes and published in *The Graphic* to commemorate the death of Charles Dickens.

When paired with its pendant *Vincent's Chair*, the painting expresses more than one artist's admiration for another: it defines the men as opposites in character and vision. Van Gogh chose a rustic, rush-bottomed chair – one of the set of twelve – as his stand-in and placed it on the bare floor. The lighter colours are brilliantly bathed in natural daylight. Gauguin's chair sits in a darkened room at night, where the radiant gaslight illuminates the jewel-toned furnishings and wall cover. In their brief time together, the camaraderie that van Gogh desired degenerated into confrontations about finances, personal habits, studio practice and the most essential ideas that fuelled their art. Gauguin quickly tired of van Gogh's overbearing company, writing to their friend, Émile Bernard, that he and his host did 'not see eye to eye'. Within a month, Gauguin was gone, and van Gogh – turning to self-mutilation in his dire depression – relinquished his dream of a community of artists in Arles.

Describing the two paintings to his brother, van Gogh noted that *Gauguin's Chair* featured a 'night effect' while his evoked 'daytime'. Taken together the two works are a study in contrasts – night and day, simple and sophisticated, bright and shadowed – portraying not just the individual perspectives of the housemates but their irreconcilable differences.

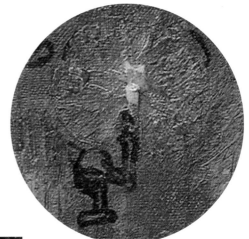

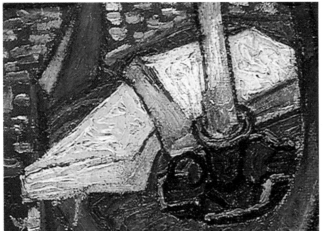

Vincent first painted a yellow-bound novel in the self-referential *Still Life with Bible*, which featured Émile Zola's *La joie de vivre* (1885, Van Gogh Museum, Amsterdam). Contemporary novels typically had an inexpensive paper covers. Here Vincent compares such writers as Zola, Joris-Karl Huysmans, and Pierre Loti with Gauguin, who shares their daring and modern perspective.

The Empty Chair, Gad's Hill – Ninth of June 1870
Luke Fildes (1843–1927)
1870
Lithograph

Van Gogh admired Charles Dickens and Luke Fildes for calling out social injustice in their art. He owned a copy of Fildes's commemorative lithograph, depicting Dickens's study where he wrote tales of contemporary life in London. The now-empty arm chair is pulled away from the desk; and the candle, on the table at the right, is extinguished.

Vincent's Chair
Vincent van Gogh
1888
Oil on canvas
91.8 c 73 cm (36.1 x 28.7 in)
National Gallery, London

In contrast to the carved and upholstered armchair, van Gogh represented himself with one of the plain, rush-seated chairs he purchased in hopes that a community of painters would gather at the Yellow House. Despite Gauguin's urging that he create from vision and memory, van Gogh persisted in working his own way: painting quickly from spontaneous observation. Throughout Gauguin's two-month stay, they argued whether inspiration was better derived from external stimulus or an individual's imagination.

Originally, Vincent did not sign the work, and the seat of the chair and the box in the back were left empty. After his release from hospital in January 1889, where he recovered from his self-inflicted wound, he added the pipe and tobacco pouch, the sprouting onions to the box, and his signature.

EVOCATIVE BUT ELUSIVE ICONOGRAPHY

Eine Kleine Nachtmusik
Dorothea Tanning (1910–2012)
1943
Oil on canvas
40.7 x 61 cm (16 x 24 in)
Tate Modern, London

Along a dimly lit, seemingly endless corridor, there are a series of numbered doors; all but one are tightly shut. Light blazes out of that narrow opening, but nothing behind the door is revealed. The atmosphere reeks of neglect. The carpet is worn, and dull, cracked paint peels off the walls. The setting evokes a tale of Gothic horror, but when the viewer tries to follow the tale, the elements don't add up. Who are the girls – one leaning against a doorframe as if transfixed, the other startled with her hair standing on end – and what are they doing in the hallway? What is the meaning of that colossal sunflower lying with a broken stem and tattered petals at the top of the stairs? It is futile to search for a literary source or to link the painting with the title's reference to a spritely composition by Wolfgang Amadeus Mozart. Dorothea Tanning's haunting imagery draws upon interior experience – perplexing dreams and the ambiguity of the unconscious – and reflects her belief that Surrealism taps into the 'limitless expanse of POSSIBILITY'.

Tanning recalled that she had been reading a lot of Gothic literature – a childhood passion – at the time. And *Eine Kleine Nachtmusik* (a little serenade) exudes the sensation of displacement and menace that she associated with tales of horror. Even the girls' garments are quaintly old-fashioned: fitted bodices, tied-back skirts and high-buttoned boots. But just as there is no clear sense of a definable time and place, there is no story, only story prompts. Viewers and critics alike have tried to assign meaning to the elusive iconography, with often frustrating results.

To Tanning, symbolic meaning is as mutable as a dream. She disregards the long-standing association of the sunflower with loyalty. The traditional meaning derives from observation of the plant's heliotropic movement; it turns to the sun with the devotion of a follower to a leader. But Tanning proclaims it as the 'most aggressive of flowers', powerful enough to embody confrontation. The battered state of the giant sunflower suggests a literal struggle, but with whom? There are ragged petals on the stairs and others clenched in the fist of the girl in the doorframe. The girl's bare torso and her surrender to reverie

hint at sexual awakening, but Tanning has been less specific, citing the confrontation as one 'between the forces of grown-up logic and the bottomless psyche of a child'. She made those comments, however, more than sixty years after conceiving the painting. At the time she offered no explanation. Perhaps these slippery symbols represent another of her beliefs, that painting should compel the viewer 'to look beyond the commonplace' and embrace 'enigma', which she regarded as 'a very healthy thing'.

The sexually charged *femme-infant* – literally a woman-child whose body and sensuality outpace her innocence – symbolized salacious desire in the work of the male Surrealists. But Tanning's portrayal is far more nuanced. The girl's body, revealed by her open bodice and drooping skirt, is that of a child, but her face suggests the kind of complete release associated with postcoital satisfaction. There is also a sense of the aftermath of a struggle, indicated by the torn sunflower petals she grips in her left hand.

With her tense shoulders and firm stance, this girl appears ready for a confrontation. But the trailing, tattered ribbons of her skirts suggest some previous scuffle. Her hair literally stands on end. Is that indicative of her rising power or that she is overwhelmed by fear?

Doors, hallways and stairways feature in many of Tanning's paintings. To her, they represented endless – and inexplicable – possibility. The vivid hue of the light that streams out of this partially opened door evokes the dangerous heat of a fire, adding to the enigmatic aura of the environment.

Dismissing traditional floral symbolism, Tanning linked her massive sunflower with aggression and confrontation. Decades after painting this work, she explained that it represented 'all the things that youth has to face or to deal with'. Does its battered state reveal that the clash is terrifying or that the girls have been triumphant?

Birthday
Dorothea Tanning
1942
Oil on canvas
102.2 × 64.8 cm (40.2 × 25.5 in)
Philadelphia Museum of Art, Philadelphia

Painted one year earlier, Tanning's self portrait shares visual elements with *Eine Kleine Nachtmusik*. The bizarre garments – an open Renaissance jacket and a draped swag-front skirt – resemble those worn by the older girl on the left. The green overskirt composed of brittle twigs and miniature writhing bodies evokes the same supernatural menace as the massive, anthropomorphic sunflower. And although these doors are open, their endless repetition only leads the viewer into ambiguous space.

PAINTED INTO HISTORY

Officer of the Hussars
Kehinde Wiley (b. 1977)
2007
Oil on canvas
304.8 x 304.8 cm (120 x 120 in)
Detroit Institute of Arts, Detroit, MI

Growing up in Los Angeles, Kehinde Wiley developed an ambivalent attraction to the Baroque and Romantic portraits that he saw in local art museums. As a young African American boy he felt a 'complete disconnect' with the long dead, European heroes, but at the same time he was 'enthralled' by their embodiment of 'history and ego'. Wiley sought to insert the experience of youth and American Blackness into the dominant tradition as a means to both expand the vision of art history and empower those who shared his identity. As seen in *Officer of the Hussars*, he revisited iconic portraits and recast them with sitters whose appearance and energy reflected his view of the contemporary world.

Wiley called his process 'street casting', and through it he brings authenticity and the sitter's involvement into each painting. He roams his neighbourhood, and when he sees someone who emanates 'a certain type of power', he invites them back to the studio. Together they page through an illustrated art-history book, and when the sitter responds to a particular portrait, Wiley has them simulate the pose wearing their own clothing so that he can photograph them. Working from the photograph, Wiley paints the portrait, filling the background with exuberant, decorative motifs. The result combines the heroic frame of reference established by art historical conventions with the dynamic infusion of a distinct individual whose presence and perspective both subverts and revitalizes the original conception.

Officer of the Hussars is part of Wiley's series 'Rumors of War' (begun 2005), featuring grand-scale, vividly painted equestrian portraits inspired by the works of such renowned painters as Peter Paul Rubens, Diego Velázquez and Jacques-Louis David. His source is Théodore Géricault's *The Officer of the Chasseurs Commanding a Charge*, which caused a sensation at its debut in Paris in 1812. Wiley recreates Géricault's depiction of the fiery, rearing horse, fitted with a gold-embellished bridle and a cheetah-skin saddle, but replaces the uniformed rider with a strapping young man dressed in an athletic T-shirt, low riding jeans and Timberland brand boots. Like Géricault's fierce and dashing officer, Wiley's sitter rises and turns in his saddle; he grasps the officer's weapon – a gleaming sabre – as an emblem of his readiness to command. Cast with sitters mostly drawn from the vicinity of 125th Street in Harlem, 'Rumors of War' engages issues of masculine power. Wiley's repertoire has expanded to other types of subject matter as well as to sitters found in other countries, women, and the first African American president of the United States. In reconciling the disconnect he felt in his youth, Wiley bridges past and present in what he regards as 'a very American conversation'.

Wiley's repeated portrayal of younger African American men mediates his boyhood experience of exclusion from art's history. He describes his heroic paintings as 'a type of self-portraiture', informed by 'looking at people who happen to look like me'.

Images of raw and refined power proclaim this sitter's authority. The chiselled muscularity of his arm is emphasized as he tightly clenches the golden hilt of his sabre. His tattoo features snakes twining around a dagger. The cheetah pelt over the saddle evokes the animal's ferocity, as well as its submission to the rider's dominant strength.

The distinctive tan, lug-soled Timberland short boot – originally marketed as utilitarian footwear – became a status symbol in hip-hop circles in the 1990s. Nicknamed 'Timbs', they were popularized by Ol' Dirty Bastard of the Wu-Tang Clan and Jay-Z, who claimed to buy a new pair every week. Wiley positioned his sitter's foot in the stirrup so that the logo near the heel is clearly displayed.

Officer of the Chasseurs Commanding a Charge
Théodore Géricault (1791–1824)
1812
Oil on canvas
346 x 266 cm (136.2 x 104.7 in)
Musée du Louvre, Paris

A friend of the painter and a lieutenant in the Chasseurs – the elite cavalry corps serving Napoleon's empire – Alexandre Dieudonné made an authentic sitter. But rather than a portrait of an individual, Géricault sought to portray the bravery possessed by an officer who controls his startled horse as he rides into the thick of the battle. Wiley appropriated the massive scale of the work, as well as the horse and the weaponry, but his rider directs his gaze to confront the viewer.

Rumors of War
Kehinde Wiley
2019
Bronze
8.2 x 4.9 m
(27 x 16 ft)
First unveiled in Times Square, NY, and now resides at the Virginia Museum of Fine Arts in Richmond, VA.

Wiley's over-life-size bronze statue grapples with a dilemma in the United States concerning public art: What to do about the monuments that glorify the Confederate Army soldiers of the American Civil War (1861–1865). Wiley's response counters them through appropriation and displacement. Here, reprising the monument to General J.E.B. Stuart – which, after 113 years was removed from its Monument Avenue site in Richmond, Virginia and placed in storage on 7 July 2020 – a proud, young Black man in braids and a hoodie is astride the horse.

7

Dress Code

IN THE VISUAL ARTS THERE IS MUCH TRUTH TO THE ADAGE 'CLOTHES MAKE THE MAN'. This commonplace saying can be traced to William Shakespeare's tragedy *Hamlet* (*c.* 1600), when the courtier Polonius sends his son to France with sound fatherly advice: listen to others, but be cautious in speech; cherish friendship and do not rush to judgement; neither lend money nor borrow it. As for attire, first impressions are significant, so choose well and wisely: 'Costly thy habit as thy purse can buy', avoiding all that is flamboyant or vulgar, 'For the apparel oft proclaims the man' (Act 1; Scene 3; lines 70–73).

In the arts, as in life, clothes provide more than modesty, warmth and ornamentation for the body. They furnish a rich and subtle language of identity through which the artist portrays age, social status and gender. Garments can accentuate the beauty of a sitter and hide physical flaws; they can be true to one's station in life or improve one's image for posterity. In a narrative representation, attire advances the story; in a portrait it can be a guide to character. Clothing has its own history and lexicon of meaning, and when an artist is fluent in that history they can use the dress code to conceal or reveal a secret.

The way we dress makes a statement about the way we see ourselves and the way we want to be perceived. We embrace fashion, follow traditions or defy conventions in a public performance of who we think we are and what we want to be. In life, clothing can speak volumes about an individual without the wearer ever having to say a word. And that wordless eloquence gains expressive power when transferred from life to art.

While an artist draws upon the references of the history of dress to indicate status, rank or character in a work of art, the depiction of clothing in art can also transcend reality, reconfigure identity and even alter history. An ermine mantel turns a mortal into a monarch; a well-fitted uniform turns a mere man into a hero. Just as an artist can improve a sitter's appearance, they can enhance the quality of their garments. A skilled painter can transform wool into silk, felt into fur, base metal into gold. An informed familiarity with the history of dress and its references becomes a potent tool to address issues and convey ideas far more complex than an individual's desire for a well-curated public image.

To unlock the dress code in a work of art, the viewer need not be an expert in the history of dress. What is needed is a willingness to see dress as more than fashion or a historical reference; we need to read what the garments reveal about the wearer and their circumstances in the context of the composition. The examples that follow illustrate just a few of the ways artists have used the codes of dress history, fashion, silhouette and style to fold meaning into their work. The glamorous attire of a foreign courtier is embroidered to define and celebrate her contribution to her husband's reign. A colourful accessory worn by a young man of privilege links the world of reality to that of allegory. A woman's dress forecasts her destiny in a moral tale with a futile hope for redemption. Transgressive dress gives another woman the power to allure and influence, while elevating her own sense of self and potential. A garment is so closely linked with an artist's public image and private identity that it asserts her presence even in her absence. And the dress code is bent to bring race, class, place and gender into a celebratory proclamation of converging cultural identities and an audacious suggestion of what clothes can make of a man.

A SYMBOL OF POTENCY AND POWER

Portrait of Eleonora of Toledo and Her Son Giovanni
Bronzino (Agnolo di Cosimo; 1503–1572)
c. 1545–1546
Oil on wood panel
115 × 96 cm (45 × 38 in)
Galleria degli Uffizi, Florence

In 1539, Leonor Álvarez de Toledo y Osorio left her home in Naples to marry Cosimo I de Medici, the recently crowned Duke of Florence. The daughter of Don Pedro Álvarez de Toledo, the Viceroy of Naples, 'Eleonora' brought wealth, prestige and the strict decorum of Spanish aristocracy to the modest Florentine court. Renowned for her elegance and beauty, Eleonora favoured the magnificent fashions worn by the female courtiers in Madrid: dresses of resplendent silks and velvets embroidered in gold and silver. The rumour that her trousseau contained an extensive cache of stunning Spanish brocades ignited widespread resentment, particularly at a time when her husband's economic plans included the increased production of Florentine silk.

The dress Eleonora wears in this portrait typifies her sophisticated style. The gown is made of thick white satin, a fabric supple enough to create the flowing skirt and puffed sleeves, but equally substantial to cover the rigid understructure of the bodice and support the elaborate embroidery in black and gold. The pattern is more than an embellishment. The motif is a golden pomegranate; with its many seeds, the hard-shelled fruit symbolized fertility in the Judeo-Christian tradition. Eleonora's dress carried a message about her husband's reign. In 1537, just two years before their

marriage, Cosimo's cousin, Duke Alessandro was assassinated and left no heir. Cosimo, elected to take the reins of the republic, assumed his cousin's title, promising a renewal of Florentine power through his alliance with Spain, as well as the perpetuation of his family's line. Bronzino's portrait affirms that promise. Within five years of marriage, Eleonora and Cosimo had two daughters and two sons, the youngest of which is seen at her side. And the silk of her gown appears to be Florentine in type rather than Spanish.

Like many official portraits of the day, Eleonora's likeness was replicated to be given as a diplomatic gift. Her image represented her husband's potency and prosperity, woven into the fabric of her gown. Eventually, Cosimo and Eleonora had eleven children, four daughters and seven sons; their eldest son, Francesco, succeeded his father as Duke, while Giovanni became a cardinal. According to contemporary accounts, Eleonora continued to wear the dress. A later portrait attributed to Bronzino's workshop, presents her in the same gown, with its distinctive embroidery and golden net partlet (a sleeveless garment worn under a bodice), as well as her magnificent strings of pearls. And tradition has it that when she died in 1562, the gown served as her shroud.

Known for her love of luxury, Eleonora was fond of pearls, as seen in the spectacular strings that enrich her ensemble and the smaller pearls woven into her golden partlet.

Giovanni de Medici, second son of Eleonora and the Duke, was two years old at the time of this portrait. Second in line to inherit his father's position, his presence alongside his mother assures the line of succession should tragedy befall his elder brother, Francesco.

The stylized pomegranate, magnificently embroidered on Eleonora's gown, proclaims the promise of abundant motherhood. In many cultures, the seeds within the fruit symbolized a large family, while its association with Persephone, whose descent into Hades brought winter to the earth, promised renewal and abundance with the onset of spring.

Portrait of Eleonora of Toledo and Her Son Giovanni
Bronzino
c. 1545–1550
Oil on wood panel
122 × 100 cm (48 × 39 in)
Detroit Institute of Arts

Portrait of Eleonora of Toledo
Workshop of Bronzino
c. 1562–1572
Oil on wood panel
78cm × 59cm (31 × 23 in)
The Wallace Collection, London

This later version of the portrait is likely to have been commissioned as a diplomatic gift, to be sent abroad to one of Florence's allies. Making such replicas was common practice and, in this case, it is believed that members of Bronzino's workshop had a hand in the completion. This panel is larger than that used in the first version, and the costly ultramarine background of the original is replaced with a muted, grey-brown hue. The boy's costume has also been modified, from a rich violet to a more modest brown.

As the beautiful wife of a powerful duke, Eleonora sat for other portraits, including a double portrait with her eldest son Francesco, also by Bronzino (*c.* 1549, Museo di Palazzo Reale, Pisa). But Bronzino's initial likeness remained her official image. This replica was a workshop creation, most likely painted after Eleonora's death from malaria in 1562. The Latin inscription at the top derives from the standard mass for holy women, and the vase to her left has been interpreted as a funerary urn.

A LUTE PLAYER'S LEGGINGS

The Pastoral Concert
Tiziano Vecellio (also known as Titian) (1488/1490–1576)
c. 1509
Oil on canvas
105 × 137 cm (41 × 54 in)
Musée du Louvre, Paris

In the brilliant light of a summer's day, two musicians sit beneath the cooling shade of a tree in a forest clearing. There is a city in the distance, high above the waters of a bay. The curve of the lute player's hand indicates that he is about to strike the strings, but at the moment only the rustle of leaves stirring in the breeze breaks the silence. In the foreground, two allegorical nudes flank the musicians. On the left is Inspiration, pouring water into a well; on the right, Echo holds a flute, ready to return the first notes that the musicians play. The pastoral setting, the suspension of action and the presence of personifications contribute to the timeless quality of Titian's rustic idyll, but the lute player's attire links the scene to present-day Venice. His bi-coloured hose mark him as a member of the Compagnie della Calza (Company of the Leggings), a confederation of wealthy young men dedicated to staging revels for the city's residents.

Founded in mid-fifteen-century Venice, the Compagnie della Calza rode the rise of the republic's economy. Its members included the sons of the most affluent citizens as well as those of noble descent. Drawing on their families' fortunes, they organized celebrations for weddings, holidays and receptions. They also contributed to such traditional festivals as boat races, *mamaria* (masked processions), and the Fèsta della Sènsa (Feast of the Ascension,

the highlight being the *Sposalizio del Mare* or the marriage of the republic and the sea). Along with raising civic spirit, the companies' activities positioned these elite young men in the centre of Venetian public life. They cut a dashing figures at every event: members dressed in the latest fashions and proudly wore the colours of their particular company affiliation on one stocking.

Titian's lute player's fine garments, as well as his green and white leggings, contrast with the simple clothes of his rural companion. Like the nudes in the foreground, the men are representations, embodying city and country life. Earlier in the decade, Venetian poet Jacopo Sannazaro had published *Arcadia* (1504), a romance in which a young aristocrat named Sincero disguises himself as a shepherd to seek a more natural existence in the countryside. Although Titian's subject is not an adaptation of Sannazaro's narrative, the spirit is the same. Both revive the pastoral ideal as defined in the classical writings of Theocritus and Virgil. Who better to personify the cultivated pleasures of urban life than an elite son of Venetian privilege, who seeks recognition through spending, extravagant clothes and public display? Titian's rustic idyll places him in a more genuine environment, countering contemporary artifice with timeless harmony.

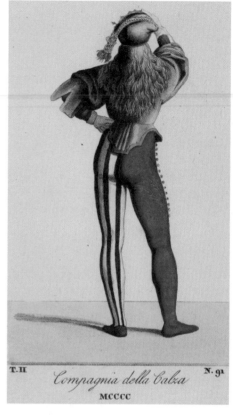

Men on a Balcony (det.), *Arrival of the English Ambassadors*
Vittore Carpaccio (*c.* 1460–1526)
from 'The Legend of Saint Ursula'
1495
Accademia, Venice

Two of the three fashionable young men in the foreground are members of the Compagnie della Calza. The man on the left wears the typical livery: one leg of his hose is vertically split into two colours. The ornate stocking of the man on the right (just behind the man in the red stockings) are embroidered and have chevron appliqué embellishing the white half. The colours, patterns and insignia represent rival companies, who, in this case, are welcoming an honoured guest.

'Young Venetian Man' from the *Compagnie della Calza*
Vittore Carpaccio (*c.* 1460–1526)
from Camille Bonnard's *Costumes Historique*
c. Fifteenth century

The livery of individual groups of the Compagnie ran from simple bisected hose to highly elaborate leggings, as in this example of a gold-embroidered scarlet stocking. The man wears a very short doublet, all the better to display his fine physique.

Just as the men's clothes are more than attire, the female nudes' lack of clothes reveal that they are more symbolic figures. Since classical times, a woman's body served to personify an abstract concept. Whether draped or nude, the attributes – in this case the pitcher and the well – identify the embodied idea.

The lute-player spared no expense in his ensemble. He wears a green leather jerkin, banded with red ribbons, over a white linen *camicia* (shirt). His voluminous silk sleeves are puffed and slashed in the latest style. His low-crowned hat, breeches and sleeves are dyed crimson, an expensive colour made from the dried and crushed bodies of the *Kermes vermilio*, an insect imported from the Middle East. With his green and white stocking proclaiming Compagno affiliation, he is the perfect embodiment of a wealthy young Venetian.

With his unruly curls and his dun-coloured, homespun garments, the musician on the right symbolizes unpretentious rural life. His legs and feet are bare; his left leg, awkwardly extended, can be seen just behind the figure of Echo.

The clothes of rural workers were serviceable and practical. The shepherd's thick, hooded cloak could be used as a blanket, and his jerkin is short, to allow freedom of motion. Rather than breeches he wears short drawers over his thickly woven hose. He, too, is a musician; he plays a rustic bagpipe as he watches over his sheep.

DRESS, DECORUM, DESTINY

The Awakening Conscience
William Holman Hunt (1827–1910)
1853
Oil on canvas
76.2 × 55.9 cm (30 × 22 in)
Tate Gallery, London

Inspired by Proverbs 25:20, 'As he that taketh away a garment in cold weather . . . so is he that singeth songs to a heavy heart', William Holman Hunt portrayed the plight of the kept woman. As a modern parallel to his biblical source, Hunt depicted a seduction, but instead of passion, the man's words – 'the idle sing song of an empty mind' – stir his mistress's recollections of her home. With a 'startled awakening', she rises from his lap intent on 'breaking away from her gilded cage'. A founding member of the Pre-Raphaelite Brotherhood, Hunt regarded painting as a moral endeavour, meant to convey 'genuine ideas'. Every object in the room, from the cheap veneer on the furniture to the lace hem of her skirt, tells a tale of a woman's fall and her potential redemption.

Hunt composed his work in adherence to the Pre-Raphaelite precept 'Truth to Nature'. He posed his models in a rented *maison de convenance* in St. John's Wood, in a building notorious for clandestine affairs. The cheap and flashy furnishings betray the transience of the couple's connection, and Hunt illustrated the woman's predicament in meticulous and meaningful detail: a cat toying with a broken winged bird, a cast-off glove, a tangle of brightly coloured yarn. The woman's attire reveals how far she has fallen. Despite the midday hour – shown on the gilded French clock – she is still in her nightdress. Made of soft cotton and trimmed with tucks and cutwork lace, the intimate garment was meant to be worn solely in the boudoir. Her tumbling hair, as well as her uncorseted body, mark her as loose. She has chosen ornaments that heighten her allure – overlarge earrings, a vivid cashmere shawl – and she wears a ring on every finger of her left hand except the one that indicates marriage.

The song sung by her seducer – the music on the piano stand is Thomas Moore's 'Oft in the Stilly Night' – laments the passing of childhood innocence. As the woman hears the words, she is transfixed by the view through a window of a verdant garden; it is reflected in the mirror behind her, but has she already fallen too far to recover her virtue? Hunt leaves the woman's future unresolved. In a defence of the painting, critic John Ruskin predicted that 'the very hem of the poor girl's dress', painted so exquisitely 'thread by thread', will soon be 'soiled with dust and rain'. Redemption is hard and hardly certain; her fate may be the same as that crumbled glove on the floor.

RIGHT Thomas Fairbairn commissioned this work to display in his home, but in 1856 he asked Hunt to repaint the woman's face. He found her grief stricken expression and streaming tears too much to bear.

BELOW Berlin work – stitching patterns in yarn on canvas – was a popular pastime for Victorian women. The decorative panels were often made into gifts for men, including cases for watch-fobs, eyeglasses and slippers. Here the unfinished work is neglected, and the brilliant yarns are in a tangle on the floor.

Versatile 'cashmeres', the finest woven of the soft hair of Kashmiri mountain goats, were worn as an indoor wrap over the shoulders or outdoors over a coat. The careless way this woman wears her cashmere reflects her character, just as the absent ring on her fourth finger indicates that her relationship flaunts moral dictates.

Worn by women of every class, nightdresses were generally made of fine linen or light cotton. The garment was meant to be worn without stays and not to be seen by anyone other than a woman's husband or her lady's maid. The woman in the painting boldly wears her richly trimmed gown in the sitting room with her suitor, breaking rules of dress decorum.

Found
Dante Gabriel Rossetti (1828–1882)
Designed 1853; begun 1859; unfinished
Oil on canvas
91.4 × 80 cm (36 × 31.5 in)
Delaware Art Museum, Wilmington, DE

Rossetti explored the subject of the fallen woman in his unfinished painting *Found*, a depiction of a farmer arriving in the city to sell his calf, only to discover his former village sweetheart plying her living on the streets. True to Pre-Raphaelite authenticity, Rossetti borrowed a farmer's smock and searched second-hand shops for an appropriately tawdry dress and a 'showy, but seedyish' mantle.

Men's kid gloves fit like a second skin. They were difficult to clean, so profligate owners discarded them once they were crumpled and soiled, making the cast-off glove an apt allusion to how this thoughtless seducer will treat his companion.

'THE DANDY IN ME'

Self-Portrait
Romaine Brooks (1874–1970)
1923
Oil on canvas
117.5 x 68.3 cm (46.3 x 26.9 in)
Smithsonian American Art Museum, Washington, DC

While staying in London in 1923, Romaine Brooks teasingly wrote to her romantic partner, poet Natalie Barney, that she was causing quite a stir. Brooks boasted of a 'string of would-be admirers', who were intrigued with her 'curly hair and white collars'. She claimed that her heightened allure had little to do with her 'inner self', but rather with a new image she had cultivated: 'They like the dandy in me'. As seen in her *Self-Portrait* of that year, Brooks had been wearing the high hats, starched collars and tailored jackets associated with masculine identity. But more than just a bold statement of her sexual orientation, Brooks appropriated men's attire – and an obsolete designation for a type of gendered elegance – to express her own sense of independence and modernity as a woman.

As a reference to sophisticated dress, the English term dandy can be traced to the late eighteenth century, but it was sharply defined a generation later by the Regency socialite George Bryan Brummell. 'Beau' Brummell practised meticulous grooming, demanded impeccable tailoring and dressed exclusively in black and white as a demonstration of his gentlemanly refinement. Over the decades, dandified dress allied with artistic identity, as seen in the garments worn by such figures as James McNeill Whistler, Oscar Wilde and Robert de Montesquiou-Fézensac. French writer Charles Baudelaire saw through the dandy's 'blasé' attitude and 'immoderate taste for the toilet and material elegance' to an 'independence of character' and 'personal originality' that was thoroughly modern. By the turn of the century, the male dandy faded into decadence, but in the early twentieth century, a select group women embraced the label in defiance of normative society and sexuality to forge their own subversive image of gender.

Brooks projects dashing self-confidence in her severe and stylish attire. The deep black of her hat and jacket, along with the pristine white of her shirt, marks a bold contrast to the misty urban setting behind her. The only flashes of colour are her scarlet lipstick, echoed by the red ribbon of the Légion d'honneur pinned to her left lapel.

During that same stay in London, she painted portraits of two other women in masculine attire: *Peter: A Young English Girl* (1923–1924) and *Una, Lady Troubridge* (1924). All three were openly gay, financially privileged, and habitués of an intellectual literary salon hosted by Brooks's partner Barney. And their preference in dress was more than a performance of appropriated identity. By choosing to wear male attire they asserted their right to masculine prerogative in every aspect of their lives.

Peter (A Young English Girl)
Romaine Brooks
1923–1924
Oil on canvas
91.9 × 62.3 cm (36.2 × 24.5 in)
Smithsonian American Art Museum, Washington, DC

Fellow painter Hannah Gluckstein signed her paintings 'Gluck', and her friends called her Peter. She had been cropping her hair and wearing men's attire since 1918, and she revelled in blurring the expectations of gendered appearance, writing to her brother 'I am flourishing in a new garb, intensely exciting'. Barney praised this portrait, telling Brooks that it made a fine addition to her 'series of modern women'.

Una, Lady Troubridge
Romaine Brooks
1924
Oil on canvas
127.3 × 76.4 cm (50.1 × 30 in)
Smithsonian American Art Museum, Washington, DC

With her bobbed hair, monocle and high-winged collar, Lady Troubridge plays on the dual references of dandified privilege: masculinity and social status. A skilled translator, she introduced the works of Colette to British audiences. After separating from her husband, Admiral Ernest Troubridge, in 1915, she partnered with Marguerite Radclyffe Hall, author of the groundbreaking novel, *The Well of Loneliness* (1928). They lived together from the early 1920s until Hall's death in 1943, raising prize dachshunds.

Her eyes nearly hidden beneath the brim of her riding hat, Brooks confronts the viewer with a bold, unwavering stare. A review in *Vogue* magazine (June 1925) admired the intelligence of her gaze, a perfect match for her 'strict *tailleur masculin*' (perfectly tailored masculine suit).

The setting of the portrait is not known, but the looming buildings and the heavy fog over the water evoke an urban dockside. Brooks cuts a dashing and unlikely figure in this rough locale. Her command of limited yet expressive tone recalls Whistler's moody nocturnes.

The bright red ribbon insignia, along with her slash of scarlet lipstick, strengthens the severity of the monochrome palette through contrast. Born to American parents, Brooks spent most of her life in Europe. In 1920, she was awarded the Croix de la Légion d'honneur from the French government for her fund-raising efforts to support the arts during the First World War.

PERFORMING AUTHENTICITY

My Dress Hangs There
Frida Kahlo (1907–1954)
1933
Oil and collage on hardboard
45.7 x 49.5 cm (19 x 19.5 in)
Private Collection

Frida Kahlo's striking appearance captivated Edward Weston when they met in San Francisco in 1930. The occasion was a photography session with her husband, famed muralist Diego Rivera. Weston noted in his daybook that the petite Kahlo, a 'little doll alongside Diego', was 'a doll in size only'. Along with her beauty, Kahlo radiated strength and confidence and looked so remarkable in her 'native costume' that people on the streets stopped 'in their tracks'. What Weston called her 'native costume' was the dress of the women of the Isthmus of Tehuantepec, in the Mexican state of Oaxaca. Kahlo's own background was Eurocentric; her Mexican mother was of Spanish descent and her father was a German immigrant. Kahlo had adopted Tehuana attire when she married Rivera in 1929, and by the time she painted *My Dress Hangs There* at the conclusion of their three-year sojourn in the United States, the square-cut cotton blouse and long skirt had become an unmistakable emblem for her own identity.

The distinctive, short-sleeved *huipil* and voluminous skirt – worn by Tehuana women for more than one hundred years – provided an essential template that could be enhanced with embroidery, lace, ribbons, tucks and flounces. This certainly appealed to Kahlo who regarded her attire as an extension of her art and her spirit. And the garments slid easily over the confining corset that she had been forced to wear after a crippling accident in 1925. But above all, Tehuana dress, associated with a strong, matriarchal indigenous society, proclaimed her *Mexicanidad* (Mexicaness). Travelling with Rivera, as he advanced his career across the United States, she was often dismissed as exotic or ornamental, no more than 'Diego's beautiful young wife'. Through Tehuana dress she linked her individuality with authenticity, all the more powerful in contrast to the crass materialism she found in the States.

My Dress Hangs There marks a rare example in which Kahlo asserts her presence without inserting her likeness. The background is a claustrophobic vision of Manhattan: a discordant display of grandiose architecture rising above a roiling mob in the streets below. Two massive but mismatched Doric columns tower above the crowds; one is topped with a sports trophy, the other with a toilet. A blue clothes line tethered between them supports Kahlo's brown and green Tehuana dress. The natural colours – earth and plant life – along with the pristine white flounce stand out against the grime of the built environment. By the time Kahlo finished the painting, she and Rivera had returned to Mexico, but she knew that she had left an indelible impression.

The gigantic poster of movie star Mae West provides a stunning contrast to the type of woman who would wear Tehuana dress. Everything about West – from her corseted curves to her peroxide-blonde hair – is over-blown and artificial. Although not Tehuana herself, Kahlo wore regional garments to express with her own sense of authentic identity.

The dress Kahlo portrays no longer survives; it may, in fact, never have existed. With its squared-off top silhouette and full, flowing skirt, the dress that hangs above Manhattan is a representation of Kahlo's signature style, so much so, it embodies her spirit even in her absence.

Kahlo clipped photographs of crowds – marching in protest, waiting at soup kitchens, trudging into factories – and pasted them on her canvas to portray the vast downtrodden sector of the American populace in the aftermath of the 1929 financial crash. Not only is this an explicit critique of American capitalism, but her use of collage is atypical

The classic Tehuana ensemble features a geometrically cut top (*huipil*) with short sleeves and either a round or squared neckline. Made of cotton, decorative elements include hand embroidery (generally patterns rather than figures), appliqué and contrasting insets, and embroidered bands. The full skirt, made of printed or solid cotton, is gathered into a band at the natural waist and similarly trimmed with embroidery and applied bands, as well as horizontal tucks near the hem, which is often augmented with a lace or pleated flounce.

Frida Kahlo in New York
Nickolas Muray
1939
Photograph
Nickolas Muray/PhotoArchive

Every aspect of Tehuana dress suited Kahlo: the comfortable style lines, the bold colour and pattern combinations, and the voluminous silhouette that allowed ease of movement. She admitted that she neither visited Tehuantepec nor had a 'relationship with its people', but declared that she dressed 'like a Tehuana' because it was her favourite of all variants of Mexican indigenous dress. And despite her own European heritage, she scoffed 'gringa women' who copied her mode 'a la Mexicana', claiming that 'the poor souls' looked like 'cabbages'.

MULTI-LAYERED MASQUERADE

Big Boy
Yinka Shonibare, CBE (b. 1962)
2002
Wax-printed cotton fabric and fibreglass
215 × 170 × 140 cm (84.6 × 66.9 × 55.1 in)
Art Institute of Chicago, Chicago, IL

Towering more than 2 m (7 ft) tall, Yinka Shonibare's *Big Boy* cuts a commanding and confident figure. His pose proclaims empowerment: shoulders back, chest expanded, forward stride. The absence of the fibreglass mannequin's head makes this physical audacity disconcerting. Without a face, it lacks the conventional symbol of identity. The clothing evokes a distant time and place; the mannequin sports impeccably tailored formal daywear that would be worn by an affluent British gentleman of the mid-Victorian era (*c.* 1870s). But the explosive colour and exuberant patterns of the textiles subvert the historic reference. Rather than plain, dark-hued wool and white linen, the ensemble – from stock to spats – is completely crafted from Dutch wax cotton, a cloth associated with West Africa.

Dutch wax cotton, also called African print or Anakara, is neither truly Dutch nor African. In the 1800s, the Dutch East India Company developed an industrial printed textile to compete with the labour intensive wax-resist batik cloth imported from Indonesia. Although produced to capitalize on the South Pacific trade, the two-sided, brightly printed textile found its best market in the ports of West Africa where it quickly evolved from a status symbol into the textile of national dress. Its popularity has endured through the decades, and although the constantly changing repertoire of prints reflects current African interests, much of the fabric is still manufactured in Europe. Shonibare, who buys his Dutch wax in London markets, calls it a 'cross-bred' cloth, and embraces its sham authenticity for a masquerade that destabilizes the presumption of a post-colonial world.

Race and nationality are only part of *Big Boy*'s subversive sentiment. Its traditionally male attire – trousers, jacket, and waistcoat – boasts an element that challenges classification as menswear. A sweeping, swallowtail train floats out from under the back skirt of the mannequin's frock coat. Like the rest of *Big Boy*'s attire, the train features the silhouette and the style lines of the 1870s. Trains were worn exclusively by women, but this train – with its tiers, puffs and flounces – is fully integrated into a male ensemble, recalling another icon of male resplendence: the peacock tail. The combination of the signature element of contemporary women's fashion with the iconic mode of masculine dress defies the rigidly binary views of the earlier era's concept of gender. Shonibare's anarchic addition is jarring but seamless; as with the colourful diversity of the textiles, the supposedly separate features of gendered dress converge into something unprecedented, alluring and audacious. Shonibare explains that fluid ambiguity is part of his purpose: 'What interests me is that area of not quite knowing whether I am celebrating difference or building a critique'.

The jacket illustrates the template of masculine tailoring: the inverted triangle of the back silhouette tapers from broad shoulders into a narrow waist, which is accentuated by a flat band, and finished with a slightly flared skirt. But here, spilling out from under the jacket is a fashionable, feminine train, augmented by ruffled tiers, a pair of bustle-like poufs and finished with five layers, each trimmed with a contrasting pleated flounce.

Whether made in the nineteenth century or manufactured today, double-sided Dutch wax cottons feature African decorative motifs. These may include traditional floral and abstract forms or pictorial ornaments, including animals, objects and human figures. The motifs reflect current interests, and in recent decades have included electronic devices, logos, celebrity portraits and even Michelle Obama's handbag.

The absence of the mannequin's head prompts multiple, and even conflicting meanings. Robbing the figure of the expected depiction of individuality and selfhood – the face – may be read as a violation of legible identity. Is this a purposeful obliteration of an outsider or an extreme mode of disguise? Ambiguity is, after all, an essential part of masquerade.

Billy Porter at the Academy Awards
Frazer Harrison
2019

Actor Billy Porter wore a 'tuxedo gown', designed by Christian Siriano, to walk the Red Carpet at the 91st Annual Academy Awards (2019). The tightly fitted velvet and silk jacket paired with a voluminous ball skirt that could be removed to reveal wide-legged trousers. Porter, star of the television series *Pose*, explained that he wanted to 'create a space' for 'dialogue about the masculine and the feminine and everything in between'.

The pattern-on-pattern aesthetic is in exact opposition to the plain severity of Victorian menswear. Shonibare celebrates the cultural clash of form and fabric as a sartorial masquerade, mocking and empowering in a singular, savvy display.

8

Unfinished, Broken, Destroyed

A TRAVELLER SEES AN ANCIENT RUIN IN THE DESERT. 'Two vast and trunkless legs of stone' and 'shattered visage' lying in the sand is all that exists of a once-towering figure. An inscription on a pedestal identifies the figure as Ozymandius, 'King of Kings', whose monument has succumbed to the ravages of time although his words still command all passersby to 'Look on my Works, ye Mighty, and despair'. In Percy Bysshe Shelley's haunting poem 'Ozymandius' (1818) the same image that comments upon the transience of human power demonstrates the enduring capacity of art to carry a powerful message, even when the work itself is crumbling into dust. Shelley's fallen figure is an ekphrasis, an imaginative description in which the art serves as a literary device. But history offers many actual works that have remained compelling despite their ruined state. The Great Sphinx of Giza's facial features have eroded beyond recognition, but this does not decrease its dignity. Many of the colossal moai (heads) on the island of Rapa Nui (Easter Island) have toppled and cracked, but their massive presence still stirs awe and admiration. Without arms, the *Venus de Milo* embodies beauty and grace; without a head the *Nike of Samothrace* expresses strength and determination. Although each has changed over time due to natural, accidental or deliberate forces, we find meaning in what survives, and we look to unlock the secrets that make the parts as intriguing as the whole.

Age is not the sole factor in works that appear to be damaged or incomplete. In his *Naturae historiae* (Natural history *c.* 77), Pliny the Elder stated that such works stir his heart for they imply the death of an artist. But an artist may abandon a work for any number of reasons. Some difficulty may have arisen in the material or the concept or the commission. The artist may put the work aside to tend to other obligations, leaving a project in a provisional state, intending, perhaps, to return to it at another time. They may have become frustrated or distracted or no longer interested in whatever they set out to create. The Italian term *non finito* (incomplete) presumes that a work of art should be brought to completion; any other state falls short of perfection, leaving the artist's idea unresolved. And yet, the condition of *non finito* raises intriguing questions about the artist's objectives and circumstances. An incomplete work can reveal as much about the artist and their art as one that is finished. From method to mind-set, an unfinished work can change our perspective on an artist's abilities and ambitions. A partial work may contain a complete idea, and even the destruction of a work may have an important story to tell.

Works that are broken, damaged or even destroyed may tempt us to imagine them as whole or pristine, but we engage with them more honestly if we accept them as complete in their unfinished state. After all, that lack of finish is integral to what we see, and it may lead us to a deeper understanding of the life of the work, as shown in the following examples. A missing part of a portrait renowned for its beauty amplifies rather than diminishes its significance. The suspension of work on a group of sculptures heightens the artist's emotional expression in ways he may not have intended. A gigantic commission is never completed due to the volatility of the times. One artist deliberately destroys another's work; another artist relies on decay to carry out the purpose of her sculptural programme. And what may have been a prank transforms a work at the very moment that it sells for a record-breaking price at an auction, raising the issue as to whether it is the same work of art or a brand new creation.

THE BEAUTIFUL ONE HAS COME

Bust of Nefertiti
Attributed to Thutmose (New Kingdom, 18th Dynasty)
c. 1348–1336/5 BCE
Painted limestone
Height 50.8 cm (20 in)
Staatliche Museen, Berlin

In 1912, when archaeologist Ludwig Borchardt uncovered an eighteenth Dynasty bust of a stunningly beautiful woman during his excavation of the ancient Egyptian capital Akhetaten (present-day Tell el-Amarna) he could not contain his astonishment. 'Describing her is useless', he declared. 'She must be seen'. The Director of the Deutsches Archäologische Institut and his crew had broken through a mud-brick wall in the workshop compound of the villa owned by Thutmose, court sculptor and master of works to King Akhenaten. Behind it they found a pantry cache; its shelves had broken over the centuries, tumbling sculptures to the floor. The bust, face down in the dust, suffered minor damage: some chipping on the rims of the ears and the upper edge of the headdress. But the naturalistic polychrome and exquisite features were fully intact, and Borchardt immediately recognized it as a portrait of Nefertiti, chief wife to the king. There was one disturbing loss. The left eye socket was empty, and Borchardt offered a £1,000 reward to anyone who could recover the missing eye.

Little is known of Nefertiti before she married Akhenaten. Together they presided over a brief but unparalleled era in ancient Egypt, during which Akhenaten (formerly Amenhotep IV; reigned 1353–1336 BCE) rejected the traditional gods and their priests, declared that the solar god Aten was his

father, and that he, the pharaoh, was the sole agent of the deity. The art created for the court emphasized a natural image of the reigning pharaoh and his family over an idealized vision of pharaonic rule. Both the queen and the king could be recognized by their distinctive facial features, as well as their royal attributes. The oval face, wide almond eyes and serene smile that were the consistent elements of Nefertiti's likeness confirmed the promise of her name: The Beautiful One Has Come.

Although ideal in its beauty, the bust is the most naturalistic of all the known imagery associated with Nefertiti. Roughly life-size, the sculpture has a vital presence; the high headdress angles back as the slender neck tilts the face forward, suggesting movement and outward engagement. Even more lifelike is the handling of the right eye. Crafted of rock crystal, with the pupil and iris painted on the inner surface, the eye was inlaid and fixed with beeswax. Its mate was never found, and further inspection revealed no evidence of carving or adhesive residue in the left socket, suggesting that the absence was deliberate. Rather than a public monument or a tomb sculpture intended to represent the queen in the afterlife, it is believed that this bust was a sculptor's model, a perfect stand in for the queen, who had more important things to do than pose for her portrait.

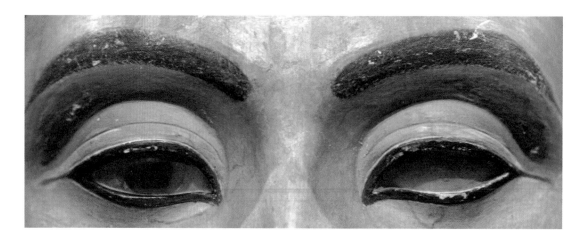

The iris and pupil painted on the inner surface of the rock crystal gives the eye credible light and depth. The outlines simulating black kohl eyeliner reflected real-life court practice for men and women throughout ancient Egyptian history, but only women tinted their lips.

Borchardt first believed that the left eye inlay fell out of the bust when it tumbled to the floor. But close inspection revealed that there had never been an eye in the socket. If the bust was in fact a sculptor's model, the socket might have been left empty to show the depth of the hollow needed for the inlay.

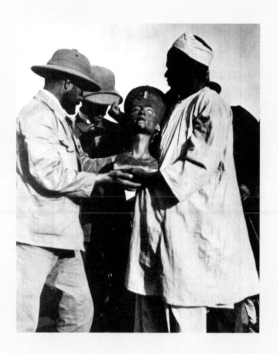

Presentation of the bust of Nefertiti on site to the Prince of Saxony by the excavation leader, Professor Ranke, in 1912.

After the death of Akhenaten, Thutmose continued to serve the court, and when the new king Tutankhaten (later Tutankhamen) overturned the beliefs of his heretic father and moved the capital back to Thebes, the sculptor followed him. Broken tools scattered throughout the workshop suggest a hasty departure, and objects associated with the old regime – unfinished sculptures, casts, portrait busts – were stored on the shelves of a pantry and sealed behind a mud-brick wall.

LEFT To avoid showing the empty socket the bust is generally photographed from the left. This view also displays the facial features associated with the queen's likeness: high cheekbones, chiselled chin and jawline, and a long lithe neck. Such individualized naturalism defied the conventions of royal depiction. In the twentieth century, the bust has come to represent ancient Egyptian beauty, inspiring poems, films, an opera and even a novel by Agatha Christie.

RIGHT Depiction of this tall blue headdress does not appear until near the end of Akhenaten's reign when it is speculated that Nefertiti served as co-regent. Resembling the crown that a king wore into battle, the headdress rests on a gold headband and features a uraeus – the rearing golden cobra – the attribute of divine authority.

STRUGGLING OUT OF THE STONE

The Atlas
Michelangelo Buonarroti (1475–1564)
c. 1520-1534
Marble
Height 334.01 cm (131.5 in)
Accademia, Florence

In a funeral oration for Michelangelo, Florentine historian Benedetto Varchi proclaimed that the late master demonstrated more brilliance in his 'unfinished works' than could be seen in the finished works of others. Michelangelo did, in fact, leave a surprising number of his sculptures in a rough state; of forty-two known works, twenty-four are regarded as *non finito* (incomplete). Over the centuries, the expressive appeal of these figures grew. They appeared to embody not just an artistic idea and a physical ideal, but the true meaning of sculpture as the act of freeing a figure from its imprisoning block of stone. This view allied with Michelangelo's own belief that the true ability of a sculptor lies not in the conception or the carving, but in his ability to recognize and release a figure placed within the stone by divine purpose. Like most in his era, he also believed that the highest standard for an artist's endeavour was *perfezione*: the balance of completeness and perfection. While his unresolved works have a raw, emotional power, this was not by intention, but by circumstance, as seen in the magnificent, struggling figure known as *The Atlas*.

Michelangelo conceived the figure as a minor part of an extensive multi-figured ensemble for the tomb of Pope Julius II. The original 1505 plan included sixteen captive figures on the first level, but the project lagged, and the design was repeatedly revised and reduced. In the years immediately after the pontiff's death in 1513, Michelangelo completed several of the planned figures, including his famed *Moses* and two of the captives, but by the end of the decade, he was deeply engaged with a large architectural and sculpture commission at San Lorenzo for the Medici family in Florence. He had been working on four more captives in his studio: none of them, including *The Atlas*, was finished.

The four Florentine captives – retrospectively named *The Awakening Captive*, *The Young Captive*, *The Bearded Captive* and *The Atlas* – reveal how Michelangelo pulled his figures out of the marble block. He began with the torso as the core of bodily motion. With its back still attached, *The Atlas* appears engaged in a struggle, its chest heaving with effort as it tries to drag its legs out of the stone. Only the left arm has emerged, and the rudimentary features of a face can be seen just above the wrist. Trapped in its rough-hewn slab, *The Atlas* conveys a powerful message of determined force, but that was not the sculptor's intent. Michelangelo planned each captive as a fully formed figure freed from its block; distracted by other projects, he just never got around to finishing them.

The torque of the figure's core sets its whole body in motion. The compressed abdominal muscles twist to the right, while the expanded ribcage pulls to the left. With a leftward swing of the elbow, the right knee spirals in the other direction, heightening the dynamic force of counterpoint.

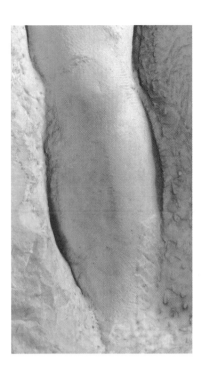

LEFT The roughed-in knee and the lower leg seem to be mired in stone. While the unfinished state can be read expressively as a commentary on human struggle, it also allows the viewer to see every stroke of Michelangelo's chisel.

BELOW The full form of the left arm is carved, but Michelangelo had yet to refine the definition of musculature or polish the surface of the marble. The hand is still just a slab, and the eyes and nose – almost hidden – are in a very rough state. The name *The Atlas* was inspired by the block of stone that the statue seems to lift; it would have been carved into the upraised right arm. Its rectangular form has prompted some to call this figure *The Blockhead*.

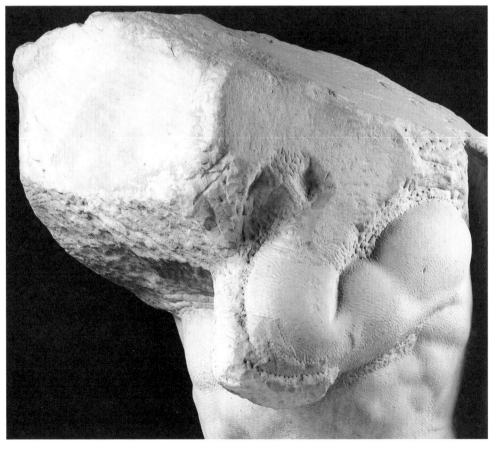

Preparatory drawing for tomb of Julius II
Michelangelo
c. 1505–1520
Pen and ink
51 × 31.9 cm (20.1 × 12.6 in)
Uffizi Gallery, Florence

In Michelangelo's original design, the sixteen captives stand on
plinths that flank niches housing personifications of Victory. Their
twisting postures portray different physical responses to bondage from
resistance to surrender. Positioned in front of a pier the individual
figures could not be seen from the back, but the drawing documents
that Michelangelo planned to carve them in the full round.

**The Awakening
Captive**
Michelangelo
c. 1520–1534
Marble
267 × 96 × 75 cm
(105.1 × 37.8 × 29.5 in)
Accademia, Florence

Deep in its block, the
figure known as *The
Awakening Captive*
arches its unseen back
and pushes against the
slab with its partially
carved right foot.
The turn of the torso
and the bent right leg
correspond with the
second figure on the
right in the preparatory
drawing. Another
parallel can be seen in
Michelangelo's sonnets
when he writes that
a 'figure grows larger
wherever the stone
decreases' (Poem 152
c. 1538–1544).

PAINTING POLITICS

The Oath of the Tennis Court
Jacques-Louis David (1748–1825)
1791
Pen, bistre wash on paper
66 × 101.2 cm (26 × 39.8 in)
Château de Versailles

The Oath of the Tennis Court portrays the newly formed National Assembly vowing to craft a constitution for the French nation. This highly finished drawing went on public display at the Louvre in 1791 to stir patriotic fervour. But more than spirited support was at stake. The drawing presented the plan for a painting commissioned by the Jacobin Club (1790), the most radical faction of the nascent government, who sought to raise funds for a monumental painting to be installed in the chamber of the National Assembly. Three thousand subscriptions were needed to cover the expense; subscribers were promised an engraved reproduction. The grandiose project typified the fierce passions of the revolution of 1789.

The depicted incident occurred on 20th June 1789. One month earlier, facing an insurmountable financial crisis, the monarchy called the Estates-General to Versailles for the first time since 1614. Composed of three elected branches – the First Estate by the clergy, the Second by the monarchy, and the Third by the common people – the current representation reflected the expansion of French franchise. There were now as many members of the Third Estate as the First and Second combined. When they protested that their influence was not proportionate to their numbers, the members of the Third Estate were locked out of the chamber. They regrouped in the palace tennis court (*jeu de paume*), renamed themselves the National Assembly and swore to remain until they wrote a viable constitution. Only one of the 577 members present refused to take the oath.

Jacques-Louis David was both ambitious and experienced in monumental history painting, but the sheer scale and import of this commission proved inherently problematic. The canvas was vast – 7 x 10 m (11 x 20 ft) – but not big enough to represent everyone, and the selection was politically fraught. In such volatile times, today's patriot could easily transform into tomorrow's traitor. A member of the Jacobin party since 1790, David allied with the extremists, and as individual members of the National Assembly fell from favour, he painted them out. In 1792, David was elected to the National Convention; he secured a position on the treacherous Public Safety Committee and voted to guillotine the king. By then David had abandoned the monumental painting and begun working on a portrait series of martyrs to the revolution, completing only his famous *The Death of Marat* (1793). Fully swept up in the Reign of Terror (1793–1794), David's fortunes failed when the Jacobin faction lost its grip on the nation. In 1794, after Jacobin leader Maximilien Robespierre was executed, David served a term in prison and subscribers to the commission finally received their engraving of *The Oath of the Tennis Court*.

The soldiers and citizens huddling in the open windows represent the public endorsement of the oath. Near the edge of the composition, an elderly woman steadies a small child who leans over the sill to get a better look. A heroic young man stands behind them. They personify the nation: past, present and future.

The radical vision of Maximilien Robespierre defined the objectives of the Jacobin Club. David awards him a prominent position – arms raised as if urging his comrades to battle – although he had yet to rise to prominence. As the architect of the Reign of Terror, he led the government through its most fanatical phase.

ABOVE When the Estates-General convened in May 1789, astronomer Jean-Sylvain Bailly was a newly elected representative of the Third Estate. He led the rebellious deputies in The Oath of the Tennis Court and served as the inaugural president of the National Assembly. A leader in progressive reform, he fell foul of the Jacobin extremists and was executed during the Reign of Terror.

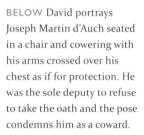

BELOW David portrays Joseph Martin d'Auch seated in a chair and cowering with his arms crossed over his chest as if for protection. He was the sole deputy to refuse to take the oath and the pose condemns him as a coward.

The Oath of the Tennis Court
(unfinished painting)
Jacques-Louis David
1791
Chalk, wash and
oil on canvas
400 × 660 cm
(157.5 × 260 in)
Château de
Versailles, Versailles

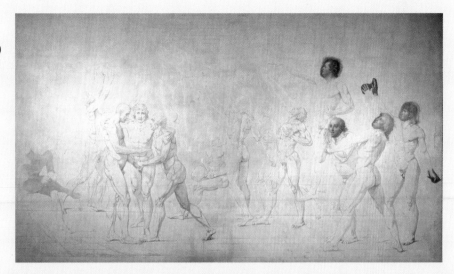

To portray a contemporary event, David employed the classical conventions of history painting. He emphasized the dramatic potential of the human body, building his composition with nude figure studies posed by professional models. It is believed that some of the assembly members sat for portrait sketches, but the number of times and duration is not known. Their faces needed to be instantly recognized, but also idealized for the sake of posterity.

Figure sketches of deputies swearing oaths
Jacques-Louis David
1791
pen, ink and wash with black chalk
49 × 60 cm (19.29 × 23.62 in)
Château de Versailles, Paris

These detailed sketches reveal how David formulated a complex composition with a large cast of characters. Each single figure and grouping presents a concise, yet highly emotional vignette. The dynamic physicality of these choreographed postures reflects David's long and successful work in interpreting classical history as exemplary of moral behaviour.

'TO SEE WHAT MAKES A PICTURE'

Erased de Kooning Drawing
Robert Rauschenberg (1925–2008)
1953
Traces of drawing media on paper with label and gilded frame
64.14 x 55.25 cm (25.3 x 21.8 in)
San Francisco Museum of Modern Art, San Francisco, CA

Robert Rauschenberg spent his first years in New York probing the boundaries of painting. He covered canvas panels in plain white housepaint with a roller. He worked in a single material – gold leaf, toilet paper, soil – to forge an 'elemental' relationship with his medium. He enlisted his friend, composer John Cage, to drive a Model A Ford through a pool of paint and then over bands of paper to create *Automobile Tire Print* (1953). His fascination with materials and surfaces led to curiosity about removing imagery, and he began to experiment with erasers. But he quickly realized that rubbing out marks that he made himself was only 'half the process'. In 1953, he asked Willem de Kooning – a pioneering master of Abstract Expressionism – for a drawing that he could erase.

Using rubber erasers, Rauschenberg methodically wiped de Kooning's pencil and charcoal marks off the sheet of paper. The results left faintly blurred lines and a soiled-looking surface; remnants of de Kooning's sketch could be seen but were rendered undecipherable. Rauschenberg then collaborated with his friend Jasper Johns to select a thin, gilded frame for the sheet and create a label reading: ERASED de KOONING DRAWING/ ROBERT RAUSCHENBERG/1953. While it is not known exactly when this final step was taken – Rauschenberg did not meet Johns until the winter of 1953–1954 – the purpose is self-explanatory. The content of the work resided in carrying out the concept rather than in the resulting object. The importance of the label can be seen in the design of the mat, which features a small, bevel-cut window for the label as well as the large window for the drawing. Often regarded as a seminal example of Conceptualism, *Erased de Kooning Drawing* stood as both a tribute and a challenge to the more visceral approach of de Kooning. In the process of incorporating de Kooning's work into his own process, Rauschenberg effaced it.

Rauschenberg's experiments with conventional visual elements also pushed against conventional assumptions. Was he the sole artist of the work, or did the creation include de Kooning and Johns? Could or should the viewer appreciate the work as an aesthetic object in its own right beyond the explanation of Rauschenberg's concept? And over the years, curiosity grew about the erased drawing; it was, after all, the work of a trailblazing twentieth-century artist. In 2010 the San Francisco Museum of Modern Art (SF MoMA) produced a digitally enhanced infrared scan of the sheet revealing a number of loose sketches from different angles, suggesting that de Kooning gave Rauschenberg a working sketch of uncertain significance. Rauschenberg did not repeat his experiment with erasure, explaining that 'the problem was solved, and I did not have to do it again'.

The surface of the erased drawing is hardly pristine. It appears roughed-up, mottled and smudged. But the aesthetic result of erasing is an accidental aspect of the object's significance. The process of creation – obtaining the drawing, erasing it, framing it – justifies the existence of the object. As in performance art, the object functions not as the end goal but as a record of what has been done.

Rauschenberg and Johns chose a simple, traditional frame. It defines the drawing, as if to remind the viewer that it is a work of art. In 1988, after the drawing was conserved, a label was affixed to the back of the frame stating: DO NOT REMOVE DRAWING FROM FRAME. FRAME IS PART OF THE WORK.

The lettering suggests the use of a pantograph or a similar mechanical writing instrument used to transfer an image and adjust its scale. Both Rauschenberg and Johns would have been familiar with this type of device from their work decorating department-store windows. The label is the key to the concept, and Rauschenberg felt it was an integral part of the work.

Digitally enhanced scan of
Rauschenberg's *Erased de Kooning
Drawing*
2010
San Francisco Museum of Modern Art

The digitally enhanced scan gave form
to the ghostly shadows and lines left
behind after Rauschenberg's erasure.
The remnants show that de Kooning
worked on the sheet from several
angles, and a figure of a woman in the
lower left corner might link the drawing
to his 'Woman' series (1950–1955). The
scan also revealed de Kooning's own use
of an eraser. Rauschenberg admired de
Kooning's work and already owned two
sketches, one a doodle on a napkin and
another that he rescued from a trash
bin in de Kooning's studio.

L.H.O.O.Q.
Marcel Duchamp (1887–1968)
1930
Graphite on photogravure
Private Collection

John Cage likened Rauschenberg's erased
drawing to Duchamp's drawing of a moustache
on a postcard image of Leonardo da Vinci's *Mona
Lisa*. But there is a difference between defacing
and erasing. Also, Rauschenberg transformed an
actual drawing by a famed artist rather than an
inexpensive reproduction of a beloved work.

SWEETNESS WITH A STING

At the Behest of Creative Time
Kara E. Walker has Confected
A Subtlety, or the Marvelous Sugar Baby, an Homage to the unpaid and overworked Artisans
who have refined our Sweet tastes from the cane fields to the Kitchens of the New World on the
Occasion of the demolition of the Domino Sugar Refining Plant
Kara Walker (b. 1969)
2014
Sugar and mixed media
10.6 × 28.9 m (35 × 75 ft)
Destroyed

Kara Walker found the subject for her first site-specific sculpture at the site itself. Creative Time, a public arts organization that sponsored the work, had secured for the venue a vast, abandoned, five-storey warehouse, part of the Domino Sugar works on the East River in Brooklyn that was slated for demolition. Given complete autonomy to select the subject, concept and medium, Walker chose to confront the benighted history of 'blood sugar', the brutal practice of the old sugar industry, fuelled by enslaved labour in the cane fields. Inspired by a nearly forgotten form of confectionary – the subtlety, a decorative sugar sculpture made to grace elite European banqueting tables from the late medieval era through the nineteenth century – she created a titanic, sphinx-like figure of a woman and coated it with a thick crust of sugar.

Building her subtlety on a colossal scale – more than 10.6 m high and 28.9 m long – Walker overturned its origins as a tabletop ornament. Using buckets, hands and shovels, Walker worked with a team of assistants to cover a carved, polystyrene core with a paste made of bleached sugar (72,575 kg/160,000 lbs provided by the Domino Sugar Company) and water. The gleaming white female figure that dominated the dark cavernous space had African features, a bandana head wrap and a powerful, graphically explicit body, crouched like a resting lion. By combining references to the ancient Egyptian sphinx and the stereotype of the domestic caretaker, or 'mammy', Walker demonstrated her belief in the 'importance to look back', not just to acknowledge history, but to unsettle its assumptions. Fifteen attendant figures, carrying baskets or bunches of bananas, surrounded Walker's formidable *Sugar Baby*. She based them on cheap, decorative figurines that she found on Amazon.com and moulded them out of sugar, syrup and water (the ingredients for caramel). The exhibition ran from 10th May to 6th July, and the rising summer heat in the poorly ventilated building played an essential role in Walker's plan.

Early in the exhibition run, several of the attendant figures melted into a pool of dark syrup that resembled blood. Walker replaced some of them with a molasses-covered version on a resin core. When pieces fell off others, she put the broken limbs in surviving figures' baskets. Over the duration, the degrading sugar mingled with the already-present odours of molasses and industrial grime, changing

the scent in the hot interior from sickly sweet to acrid. Walker regarded the effects of decomposition as part of the experience, stating, 'it was important to me to have the figures made out of a substance that was so temporal, so subject to change'. During the last five minutes on the closing day, visitors were allowed to touch the works. Then, the imposing *Sugar Baby* was disassembled, the polystyrene blocks were recycled, and the remnants of the installation were bulldozed with the rest of the building.

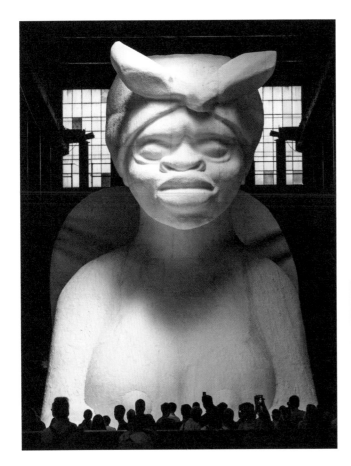

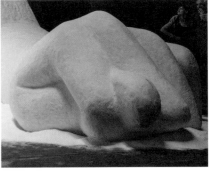

Throughout the exhibition visitors were encouraged to take photographs and post them on Instagram at #KaraWalkerDomino. Creative Time also supported a website featuring a three-dimensional *Digital Sugar Baby* that could be rotated by moving a cursor. This allowed remote viewers to track the decomposition of the sugar crust and view visitors' uploaded photographs.

The *Sugar Baby*'s fingers are curled, echoing a sphinx's lion paws. But these large, capable hands belong to a working woman. At the close of the exhibition, before the figure was dismantled, the left hand was carefully removed and delivered to Walker's studio.

Walker deliberately invoked the southern American stereotype of the mythic 'mammy', the big-hearted, passive worker whose duties ranged from cooking and cleaning to childcare and field work. But the impressive physicality of the figure, along with its proud posture and stern dignity, undermines the trope of the dutiful black domestic, turning a cliché of submission into an embodiment of power.

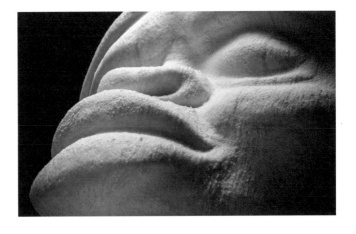

ABOVE The design for the colossal figure started as a small, clay model. The model was scanned and digitized; carving robots read the information to cut the polystyrene blocks, which were then refined by hand. The sugar paste was also applied by hand, using bleached sugar. Raw sugar is brown, and Walker wanted her figure to have the gleaming white surface of a refined confectionary.

LEFT At 1.5 m (5 ft) tall, the boy attendants seemed to mingle with the visiting crowds. Like the imposing *Sugar Baby,* they mock a stereotype: the exotic boy servant ever compliant and ready to please.

GOING, GOING, GONE

Love is in the Bin (originally *Girl with Balloon*)
Banksy (b. 1974)
2018
Aerosol paint, acrylic paint, canvas board
101 × 78 cm (40 × 38 in)
Private Collection

Anticipation ran high at Sotheby's on 5th October 2018 as the final lot in the Evening Contemporary Art Sale was carried into the sales room. It was a unique version of Banksy's best-known – and most-loved – motif, *Girl with Balloon*. The artist/activist had introduced the appealing depiction of a small girl reaching towards the string of a heart-shaped balloon in 2002, and, through multiple iterations it had earned iconic status in the world of street art and popular media, as well as in his repertoire. Once the bidding began, the £200,000–300,000 estimate for the work – a stencil image sprayed with acrylic paint on canvas and housed in an ornate gilded frame – rapidly escalated. The lot closed slightly above a record-shattering £1,000,000. But as the hammer came down, the work within the frame began to slide, and a fringe of shredded canvas emerged from the bottom. Banksy, who stipulated that the frame was integral to the work, had hidden a mechanical paper shredder in the frame's lower bar. In the wake of general astonishment, Alex Branczik, Sotheby's head of contemporary art for Europe, observed: 'It appears we just got Banksy-ed'.

Over a two decade-career, Banksy has drawn wide attention and critical acclaim, while protecting his anonymity, for socially conscious street art and installations, as well as artfully droll pranks. His motif of *Girl with Balloon* expresses an uncharacteristic poignancy. From its first appearance in 2002, on a shop wall in London's Shoreditch and then near a stairway on Waterloo Bridge, it had a broad appeal. Banksy repeated the motif in other locations until 2006; he then released it in a series of limited-addition prints as well as other, more affordable products. The singularity of the canvas version made it all the more desirable as well as heightening the shock at its destruction. And, when Banksy posted on Instagram, 'Going, going, gone', there was no doubt that the prank went as planned.

The smoothness of the prank – someone on site had to activate the shredder with a remote-controlled device – raised suspicions about collusion between Sotheby's and the artist. But Sotheby's has denied any prior knowledge or involvement. Defining the work as irreversibly altered, the auction house required a new certificate of authenticity, which they were granted from Pest Control, a service Banksy created in 2009 to authenticate his works. And reflecting his belief that the 'urge to destroy' was itself a creative process, Banksy gave the work a new name: *Love is in the Bin*. The buyer, whose identity is unknown, fully agrees. Although she confessed to her initial shock at the shredding, she now regards the circumstances around her purchase as an essential part of its history.

The canvas stopped sliding about halfway through the shredder raising speculation, in retrospect, that it had jammed. After the sale Banksy released a video of completely shredding a replica, but he neither confirmed nor denied how much of the canvas he had intended to shred.

The mechanical paper shredder was hidden within the lower bar of the frame. It is not typical of Banksy to frame his work, let alone use such an ornate design. And the shredder would have made the object extraordinarily heavy. But Sotheby's took no notice of these unusual factors. The artist had chosen the frame and it was regarded as part of the work.

The buyer went ahead with her purchase and, along with Banksy and Sotheby's, regards the change as part of the object. Redefining the prank as performance adds history as well as value. Sotheby's Alex Branczik now describes it as 'the first artwork to have been created live during an auction'.

Girl with Balloon, Waterloo Bridge
2004

Banksy debuted *Girl with Balloon* on two sites
in London: first on a shop wall in Shoreditch
and soon after, on the stairway at Waterloo
Bridge. Exposed to the elements, as well as to
the whims of other artists and vandals, street art
is not meant to last in pristine condition. Here,
other hands have added tags, words and the
heartening sentiment: 'There is always hope'.

Girl with Balloon
Banksy
2006
Spray paint and acrylic on canvas

As a motif *Girl with Balloon* strikes a delicate
balance between hope and wistfulness. Will
the girl be able to grab the string or will the
balloon be forever beyond her reach? Widely
reproduced, marketed and even modified by
the artist for varied political messages, the
image is one of the most recognized in Banksy's
repertoire. This version, sprayed on canvas, was
all the more desirable because it was unique.

INDEX

SOURCES

INTRODUCTION
page 10, descriptions of work, as quoted in Gary Schwartz, *The Night Watch*. Amsterdam: Rijksmuseum, 2002, page 5. • page 11: 'admirable' and following, Jan van Dijk, as quoted in Schwartz, page 32.

CHAPTER 1
The Lady with an Ermine: page 22: 'one of your stars', Bernardo Bellincioni, as quoted in Janice Shell and Grazioso Sironi, 'Cecilia Gallerani: Leonardo's Lady with an Ermine', *Artibus et Historiae* 13:25 (1992). • page 22: 'painted when...', Cecilia Gallerani to Isabella d'Este, 29 April 1498, as quoted in Józef Grabski and Janusz Walek (eds.), 'Leonardo da Vinci (1452–1519) Lady with an Ermine', Vienna/Cracow: IRSA, 1991, 11.

The Blue Boy: page 24: 'Gainsborough is beyond...', Mary Moser to Henry Fuseli (1770), as quoted in Robert R. Wark, *The Blue Boy and Pinkie*. San Marino, CA: The Huntington Library, 1998, page 19. • page 24: 'a Master Brutall...', Edward Edwards, *Anecdotes of Painters* (1808), as quoted in Wark, page 9.

Harvard Art Mural Triptych: page 32: 'between the idea...', Mark Rothko, as quoted in Jeffrey Weiss, *Mark Rothko*. New Haven and London: Yale University Press, 1998, page 342. • page 32: 'close quarters', Mark Rothko as quoted in Weiss, page 345.

CHAPTER 2
Girl reading a Letter at an Open Window: page 44: 'picture of Cupid', as quoted in, Walter Liedtke, *Vermeer and the Delft School*. New York: Metropolitan Museum of Art, 2001, page 149.

Man with a Leather Belt: page 49: 'independent sense...', Gustave Courbet (1855), as quoted in David Bomford, 'Rough Manners: Reflections on Courbet and Seventeenth-Century Painting', Papers from the Symposium Looking at the Landscapes: Courbet and Modernism, J. Paul Getty Museum, 18th March 2006. J. Paul Getty Trust, 2007, page 7.

White Flag: page 56: 'I dreamt one night...', Jasper Johns, as quoted in, Morgan Meis, 'Taking Aim: Jasper Johns: An Allegory of Painting', *The Virginia Quarterly Review* 83:2 (Spring 2007), page 108. • page 56: 'things that the mind...', Jasper Johns, as quoted in James Rondeau and Douglas Druick, *Jasper Johns: Grey*. New Haven and London: Yale University Press, 2007, page 1. • page 59: 'seen and looked at...', Jasper Johns, as quoted on Whitney Museum of American Art website https://whitney.org/collection/works/1060

CHAPTER 3
Swans Reflecting Elephants: page 82: 'the world of...', as quoted in, David Spurr, 'Paranoid Modernism in Joyce and Kafka', *Journal of Modern Literature* 34:2 (Winter 2011), page 178.

Movement in Squares: page 86: 'was there...' and 'new pictorial identity', Bridget Riley, 'At the end of my pencil', *London Review of Books*. 31:19 (8 October 2009). • page 86: 'closest historical relatives', Bridget Riley, as quoted in Cornelia Butler and Alexandra Schwartz (eds.), *Modern Women: Women Artists at the Museum of Modern Art*. New York: Museum of Modern Art, 2010, page 256. • page 89: 'it will take twenty years...', Bridget Riley, as quoted in Michael Kimmelman, 'Not so square after all', *The Guardian* 27th September 2000.

CHAPTER 4
Bernardino Campi painting Sofonisba Anguissola: page 96: 'vain'; 'frivolous', Baldassare Castiglione, as quoted in Anthony Bond and Joanna Woodall, *Self-Portrait: Renaissance to Contemporary*. London: National Portrait Gallery, 2005, page 91. • page 96: 'any other woman...', Giorgio Vasari, *The Lives of the Most Excellent Painters, Sculptors and Architects* (1568), trans. Gaston du C. Vere. New York: The Modern Library, 2006, page 305. • page 97: 'I, the maiden Sofonisba...' as quoted in Frances Borzello, *A World of Our Own: Women Artists Since the Renaissance*. New York: Watson-Guptill, 2000, page 46.

David with the Head of Goliath: page 98: 'half-length...' and 'Caravaggio's...', Giovanni Pietro Bellori, as quoted in, David M. Stone, 'Self and Myth in Caravaggio's David and Goliath', in, *Caravaggio: Realism, Rebellion, Deception* (ed. Genevieve Warwick). Newark, DE: University of Delaware Press, 2006, page 37. • page 100: 'Jacopo Manilli, *suo Caravaggino*', as quoted in, Catherine Puglisi, *Michelangelo Merisi da Caravaggio*. London: Phaidon Press Limited, 2000, page 363.

Las Meninas: page 103: 'Retrato...', as quoted in Javier Partús (ed.), *Velázquez: Las Meninas and the Late Portraits*. London: Thames & Hudson, 2014, page 126.

Untitled (Woman in Mask): page 106: 'mask than a man', Ralph Waldo Emerson, journal entry 24 October 1841, as quoted in Merry A. Foresta and John Wood, *Secrets of the Dark Chamber: The Art of the American Daguerreotype*. Washington, D.C.: Smithsonian Institution Press, 1995, page 23. • page 106: 'a transcript...', Marcus Root, 'The Various Uses of the Daguerrrean Art', *Photographic Art-Journal* (December 1852), as quoted in Foresta and Wood, page 263. • page 106: 'is everything...', Albert S. Southworth, 'Suggestions to Ladies Who Sit for Daguerreotypes', *Lady's Almanac* (1854), as quoted in Foresta and Wood, page 282.

Untitled Film Still #14: page 110: 'In fact . . .', Cindy Sherman, as quoted in Eva Respini, *Cindy Sherman*. New York: The Museum of Modern Art, 2012, page 18. • page 110: 'I am the one...', Cindy Sherman, as quoted in Betsy Berne, 'Studio: Cindy Sherman', *Tate Arts and Culture Magazine* 5 (May/June 2003). • page 112: 'I wanted them...', Cindy Sherman as quoted in Respini, pages 21–22.

Portrait of the Artist as a Shadow of His Former Self: page 114: 'pushing around paint' and 'dead end', Kerry James Marshall, as quoted in Helen Molesworth (ed.), *Kerry James Marshall: Mastry*. New York: Skira Rizzoli, 2016, page 49. • page 114: 'I am invisible...', Ralph Ellison, *The Invisible Man*, 1952. • page 114: 'simultaneous presence and absence', Kerry James Marshall, as quoted in, Molesworth, page 49. • page 114: 'I was aware...', Kerry James Marshall, as quoted in, Antwaun Sargent, 'Kerry James Marshall's Mastry', *Interview Magazine* 22 April 2016. • page 114: 'idea of those paintings...', Kerry James Marshall, as quoted in Wyatt Mason, 'Kerry James Marshall is Shifting the Color of Art History', *The New York Times Style Magazine* (17th October 2016).

CHAPTER 5
Phyllis and Demophoön: page 126: 'want of sympathy...' and 'absolute freedom', Edward Burne-Jones, as quoted in Georgiana Burne-Jones, *Memorials of Edward Burne-Jones*. Freeport, NY: Books for Libraries Press, 1904 (1971), volume 2; page 12. • page 128: 'love chase' and 'woman follower', Tom Taylor, *The Times* (27 April 1870): page 4. • page 129: 'would have done for a portrait' and 'glorious head', Edward Burne-Jones to Helen Mary Gaskell (1893), as quoted in Fiona MacCarthy, *The Last Pre-Raphaelite: Edward Burne-Jones and the Victorian Imagination*. Cambridge, MA: Harvard University Press, 2011, page 220.

Man at the Crossroads...: page 130: 'cultural vandalism', Diego Rivera, as quoted in, 'Rivera RCA Mural is Cut From Wall', *The New York Times*, 13th February 1934.

Untitled photograph, possibly related to Wife and Child of a Sharecropper: page 136: 'to collect documents', Roy E. Stryker, as quoted in, Lisa Helen Kaplan, ' "Introducing America to Americans": FSA Photography and the Construction of Racialized and Gendered Citizens', PhD thesis, Bowling Green State University, December 2015, page 41. • page 136: 'barbaric', Edwin Rosskam, as quoted in, Allen C. Benson, 'Killed Negatives: The Unseen Photographic Archives', *Archivaria, The Journal of the Association of Canadian Archivists* 68 (Fall 2009), page 19. • page 136: 'duplicates' 'weren't the best', Arthur Rothstein, as quoted in Benson, page 4. • page 136: 'a little bit...' Ben Shahn, as quoted in Benson, page 19. • page 136: 'needy families...' Roy Stryker Papers, as quoted in Kaplan, page 47.

What is the Proper Way to Display a US Flag?: page 147: 'walk on...', as quoted in Robert Justin Goldstein, *Burning the Flag: The Great 1989–1990 American Flag Desecration Controversy*. Kent, OH : The Kent State University Press, 1996, page 79. • page 147: 'propel history forward', Dread Scott, as quoted in Louis P. Masur, *The Soiling of Old Glory: The Story of a Photograph that Shocked America*. New York: Bloomsbury Press, 2008, page 172. • page 147: 'I'm not...', Dread Scott, as quoted in Emily Mantell, 'Political Art Censorship: A productive Power', MA Thesis, Ohio University, April 2017, page 87. • page 148: 'I don't know...', Bob Dole, as quoted in William E. Schmidt, 'Disputed Exhibit of Flag is Ended', *The New York Times* (17 March 1989). • page 148: 'In Russia, Ledger Entry, as quoted in Dread Scott website, https://www.dreadscott.net/works/what-is-the-proper-way-to-display-a-us-flag/ • page 148: 'moment of self-awareness', Ledger Entry, as quoted in Dread Scott website, https://www.dreadscott.net/works/what-is-the-proper-way-to-display-a-us-flag/ • page 149: 'One, two...', Protestors' chant, as quoted in Goldstein, page 82.

CHAPTER 6

The Arnolfini Portrait: page 154: 'A large picture', as quoted in Lorne Campbell, *The Fifteen Century Netherlandish Paintings*. London: National Gallery Company, 1998, page 134. • page 154: Karel van Mander, as quoted in, Erwin Panofsky, 'Jan van Eyck's Arnolfini Portrait', *Burlington Magazine for Connoisseurs*. 64:372 (March 1934), page 117. • page 154: 'pictorial marriage certificate', Panofsky, page 124. • page 154: 'Nuptial chamber' and 'affidavit', Panofsky, page 126.

Gauguin's Chair: page 162: 'nature under a brighter...', Vincent van Gogh, to Theo van Gogh, *The Complete Letters of Vincent van Gogh*, 3 vols. Boston/New York Graphic Society, 1958, letter 605. • page 162: 'dainty', Vincent van Gogh to Theo van Gogh, Vincent van Gogh, *The Letters of Vincent van Gogh*. London: Constable & Robinson Ltd., 2003, Letter 534. • page 162: 'eye to eye', Paul Gauguin to Émile Bernard, (around 23rd November 1888), as quoted in Douglas W. Druick and Peter Kort Zegers, *Van Gogh and Gauguin: The Studio of the South*. London : Thames & Hudson, 2001, page 206. • page 164: 'night effect' and 'daytime', Vincent van Gogh to Theo van Gogh (November 1888), as quoted in, Martin Gayford, *The Yellow House: Van Gogh, Gauguin and Nine Turbulent Weeks in Provence*. Boston: Houghton, Mifflin Company, 2008, page 159.

Eine Kleine Nachtmusik: page 166: 'Limitless expanse...', Dorothea Tanning (1936), as quoted in Jean Christophe Bailly, *Dorothea Tanning*. New York: George Braziller, Inc., 1995, page 166. • page 14: 'most aggressive', Dorothea Tanning (1999), as quoted in a letter to the Tate Gallery, https://www.tate.org.uk/art/artworks/tanning-eine-kleine-nachtmusik-t07346 • page 166: 'between the forces...', Dorothea Tanning (2005), as quoted in Alyce Mahon, *Dorothea Tanning*. London: Tate Publishing, 2018, page 7. • page 166: 'to look beyond...' and following, Dorothea Tanning (1991), as quoted in Mahon, page 15. • page 169: 'all the things...' Dorothea Tanning (1999), as quoted in a letter to the Tate Gallery, https://www.tate.org.uk/art/artworks/tanning-eine-kleine-nachtmusik-t07346

Officer of the Hussars: page 170: 'complete disconnect', Kehinde Wiley, as quoted in Thelma Golden, *Kehinde Wiley*. New York: Rizzoli, 2012, page 24. • page 170: 'enthralled', and 'history and ego', Kehinde Wiley, as quoted in Vinson Cunningham, 'Kehinde Wiley on Painting Masculinity and Blackness from President Obama to the People of Ferguson', *The New Yorker* (22 October 2018). • page 170: 'a certain type of power', Kehinde Wiley, as quoted in, Golden, page 48. • page 170: 'a very American conversation', Kehinde Wiley, as quoted in Cunningham. • page 172: 'a type of self-portraiture' and 'looking at people...', Kehinde Wiley, as quoted in Cunningham.

CHAPTER 7

The Awakening Conscience: page 187: 'the idle sing song...' and following, *William Holman Hunt, Pre-Raphaelitism and the Pre-Raphaelite Brotherhood*. New York: London: Macmillan & Company, 1905, vol. 2; pages 429–430. • page 187: 'genuine ideas', William Michael Rossetti, in Angela Thirlwell (introduction), *The Pre-Raphaelites and their World: A Personal View*. From 'Some Reminiscences' and other writings of William Michael Rossetti. London: The Folio Society, 1995, page 46. • page 187: 'the very hem...' and following, John Ruskin, 'To the Editor of The Times (4th May 1854), in Linda Nochlin (ed.), *Realism and Tradition in Art, 1848–1900*. Englewood Cliffs, NJ: Prentice-Hall, Inc., 1966, page 127. • page 189: 'showy but seedyish', Dante Gabriel Rossetti to Henry Treffry Dunn (1873), as quoted in Leonée Ormond, 'Dress in the Painting of Dante Gabriel Rossetti', *Costume: The Journal of the Costume Society* 8 (1974): page 26.

Self-Portrait: page 190: 'string of...' and following, Romaine brooks to Natalie Barney, 23rd June 1923, as quoted in Joe Lucchesi, '"The Dandy in Me", Romaine Brooks's 1923 Portraits', Susan Fillin-Yeh (ed.), *Dandies: Fashion and Finesse in Art and Culture*. New York: New York University Press, 2001, page 153. • page 190: 'blasé' and following, Charles Baudelaire, 'The Dandy', in *The Painter of Modern Life* (1863), in *The Painter of Modern Life and other Essays* (trans. and ed. Jonathan Mayne). London: Phaidon Press Limited, 2000, pages 26–27. • page 192: I am flourishing...' Hannah Gluckstein to her brother, 1918, as quoted on exhibition label, Smithsonian American Art Museum https://americanart.si.edu/artwork/peter-young-english-girl-2909 • page 192: 'series of modern women', Natalie Barney to Romaine Brooks, n.d. 1923, as quoted in Lucchesi, page 155. • page 193: 'strict tailleur masculin', *Vogue*, June 1923.

My Dress Hangs There: page 194: 'little doll' and following, Edward Weston, as quoted in Claire Wilcox and Circe Henestrosa (eds.), *Frida Kahlo: Making Herself Up*. London: V&A Publishing, 2018, pages 146; 149. • page 194: 'Diego's...', Helen Appleton Read, Boston Evening Transcript (22nd October 1931), as quoted in Claire Wilcox and Circe Henestrosa, page 146. • page 197: 'relationship with its people' and 'like a Tehuana', Frida Kahlo, as quoted in Alba F. Aragón, 'Uninhabited Dresses: Frida Kahlo, from Icon of Mexico to Fashion

Muse', *Fashion Theory: The Journal of Dress, Body & Culture*, 18:5 (2018), page 544 n 25. • page 197: 'gringa women', and following, Frida Kahlo, as quoted in Hayden Herrera, Frida *A Biography of Frida Kahlo*. New York: Harper and Row, 1983, page 143.

Big Boy: page 198: 'cross bred', Yinka Shonibare, as quoted in Robb Young, 'Africa's Fabric is Dutch', *The New York Times* (14th November 2012). • page 198: 'What interests me...' Yinka Shonibare, as quoted in Lisa Dorin, '*Big Boy*', Art Institute of Chicago Museum Studies 32: 1 (2006): page 43. • page 201: 'create a space' and 'dialogue...' Billy Porter, as quoted in Erica Gonzales, 'Billy Porter Slays in a Christian Siriano Tuxedo Dress on the Oscars Red Carpet', *Bazaar* (24th February 2019).

CHAPTER 8

Bust of Nefertiti: page 206: 'Describing her...', Ludwig Borchardt, as quoted in, Samir Raafat, *Cairo Times*, 1st March 2001.

The Atlas: page 210: 'unfinished works' and follows, as quoted in Creighton E. Gilbert, 'What is Expressed in Michelangelo's "Non-Finito"', *Artibus et Historiae*, 24: 48 (2003), page 59. • page 215: 'figure grows larger...', Michelangelo, Poem 152, as translated in, James M. Saslow, *The Poetry of Michelangelo: An annotated translation*. New Haven and London, Yale University Press, 1991, page 304.

Erased de Kooning Drawing: page 220: 'To see...', Robert Rauschenberg, as quoted in Calvin Tompkins, 'Moving Out', *The New Yorker*, 29th February 1964, pages 39–40. • page 220: 'elemental', from his term 'Elemental painting', Catherine Craft, *Robert Rauschenberg*. London: Phaidon Press, 2013, page 27. • page 220: 'half the process', Robert Rauschenberg, as quoted Calvin Tompkins, page 66. • page 220: 'the problem...', as quoted in Tompkins, page 71.

Sugar Baby: page 224: 'blood sugar', Kara Walker, in an interview with Audie Cornish, 'Artist Kara Walker Draws Us Into Bitter History with Something Sweet', WBUR News, 16th May 2014. https://www.wbur.org/npr/313017716/artist-kara-walker-draws-us-into-bitter-history-with-something-sweet • page 224: 'importance to look back', Kara Walker, Museum of Modern Art, video https://www.moma.org/artists/7679 • page 225: 'it was important...', Kara Walker, as quoted in, Rebecca Peabody, *Consuming Stories: Kara Walker and the Imaging of American Race*. Oakland: University of California Press, 2016, pages 156–157.

Love is in the Bin: page 228: 'It appears...', Alex Branczik, as quoted in Scott Reyburn, 'Banksy Painting Self-Destructs After Fetching $1.4 Million at Sotheby's', *The New York Times*, 6th October 2018. • page 228: 'Going, going, gone', Banksy, as quoted in Reyburn 6th October 2018. • page 228: 'urge to destroy', Banksy, as quoted in Scott Reyburn, 'Winning Bidder for Shredded Banksy Painting Says She'll Keep It', *The New York Times*, 11 October 2018. • page 230: 'the first artwork...', Alex Branczik, as quoted in Reyburn, 11th October 2018.

PICTURE CREDITS

3 Heritage Images/Getty 6–9 VCG Wilson/Corbis via Getty Images 12–13 The Huntington Library, Art Museum, and Botanical Gardens 17–18 Historic Royal Palaces 19t Mark Beton/London/Alamy 19b Historic Royal Palaces 21–22 PAINTING/Alamy 23t Sipa Press 23b Bridgeman Images 25–26 The Huntington Library, Art Museum, and Botanical Gardens 27t The Huntington Library, Art Museum, and Botanical Gardens 27b © The National Trust, Waddesdon Manor 29 agefotostock/Alamy 30t The Metropolitan Museum of Art/Art Resource/Scala, Firenze 30b Smithsonian Institution, Archives of American Art 31t The Metropolitan Museum of Art/Art Resource/Scala, Firenze 31b Harvard Art Museums/Fogg Museum, Bequest of Grenville L. Winthrop © President and Fellows of Harvard College 32–35 Harvard Art Museums/Fogg Museum, Transfer from Harvard University, Gift of the Artist ©President and Fellows of Harvard College 36–37 Heritage Images/Getty 41–43 Mount Holyoke College Art Museum 45 Heritage Images/Getty 46tl c, br Heritage Images/Getty 46tr, bl, Gemäldegalerie Alte Meister, Staatliche Kunstsammlungen Dresden 47t Getty Research Institute 47b Fine Art/Getty 48–50 Imagno/Getty 51t classicpaintings/Alamy 51b The Print Collector/Alamy 53, 54, 55t, 55bl © Solomon R. Guggenheim Foundation, New York. All Rights Reserved © 2018 Estate of Pablo Picasso/Artists Rights Society (ARS), New York 55r Gift of the Hanna Fund/Bridgeman 57, 58, 59t The Metropolitan Museum of Art/Art Resource/Scala, Florence 59b Whitney Museum of American Art/Scala, Florence 60–61 DEA/G.DAGLI ORTI/Getty 64 DEA/M. CARRIERI/Getty 66t Raffaello Bencini/Bridgeman 66b DEA/M. CARRIERI/Getty 67 DEA/M. CARRIERI/Getty 69, 70, 71, 72tl, 72tr Fine Art/Getty 72c Heritage Images/Getty 72b, 73t Fine Art/Getty 73b Sepia Times/Getty 75–76 Bridgeman 77t akg-images 77b The Stapleton Collection/Bridgeman 79–80 Smithsonian American Art Museum/Gift of Nathaly Baum in memory of Harry Baum 81 Tate, London/Photo Scala, Florence 83, 84, 85l DEA/G.DAGLI ORTI/Getty 85r Gift of Mrs. Charles B. Goodspeed/Bridgeman 87–88 Arts Council Collection, Southbank Centre, London © Bridget Riley 2019. All Rights Reserved 89 Mirrorpix/Getty 90–91 GL Archive/Alamy 95–96 Scala, Florence 97 Ali Meyer/Getty 99–100 Wiki commons 101t Photo Scala, Florence 101b Heritage Image Partnership Ltd/Alamy 102–104 GL Archive/Alamy 105t Leemage/Getty 105b GL Archive/Alamy 107–108 The Art Institute of Chicago/Art Resource, NY/Scala, Florence 109 Granger Historical Picture Archive/Alamy

111–113 Courtesy of the artist and Metro Pictures, New York 115–116 Matthew Fried, © MCA Chicago 117t The Art Institute of Chicago/Art Resource, NY/Scala, Florence 117b © Kerry James Marshall. Courtesy of the artist and Jack Shainman Gallery, New York 118–119 Heritage Images/Getty 122, 124l Mondadori Portfolio/Getty 124r Photo Scala, Florence/Fondo Edifici di Culto - Min. dell'Interno 125 Mondadori Portfolio/Getty 127–128 Heritage Images/Getty 129t Peter Barritt/Alamy 129b Artmedia/Alamy 131 Library of Congress 132–135 Bjanka Kadic/Alamy 137, 138, 139t Library of Congress 139b GraphicaArtis/Getty 140–141 Library of Congress 143–144 © Ulay / Marina Abramović / Ph: Giovanna dal Magro: Courtesy of Marina Abramović Archives 145t Shelby Lessig 145b Marius Becker/picture-alliance/dpa/AP Images 146–148 Dread Scott 149 Keith Philpott/Getty 150–151 Tate, London/Photo Scala, Florence 155–156 Universal History Archive/Getty 157t Wiki commons 157b Universal History Archive/Getty 159, 160, 161t Petegorsky/Gipe/Mount Holyoke College Art Museum, South Hadley, Massachusetts 161b Peter Horree/Alamy 163, 164tl, 164tr, 164c Picturenow/Getty 164b Historic Images/Alamy 165 Fine Art/Getty 167, 168, 169tl, 169 bl Tate, London/Photo Scala, Florence 169r The Philadelphia Museum of Art/Art Resource/Scala, Florence 171–172 DIA/Bridgeman 173t The Picture Art Collection/Alamy 173b Spencer Platt/Getty 174–175 Christie's Images/Bridgeman 179–180 Picturenow/Getty 181l DIA 181r The Picture Art Collection/Alamy 183 Fine Art/Getty 184l The Picture Art Collection/Alamy 184r DEA/BIBLIOTECA AMBROSIANA/Getty 185 Fine Art/Getty 186, 188, 189b Christophel Fine Art/Getty 189tl DEA PICTURE LIBRARY/Getty 189tr The Metropolitan Museum of Art/Gift of the Misses Dorcas & Katherine Beer, 1941 191–193 Photo Smithsonian American Art Museum/Art Resource/Scala, Florence 195–196 Christie's Images/Bridgeman 197t Museo Frida Kahlo 197b Photo by Nickolas Muray © Nickolas Muray Photo Archives 199, 200tl The Art Institute of Chicago/Art Resource, NY 200tc, 200tr, 200b Michael Tropea at The Richard H. Driehaus Museum, Chicago, 2019 201tl, 201bl The Art Institute of Chicago/Art Resource, NY 201r Frazer Harrison/Getty 202–203 Photo Josse/Leemage/Getty 207, 208br DEA PICTURE LIBRARY/Getty 208t OLIVER LANG/Getty 208bl Werner Forman/Getty 209t Photo Scala, Florence/bpk, Bildagentur fuer Kunst, Kultur und Geschichte, Berlin 209b OLIVER LANG/Getty 211, 212, 213b Alinari Archives/Getty 213t DEA/G. NIMATALLAH/Getty 214 Alinari Archives/Getty Leemage/Getty 217–218 Photo Josse/Leemage/Getty 219t akg-images 219b RMN-Grand Palais (Palace of Versailles)/image RMN-GP 221–222 Collection SFMOMA Purchase through a gift of Phyllis C. Wattis © Robert Rauschenberg Foundation 223t Collection SFMOMA 223b Cameraphoto Arte Venezia/Bridgeman 225, 226, 227t Andrew Burton/Getty 227b Karla Rosenberg/Alamy 229–230 © Sotheby's/Banksy 231t akg-images/Album 231b Banksy

ACKNOWLEDGEMENTS

In writing this book, I benefitted from the support of a number of people, and I would like to thank them. For reading suggestions and response to my queries, I thank Paul B. Jaskot, Professor of Art, Art History, and Visual Culture at Duke University in Durham, North Carolina, and Ellen M. Alvord, Weatherbie Curator of Education and Academic Programs, at the Mount Holyoke College Art Museum, in South Hadley, Massachusetts. For sharing their interpretations and facilitating access to the collection, I thank staff members of the Department of Photography at the Art Institute of Chicago, especially Elizabeth Siegel, Curator of Photography, Michal Raz-Russo, the David C. and Sarajean Ruttenberg Associate Curator of Photography, and Jacqueline Lopez, Research Assistant. I am grateful to the Newberry Library for their ongoing support of my work as a Scholar-in-Residence. At the White Lion Publishing I thank Joe Hallsworth for his editorial work on the manuscript and the illustrations and Paileen Currie for the design. And my deep and genuine gratitude goes to Nicki Davis for sharing her encouragement, ideas, and insights from the launch of this project to its conclusion.

This book is dedicated to Donald L. Hoffman and Melvin L. Askew, who love to share secrets.

Brimming with creative inspiration, how-to projects and useful information to enrich your everyday life, Quarto Knows is a favourite destination for those pursuing their interests and passions. Visit our site and dig deeper with our books into your area of interest: Quarto Creates, Quarto Cooks, Quarto Homes, Quarto Lives, Quarto Drives, Quarto Explores, Quarto Gifts, or Quarto Kids.

First published in 2021 by Frances Lincoln,
an imprint of The Quarto Group.
The Old Brewery, 6 Blundell Street
London, N7 9BH,
United Kingdom
T (0)20 7700 6700
www.QuartoKnows.com

Text © 2021 Debra N. Mancoff

A catalogue record for this book is available from the British Library.

ISBN 978 0 7112 4874 8
Ebook ISBN 978 0 7112 6189 1

10 9 8 7 6 5 4 3 2 1

Design by Sally Bond

Printed in Singapore

MIX
Paper from responsible sources
FSC™ C007207